P9-CRW-630
3 5674 03301944 8

CHILDREN'S ATLAS of the WORLD

CHILDREN'S ATLAS of the WORLD

Written by

PHILIP STEELE

FRANKLIN WATTS
A Division of Grolier Publishing
Danbury, Connecticut
New York London Hong Kong Sydney

Produced in association with **ticktock** *Publishing Ltd.*

Writer: *Philip Steele*
Editor: *Felicity Trotman*
Managing Editor: *Penny Worms*
Designers: *Graham Rich, Elaine Wilkinson*
Artwork: *Peter Bull Art Studio*

SOURCES

This atlas has been compiled using the following sources:
North American State and land areas: *Webster's Geographical Dictionary*
Other land areas: *Times Atlas of the World 1994 ed.*
Population statistics: *World Population Data Sheets* produced by
Population Reference Bureau, Washington D.C.
Languages: *Ethnologue – Languages of the World 13th ed. 1996**
Religions: adherents.com and *Encyclopedia Britannica CD99**

Hutchinson 1999 Almanac, *Statesman's Yearbook*, *Statesman's Yearbook World Gazetteer*, *Economist Pocket World in Figures 1998*, *Dorling Kindersley World Reference Atlas*, *Encyclopedia Britannica CD99* and *World Book Encyclopedia* were used for world resources, farming and other general information.

In some instances it has been necessary to approximate statistics due to recent developments or where no statistics were available from reliable sources.
** Languages and religions can be particularly speculative due to lack of reliable data.*

Library of Congress Cataloging-in-Publication Data

Steele, Philip, 1948-
The children's atlas of the world / by Philip Steele.
p.cm.
Includes index.
Summary: An atlas of the world with general and specific maps of each region, as well as text, photographs, charts, and graphs presenting the political, cultural, ethnic, religious, and linguistic characteristics of the world's peoples and the physical features of the continents.
ISBN 0-531-11775-8 (Lib. Bdg.) 0-531-16551-5 (Pbk)
1. Children's atlases.
[1. Atlases. 2. Geography.]
I. Title

G1021 .S677 2000
912—dc21
99-462208

Printed in the United States of America and Canada
1 2 3 4 5 6 7 8 9 10 R 09 08 07 06 05 04 03 02 01 00

CONTENTS

OUR PLANET

Our world is a ball of rock flying through space. It is one of nine planets that travel round our star, the Sun. The planets cannot escape from the gravity, or pulling power, of the Sun. Gravity keeps them on an elliptical, or oval-shaped, course called an orbit. It takes the Earth 365 days, 6 hours, 9 minutes and 10 seconds to complete one orbit of the Sun. We call each period of 365 days a "year." Every four years we add up the extra time and put another day into the calendar. This makes a "leap year" of 366 days. As the Earth travels in its orbit, it rotates, or spins around. One rotation takes almost a day—23 hours, 56 minutes and 4 seconds.

THE SOLAR SYSTEM

Nine planets travel around the Sun. Smaller bodies, known as moons, orbit seven of the planets. The planets, moons, chunks of rock, streams of dust, and clouds of gas that orbit the Sun make up the Solar System. The planets are Mercury, Venus, Earth, Mars, Jupiter, Saturn, Uranus, Neptune, and Pluto. To remember their order from the Sun, you can learn the phrase: My Very Easy Method—Just Set Up Nine Planets!

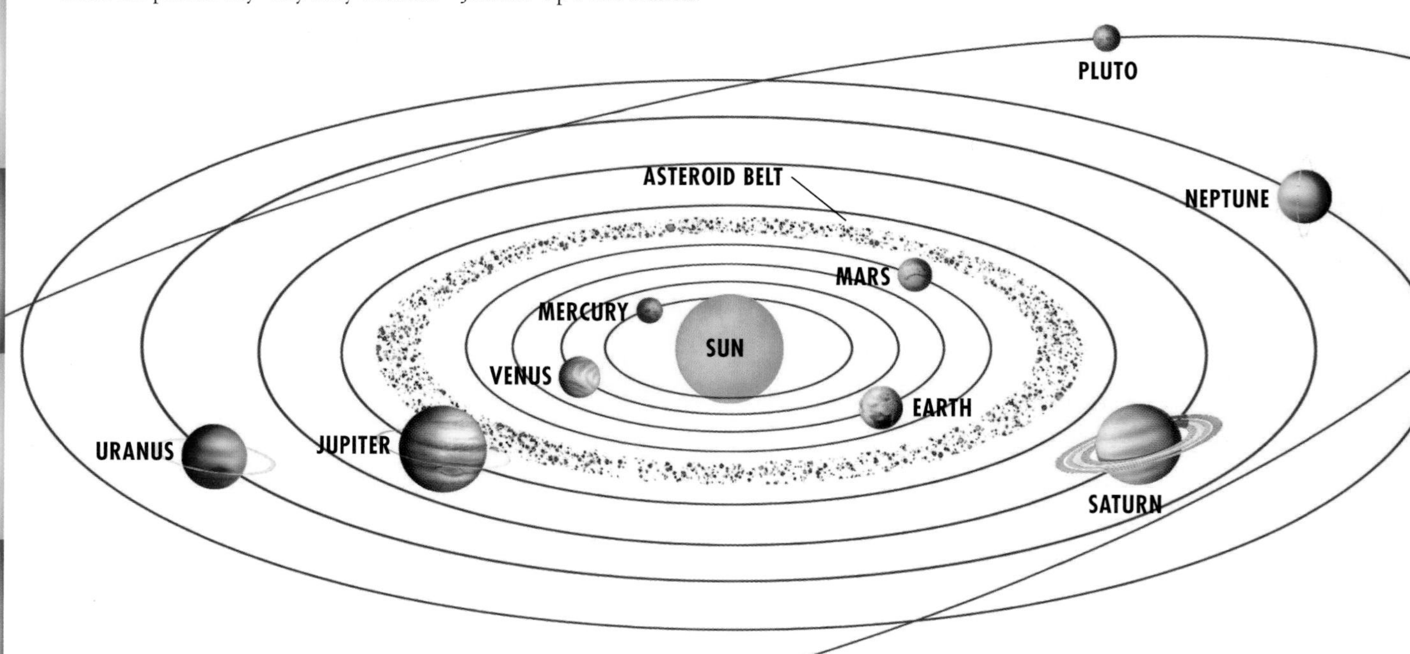
PLUTO
ASTEROID BELT
NEPTUNE
MARS
MERCURY
SUN
VENUS
EARTH
URANUS
JUPITER
SATURN

THE EARTH IN SPACE

Seen from space, Earth is colored blue, brown and white. The blue is the color of the oceans, which cover 71 percent of the planet's surface. The brown is the color of the landmasses, big areas of dry land. People divide these into seven continents, North America, South America, Europe, Asia, Africa, Oceania, and Antarctica. The regions around the North and South Poles are always covered in thick ice.

White clouds swirl around the Earth. They are formed by water droplets and ice crystals. The clouds hang in the atmosphere, the layer of air which surrounds our planet. Air is a mixture of gases. They are nitrogen, oxygen, carbon dioxide, argon, and water vapor. Oxygen is the gas which allows us to breathe and keeps us alive.

INSIDE OUR PLANET

CRUST
MANTLE
OUTER CORE
INNER CORE

The surface of the Earth is called the crust. Its rock may be about thirty kilometers thick under the continents but as little as five kilometers thick beneath the oceans. The crust is cracked into sections called plates, which rest on the mantle. This layer of rock is partly solid and partly melted into a semi-solid, red-hot, gooey mass. The center of the Earth is called the core. The outer core is molten iron, cobalt and nickel. The inner core is solid iron.

WHY DO WE HAVE SEASONS?

The spinning Earth does not move in an upright position. It is tilted. During the year, Earth's position in relation to the Sun changes. When the northern hemisphere (above the Equator) is nearest to the Sun, it has summer. At the same time, the southern hemisphere (below the Equator) is farthest from the Sun and has winter. As Earth continues its orbit, the southern hemisphere tilts towards the Sun, and has summer. The northern hemisphere has winter. The Earth's tropical regions remain at a steady distance from the Sun. The temperature does not change much, but the tropics have dry and wet seasons.

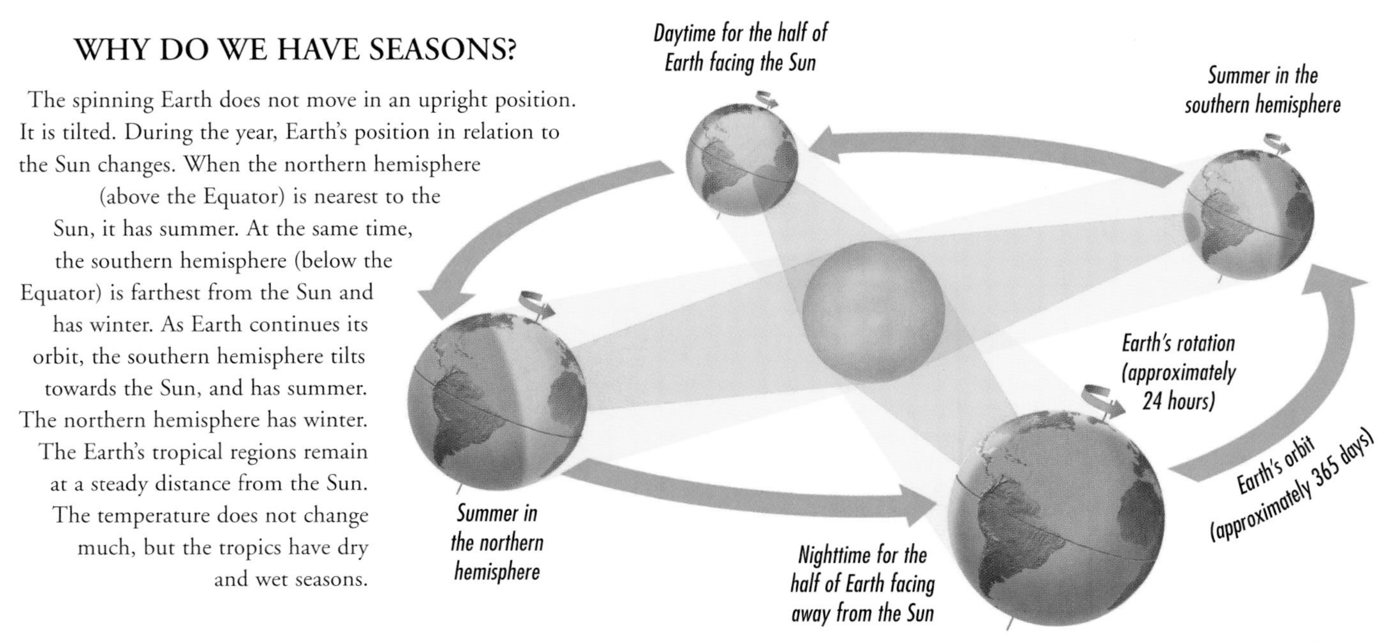
Daytime for the half of Earth facing the Sun
Summer in the southern hemisphere
Earth's rotation (approximately 24 hours)
Earth's orbit (approximately 365 days)
Summer in the northern hemisphere
Nighttime for the half of Earth facing away from the Sun

MAKING MAPS

Maps are plans we make of the Earth's surface. They can show coastlines and oceans, mountains and plains, rivers and lakes. They can show villages, towns, countries, or borders. Maps can also show other useful information, such as population, vegetation, ocean currents, or climate. A criss-cross grid is normally drawn over a map. The grid lines are given numbers or letters, which are used to find any particular spot. On many maps the grid lines show degrees of longitude (north-south) and latitude (east-west).

CARTOGRAPHERS

Map-making, or cartography, is an ancient skill. It requires accurate measurement of landscapes, effective projections, and clear design. Maps were once drawn out, colored in, and labeled carefully by hand. Today, computers may be programmed with a variety of projections and very precise measurements. Data about place names or borders can be constantly updated. This makes it possible for cartographers to produce all kinds of maps at high speed.

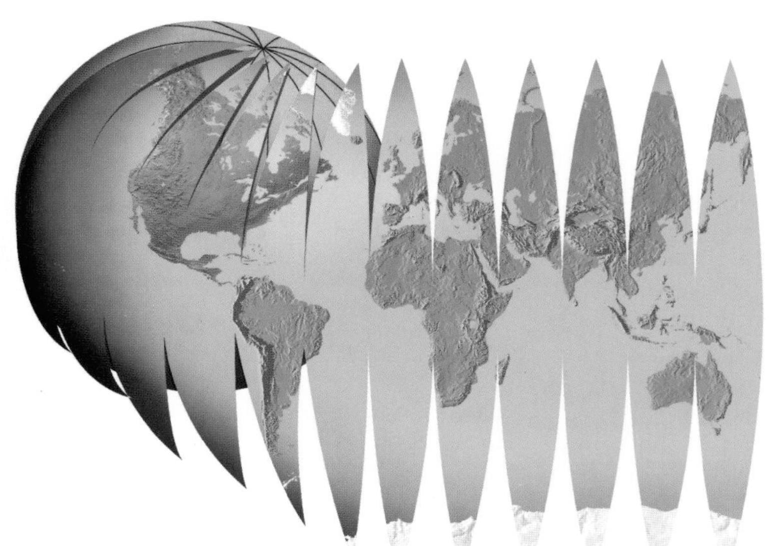

PEELING THE WORLD

The world is round. It has three dimensions, length, breadth and depth. It can be shown accurately on a globe. However, in an atlas a map is flat. It has only two dimensions, length and breadth. So making a map is a bit like having to peel an orange and lay the skin out flat.

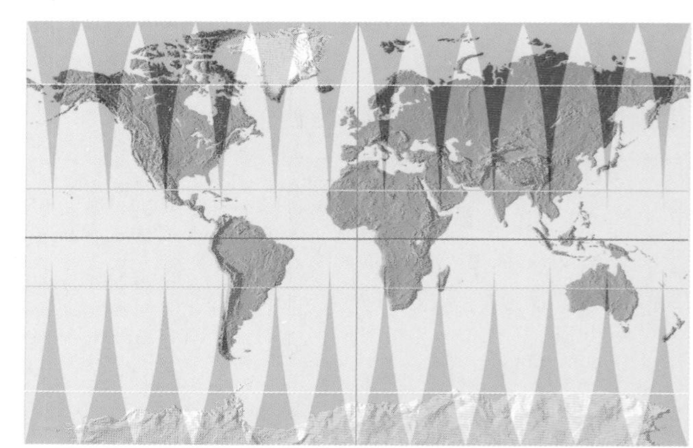

MAP PROJECTIONS

Map-makers have invented many clever ways of converting the curved surface of Earth into a flat image. These are called projections. Projections distort or stretch the true image, but even so they can be accurate enough to be useful. In some projections, the lines of latitude and longitude are matched up to a grid drawn onto imaginary shapes such as cylinders or cones.

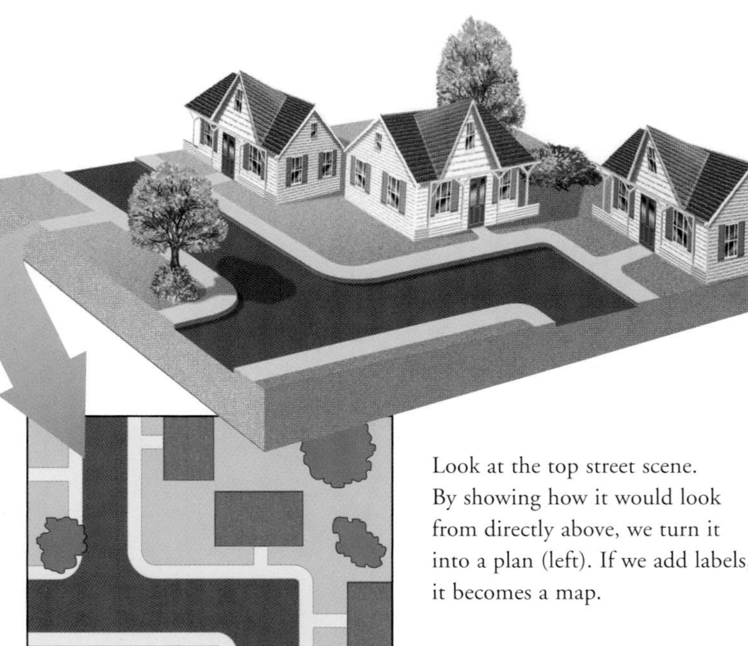

Look at the top street scene. By showing how it would look from directly above, we turn it into a plan (left). If we add labels, it becomes a map.

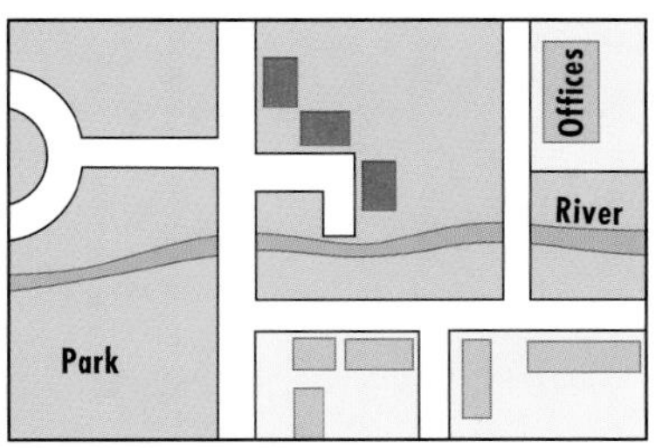
Offices
River
Park

Looking down from a greater height, the map now appears on a smaller scale. Streets and buildings appear as rectangles and lines. Colors show how land is used. This is a street plan.

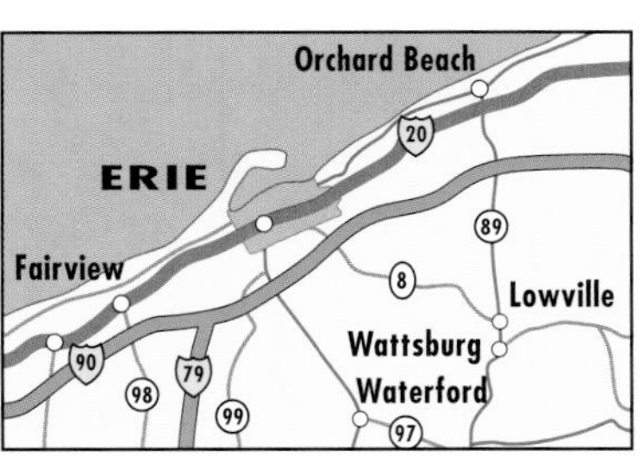
Orchard Beach
ERIE
Fairview
Lowville
Wattsburg
Waterford
20
89
8
90
98
79
99
97

Zoom back to a smaller scale, and we can now see road networks and a lake. Towns are shown by a dot. Map-makers use all sorts of symbols to show different features.

Lake Ontario
NEW YORK
Syracuse
Rochester
Albany
Buffalo
Erie
Scranton
PENNSYLVANIA
Harrisburg
Pittsburgh
Baltimore
Washington
Annapolis
MARYLAND
WEST
Concord
MASSACHUSETTS
Boston
Cape Cod
Providence
Hartford
RHODE ISLAND
CONNECTICUT
New York
NEW JERSEY
Trenton
Philadelphia
Wilmington
Dover
DELAWARE
ATLANTI
OCEAN

Zoom back again. We can now see the whole region. This map shows the northeastern United States, state borders and cities. It also shows physical relief, giving an impression of mountains and landscape.

UNITED
STATES OF
AMERICA
GULF OF
MEXICO
MEXICO
CUBA

Zoom back again. The image of the whole of the United States mainland now comes into view, showing coastlines and national land borders. What uses might you find for a large-scale map? What uses for medium-scale and small-scale maps?

IMAGES FROM SPACE

The Earth's surface may be surveyed from land, sea or air. Accurate measurements can also be taken from satellites in space. This space image shows the continent of Africa.

MEASURING DISTANCE

Atlases and maps normally indicate the scale of the map. They may have a bar like the one below, which compares the distance on the map with the real distance, in kilometers or miles.

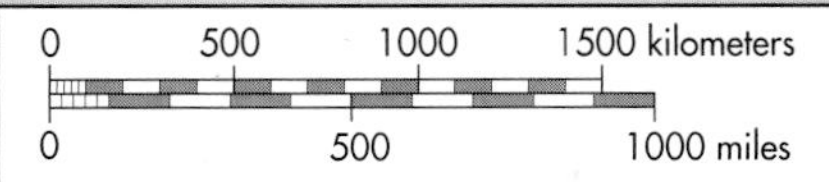
0
500
1000
1500 kilometers
0
500
1000 miles

On this scale 36 mm equals 1,500 kilometers and $1\frac{9}{16}$ inches equals 1,000 miles. Using a ruler you can measure the distance between two points.

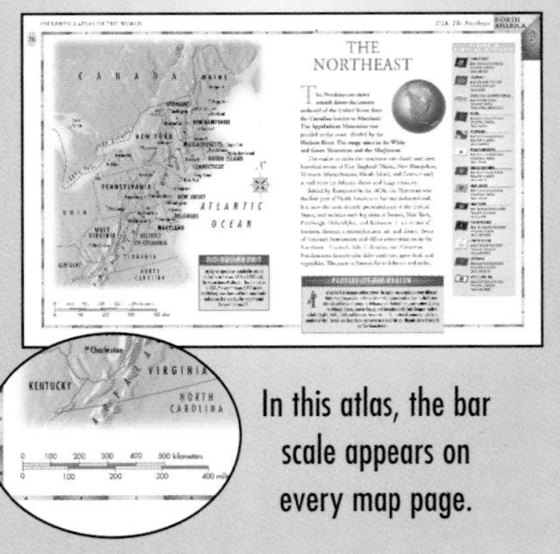
THE
NORTHEAST
ATLANTIC
OCEAN
KENTUCKY
VIRGINIA
NORTH
CAROLINA

In this atlas, the bar scale appears on every map page.

OUR WORLD: POLITICAL

Political maps are ones that show nations, territories, borders, states and capital cities. The number of countries in the world changes often. Large countries divide into smaller ones. Small countries link up to form larger ones. Countries which rule themselves are called independent nations. Countries ruled by others are usually known as dependencies, colonies or overseas territories. Within a single country there may be a mixture of peoples, languages, customs, and religions. Many countries join together to form political, regional or economic unions. Most countries are members of the United Nations (UN). This is an organization which tries to keep the world a peaceful, healthy and prosperous place.

ALASKA
CANADA
UNITED STATES OF AMERICA
MEXICO
GULF OF MEXICO
HAWAII
CUBA
DOMINICAN REPUBLIC
JAMAICA
HAITI
PUERTO RICO
BELIZE
GUATEMALA
HONDURAS
CARIBBEAN SEA
EL SALVADOR
NICARAGUA
COSTA RICA
PANAMA
TRINIDAD & TOBAGO
VENEZUELA
GUYANA
SURINAME
FRENCH GUIANA
COLOMBIA
GALAPAGOS IS
ECUADOR
PACIFIC OCEAN
BRAZIL
PERU
BOLIVIA
PARAGUAY
CHILE
URUGUAY
ARGENTINA
FALKLAND/MALVINAS ISLANDS
NORTH ATLANTIC OCEAN
ARCTIC OCEAN
GREENLAND (KALAALLIT NUNAAT)

RUSSIAN FEDERATION
ARCTIC CIRCLE
FINLAND
NORWAY
SWEDEN
ESTONIA
LATVIA
LITHUANIA
DENMARK
RUSSIA
BELARUS
UNITED KINGDOM
IRELAND
NETHERLANDS
POLAND
UKRAINE
BELGIUM
GERMANY
CZECH REP.
SLOVAK REP.
LUXEMBOURG
AUSTRIA
HUNGARY
MOLDOVA
SWITZERLAND
SLOVENIA
ROMANIA
FRANCE
CROATIA
SERBIA
BOSNIA-HERZEGOVINA
MONTENEGRO
BULGARIA
BLACK SEA
GEORGIA
ANDORRA
MACEDONIA
ARMENIA
AZERBAIJAN
PORTUGAL
SPAIN
ITALY
ALBANIA
GREECE
TURKEY
MEDITERRANEAN SEA
TUNISIA
CYPRUS
SYRIA
LEBANON
ISRAEL
JORDAN
IRAQ
IRAN
KAZAKHSTAN
MONGOLIA
UZBEKISTAN
KYRGYZSTAN
TURKMENISTAN
TAJIKISTAN
AFGHANISTAN
CHINA
NORTH KOREA
SOUTH KOREA
JAPAN
TROPIC OF CANCER
MOROCCO
ALGERIA
LIBYA
EGYPT
KUWAIT
SAUDI ARABIA
QATAR
UNITED ARAB EMIRATES
PAKISTAN
NEPAL
BHUTAN
BANGLADESH
INDIA
TAIWAN
PACIFIC OCEAN
MAURITANIA
MALI
NIGER
CHAD
SUDAN
OMAN
ERITREA
YEMEN
ARABIAN SEA
BAY OF BENGAL
BURMA
LAOS
THAILAND
VIETNAM
CAMBODIA
PHILIPPINES
BURKINA FASO
GUINEA
NIGERIA
DJIBOUTI
SOMALIA
IVORY COAST
GHANA
TOGO
BENIN
CENTRAL AFRICAN REPUBLIC
ETHIOPIA
LIBERIA
CAMEROON
SRI LANKA
BRUNEI
MALAYSIA
SINGAPORE
EQUATORIAL GUINEA
GABON
REPUBLIC OF CONGO
DEMOCRATIC REPUBLIC OF CONGO
UGANDA
KENYA
RWANDA
BURUNDI
TANZANIA
EQUATOR
INDIAN OCEAN
INDONESIA
PAPUA NEW GUINEA
SOLOMON ISLANDS
ANGOLA
ZAMBIA
MALAWI
MOZAMBIQUE
NAMIBIA
ZIMBABWE
BOTSWANA
MADAGASCAR
MAURITIUS
RÉUNION
VANUATU
FIJI
NEW CALEDONIA
AUSTRALIA
SOUTH ATLANTIC OCEAN
SWAZILAND
LESOTHO
SOUTH AFRICA
TROPIC OF CAPRICORN
NEW ZEALAND
SOUTHERN OCEAN
ANTARCTIC CIRCLE
ANTARCTICA

FINDING PLACES

Look up the place you want to find in the index at the back of the atlas. There you will see a letter and number code, and also a page number. Turn to the correct page and look for the number and letter on the grid at the edges of the page. Follow the two tracks with your fingers. You will find your location in the region where they meet.

OUR WORLD: PHYSICAL

Physical maps are ones that show mountains, rivers, lakes, and other natural features. The landmasses are shaped by great movements of the continental plates underneath them, by volcanoes, and by earthquakes. Mountain ranges are pushed up high. They fold over and slip and slide. They are worn down again, or eroded, by rivers, oceans, glaciers, wind, and frost. The climate turns some regions of the world into dry deserts, into wildernesses of ice, or marshy wetlands. The vegetation changes with the climate too, creating conifer forests, woodlands, grasslands, or tropical rainforests.

ARCTIC OCEAN
GREENL
GULF OF ALASKA
ROCKY MOUNTAINS
NORTH AMERICA
NORTH ATLANT
OCEAN
GULF OF MEXICO
CARIBBEAN SEA
AMAZON BASIN
ANDES
SOUTH AMERICA
PACIFIC OCEAN

DID YOU KNOW?

Look at a map of South America and a map of West Africa. The two landmasses could fit together like pieces of a jigsaw puzzle. That is because about 100 million years ago they really were joined together. Since then, the continents have drifted apart, separated by the widening Atlantic Ocean.

J
K
L
M
N
O
P
1
2
3
4
5
6
7
8
N
SIBERIA
URAL MOUNTAINS
ARCTIC CIRCLE
EUROPE
ALPS
ASIA
GOBI DESERT
BLACK SEA
MEDITERRANEAN SEA
HIMALAYAS
PLATEAU OF TIBET
PACIFIC OCEAN
TROPIC OF CANCER
SAHARA
SAHEL
RED SEA
ARABIAN PENINSULA
ARABIAN SEA
BAY OF BENGAL
AFRICA
EQUATOR
INDIAN OCEAN
KALAHARI DESERT
OUTH
LANTIC
CEAN
OCEANIA
TROPIC OF CAPRICORN
SOUTHERN OCEAN
ANTARCTIC CIRCLE
ANTARCTICA

MAP KEY

Certain symbols appear on the maps in this book. These symbols represent cities and towns; country borders and geographical features. Here each symbol shows what it represents.

VEGETATION

Mountains | Ice | Forest | Grassland | Desert | Tundra

- Cities & major towns
- Capital cities
- Lakes, seas & oceans
- Rivers
- State & provincial borders
- Country borders
- Mountains

NORTH AMERICA

A mask used by the Iroquois peoples of the American Northeast to turn away unkind spirits.

The North American continent lies between the Pacific and Atlantic Oceans. It stretches south from the Arctic ice pack to the warm lands of Central America. The Bering Strait, only 85 kilometers (53 miles) wide, separates Alaska from the Siberian region of Asia.

Arctic North America is made up of icy plains called tundra. Great forests cross the north, giving way toward the south to milder regions—temperate woodlands and prairie grasslands. There are hot deserts in the southwest, a massive mountain range—the Rocky Mountains—running from north to south, and lush tropical forests in the southernmost region.

North America includes Canada, the United States of America, Mexico, and the countries of Central America—from Guatemala through Panama. The continent also includes Greenland (a self-governing territory of Denmark), the tiny French islands of St.-Pierre and Miquelon, and the many islands of the Caribbean Sea.

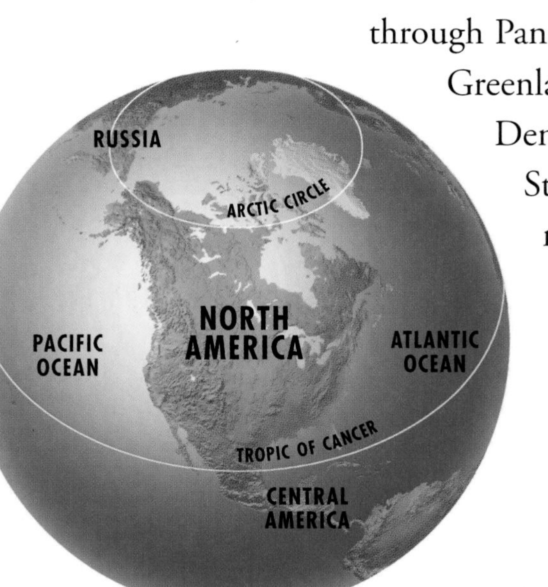
RUSSIA
ARCTIC CIRCLE
PACIFIC OCEAN
NORTH AMERICA
ATLANTIC OCEAN
TROPIC OF CANCER
CENTRAL AMERICA

THE PEOPLING OF NORTH AMERICA

Nobody is sure exactly when the first humans entered the Americas, but between 30,000 and 12,000 years ago, waves of hunters crossed into North America from Siberia. At that time the continents of Asia and America were probably joined by a bridge of land. Later, ancestors of the Inuit peoples came from Asia, and settled on Arctic coasts. Inuit, Native Americans, and First Peoples still live in Canada, Greenland, the United States and the rest of North America.

ARCTIC OCEAN
SIBERIA
CHUKCHI SEA
St. Lawrence Island
BERING SEA
Alaska (USA)
ALEUTIAN ISLANDS
Kodiak Island
GULF OF ALASKA
QUEEN CHARLOTTE ISLANDS
VANCOUVER ISLAND
BEAUFORT SEA
QUEEN ELIZABETH ISLANDS
Ellesmere Island
GREENLAND (KALAALLIT NUNAAT)
North Magnetic Pole
Victoria Island
Baffin Bay
Baffin Island
LABRADOR SEA
Hudson Bay
Belcher Is.
Labrador
Newfoundland
CANADA
St.-Pierre & Miquelon
KAUAI
OAHU
MOLOKAI
MAUI
HAWAII
UNITED STATES OF AMERICA
BERMUDA
ATLANTIC OCEAN
BAHAMA IS.
GULF OF MEXICO
DOMINICAN REPUBLIC
CUBA
HAITI
PUERTO RICO
MEXICO
PACIFIC OCEAN
JAMAICA
BELIZE
CARIBBEAN SEA
GUATEMALA
HONDURAS
EL SALVADOR
NICARAGUA
VENEZUELA
COSTA RICA
PANAMA
COLOMBIA
0 500 1000 1500 kilometers
0 500 1000 miles

IN YOSEMITE

Yosemite Valley, in California, attracts many climbers and walkers. It was shaped by the Merced River and by glaciers that ground their way through the region about 10,000 years ago. Sheer walls of granite rise from the valley floor. Yosemite became a protected area in 1864. It was made a national park 26 years later.

DID YOU KNOW?

The northern half of North America is full of holes. Canada and the northern United States have been scraped and broken up into ragged shores and islands, and pitted with many thousands of lakes. This is the result of great movements of ice, which advanced southward in the last great Ice Age, only to retreat about 10,000 years ago.

THE NEWCOMERS

About 1,000 years ago, Viking seafarers from northern Europe briefly visited Labrador and Newfoundland. Europeans explored and began to settle in North America in the 1500s and 1600s. The Spanish, French, Dutch, and British founded colonies on the eastern and southern sides of the continent. It was the start of a flood of settlement that almost overwhelmed the native inhabitants.

NORTH AMERICA

North America is the third largest continent in the world. Its Arctic regions are very sparsely populated. Much of the continent is famed for its natural beauty, but over three-quarters of Canadians and Americans, and almost two-thirds of people in Mexico and Central America live in towns and cities. The continent is rich in resources, but the standard of living can differ greatly from region to region.

• GENERAL FACTS •

HIGHEST POINT
MT. MCKINLEY, DENALI, 6,194 M (20,321 FT), ALASKA, U.S.A.

LOWEST POINT
BADWATER, DEATH VALLEY, -86 M (-282 FT), CALIFORNIA, U.S.A.

LONGEST RIVER
MISSISSIPPI-MISSOURI RIVER, 6,019 KM (3,740 MI), U.S.A.

BIGGEST LAKE
LAKE SUPERIOR, 82,409 SQ KM (31,818 SQ MI), U.S.A.-CANADA

HIGHEST WATERFALL
RIBBON FALL, YOSEMITE, 491 M (1,611 FT), CALIFORNIA, U.S.A.

BIGGEST ISLAND
GREENLAND, 2,175,600 SQ KM (840,000 SQ MI), ARCTIC OCEAN-ATLANTIC OCEAN

BIGGEST DESERT
GREAT AMERICAN (GREAT BASIN-MOJAVE-SONORA-CHIHUAHUA), 800,000 SQ KM (308,880 SQ MI), U.S.A.-MEXICO

POPULATION OF CONTINENT
475 MILLION (1999)

MOST POPULOUS COUNTRY
UNITED STATES OF AMERICA, 272.5 MILLION (1999)

MOST DENSELY POPULATED COUNTRY
PUERTO RICO, 433 PER SQ KM (167 PER SQ MILE)

MOST POPULOUS CITY
MEXICO CITY, MEXICO, 20 MILLION (1998)

POPULATION LIVING IN CITIES
72 PERCENT

INFANT MORTALITY
7 DEATHS PER 1,000 CHILDREN UNDER AGE 1

LIFE EXPECTANCY
MALE 70 YEARS; FEMALE 75 YEARS

WEALTH
GROSS DOMESTIC PRODUCT PER PERSON U.S. $15,630 (1997)

LITERACY RATE
88 PERCENT MALE; 84 PERCENT FEMALE

• VEGETATION •

The surface of the Arctic tundra, frozen over for most of the year, springs to life during the short Arctic summer. To the south, vast evergreen forests extend across Canada. On either side of the U.S.-Canadian border lie prairie grasslands. Deserts occupy the southwest. Mountain vegetation runs down the Rockies. Woodlands in the eastern states change color in the Fall. The south is hot and humid—a land of deltas, swamps and bayous. Northern Mexico has deserts. The rainforest zones of the south extends through Central America, although logging has destroyed much of the original forest cover.

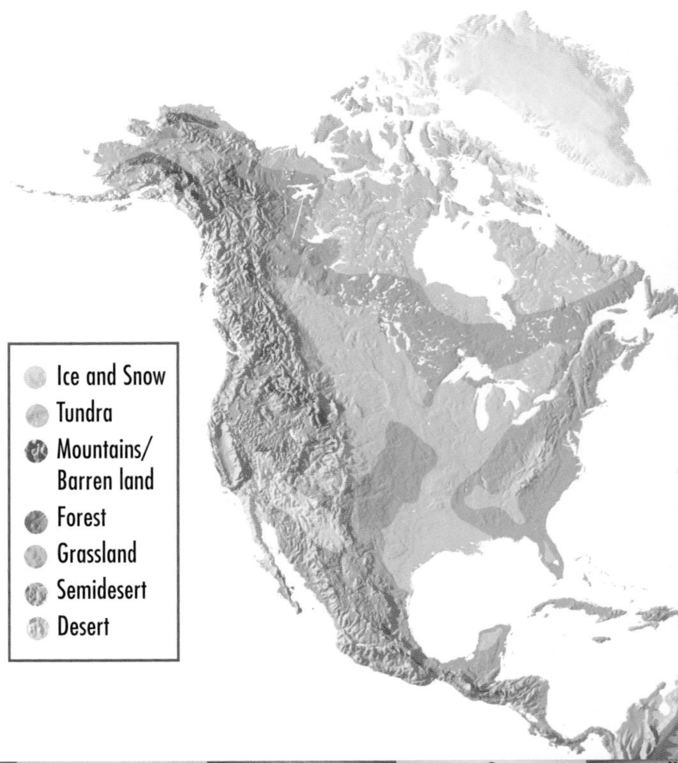

Ice and Snow
Tundra
Mountains/Barren land
Forest
Grassland
Semidesert
Desert

• LANGUAGE •

In the northern lands of North America, English is the most widely spoken language, with French as a major language in Canada. Native American and Inuit languages are spoken by small communities, and various Asian and European languages may also be heard. In Mexico and Central America, Spanish is most common. Some Caribbean islands are Spanish-speaking, while many others use dialects of English or French.

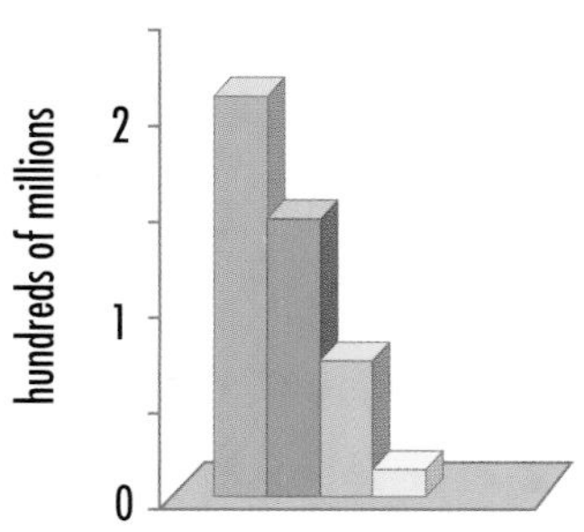
hundreds of millions
2
1
0

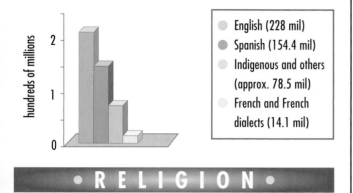

- English (228 mil)
- Spanish (154.4 mil)
- Indigenous and others (approx. 78.5 mil)
- French and French dialects (14.1 mil)

• RELIGION •

Christianity is followed by the great majority of North Americans, with Roman Catholic, Protestant, Orthodox, and many other Churches. Judaism, Islam, and other faiths have their followers also. In some regions, especially in Central America, indigenous beliefs overlap with Christianity. In the Caribbean islands, some African traditions also survive.

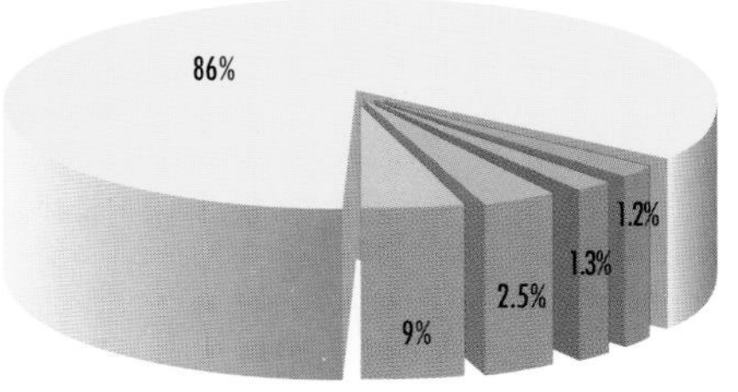
86%
9%
2.5%
1.3%
1.2%

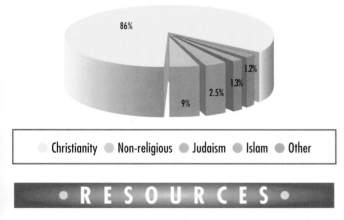

Christianity • Non-religious • Judaism • Islam • Other

• CLIMATE •

North America extends into the bitterly cold regions of the Arctic. Much of Canada experiences harsh winters. The United States' climate varies greatly according to latitude, altitude and distance from the sea. Hot summers and cold winters are common in the Midwest, Great Lakes and Central Plains. The South, including Central America, is hot and humid, with hurricanes common along the coast.

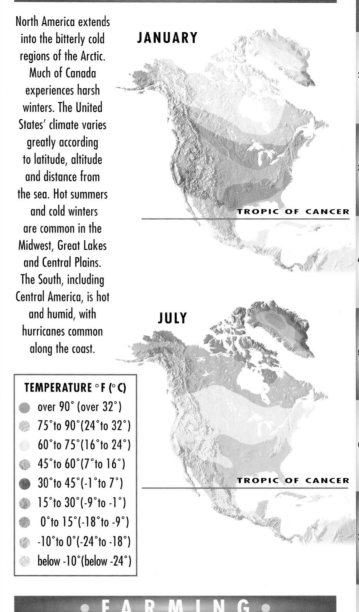

JANUARY
TROPIC OF CANCER

JULY
TROPIC OF CANCER

TEMPERATURE °F (°C)
- over 90° (over 32°)
- 75° to 90° (24° to 32°)
- 60° to 75° (16° to 24°)
- 45° to 60° (7° to 16°)
- 30° to 45° (-1° to 7°)
- 15° to 30° (-9° to -1°)
- 0° to 15° (-18° to -9°)
- -10° to 0° (-24° to -18°)
- below -10° (below -24°)

• RESOURCES •

Canada is the world's largest producer of zinc, and a major supplier of lead, copper, nickel, and oil. Copper and zinc mining are major industries in the United States, which also produces oil, iron ore, bauxite, and uranium. Timber is a vital resource in both Canada and the U.S.A., and the continent's many lakes and rivers provide hydroelectric power.

COPPER: *Canada, Mexico, Nicaragua, U.S.A.*

FISHERIES: *Greenland, Canada, Mexico, U.S.A.*

OIL AND NATURAL GAS: *Canada, Mexico, Trinidad, U.S.A.*

TIMBER: *Belize, Canada, Honduras, U.S.A.*

ZINC: *Canada, Mexico, Nicaragua, U.S.A.*

• FARMING •

Wheat and cattle ranching are the mainstay of the prairies, on both sides of the Canadian-U.S. border. The varied climate of the United States makes it possible to grow many different crops, from grapevines and citrus fruit in California, to corn and soybeans in the Midwest. Bananas, coffee, and sugarcane are grown in Central America and the Caribbean.

BANANAS: *Belize, Honduras, Windward Islands*

CATTLE: *Canada, Nicaragua, U.S.A.*

CORN: *Canada, U.S.A.*

SUGARCANE: *Barbados, Belize, Guatemala, Jamaica, Mexico, U.S.A.*

WHEAT: *Canada, U.S.A.*

NORTH AMERICA: *The Melting Pot*

North America has been settled by people from so many parts of the world that it has sometimes been called a "melting pot" of cultures. The Inuit are a people of the Arctic. They have their own territory in Canada, called Nunavut, and self-rule in Greenland. Other indigenous groups may be divided into various geographical areas—Subarctic, Northeast, Southeast, Plains, Plateau and Great Basin, Northwest, Southwest, California, Mexico, Mesoamerica (and Central America), and Caribbean coasts. Scattered, persecuted and attacked since the arrival of European settlers, they have nonetheless survived and protected their traditions.

European settlers in the 1500s and 1600s included the Spanish, French, English, and Dutch. The British eventually gained control of Canada, where there remains a large population of French descent. Farther south, the colonists broke away from British rule to found the United States of America in 1776. This new country grew and grew, purchasing or conquering territory from native people and from the French, Spanish, Mexicans, and Russians. In the 1600s and 1700s many Africans were brought to North America as slave labor. They won their freedom only gradually, beginning in Haiti in the 1790s and ending in the United States in the 1860s. From the 1820s into the twenty-first century, millions of newcomers poured into North America from Europe and the Far East.

POLYNESIAN AMERICANS

Hawaii lies far to the west of the American mainland. Hundreds of years ago it was settled by Polynesians, a seafaring people who colonized a vast area of the Pacific Ocean. The volcanic islands attract many tourists, who come to view the natural beauty and such local customs as the dance shown here.

SAGUARO LAND

The saguaro cactus is a symbol of the Sonoran Desert around Tucson, Arizona. The world's biggest cactus, it grows to over 15 meters (50 feet) and can live more than 200 years. With its spreading roots, the cactus is designed to soak up every last drop of moisture from a very harsh environment. Water is stored in its fleshy stem and branches, which are protected by sharp spines.

GROWING UP THE HARD WAY

In Mexico and its Central American neighbors, a few people are wealthy and many are very poor. These are lands of cactus and dusty roads, of green forested highlands and humid coastal lagoons, of small farms and large, often polluted cities. Some young children face problems getting proper health care, good food or education.

IN THE CANADIAN ROCKIES

Banff National Park, in Alberta, was the first national park in Canada. It was established in 1887. It has some of the finest mountain scenery in all the Rockies. Snow-capped peaks tower over blue lakes and conifer forests. Backpackers can explore over 1,500 kilometers (930 miles) of trails.

NATIVE AMERICANS

The Shoshone peoples and the Bannock are Native Americans of the Great Basin. At the height of their power, in about 1800, the Shoshone language could be heard from the Northern Plains almost all the way down to Mexico.

THRILLS ON ICE

The rules for ice hockey were first drawn up in the Canadian city of Montreal in 1879. This fast, tough sport quickly became the national game of Canada, and spread to the United States and other lands. Today, both Canadian and American teams compete in the North American National Hockey League (NHL).

COUNTRIES & DEPENDENCIES

CANADA
AREA: 9,976,185 SQ KM (3,851,805 SQ MI)
POPULATION: 30.6 MILLION
CAPITAL: OTTAWA

GREENLAND (KALAALLIT NUNAAT)
OVERSEAS TERRITORY OF DENMARK
AREA: 2,175,600 SQ KM (839, 999 SQ MI)
POPULATION: 57,000
CAPITAL: GODTHÅB (NUUK)

ST.-PIERRE & MIQUELON
FRENCH DEPENDENCY
AREA: 241 SQ KM (93 SQ MI)
POPULATION: 6,500
CAPITAL: ST. PIERRE

CANADA & GREENLAND

Greenland is a dependency of Denmark, but since 1993 it has controlled all its own affairs apart from foreign policy and defense. Most of its people are of Inuit or mixed Danish-Inuit descent.

The Canadian nation was created by European invaders who explored, traded with, and then occupied the land of the First Peoples. These included the Inuit of the Arctic and the Native American peoples whose land stretched far to the south, across what is now the United States border. The French and the British both seized large areas, but from 1763 Britain came to rule all Canada. Canadian territory gradually spread westward across the prairies to the Pacific.

Canada became completely independent in 1931. Canada's Quebec province remains a stronghold of French language and culture. Many Quebecois campaign for independence. The large cities of modern Canada are home to people of many other ethnic groups, including Ukrainian, Dutch, German, Vietnamese, and Afro-Caribbean.

Canadians share many interests with their American neighbors, but are proud of their own separate heritage. Canada is a major economic power and plays an important part in world affairs.

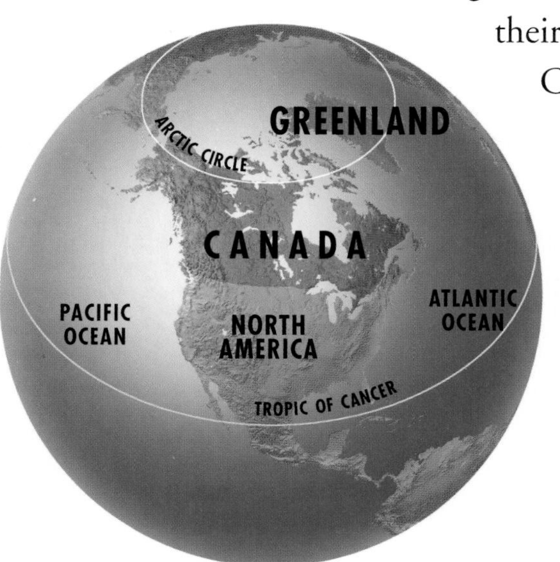
GREENLAND
ARCTIC CIRCLE
CANADA
PACIFIC OCEAN
NORTH AMERICA
ATLANTIC OCEAN
TROPIC OF CANCER

TOTEM POLES

The native peoples of the British Columbian coast carved tall pillars of cedarwood with mythical beings and the badges of their clan, or family group. They are called totem poles. Canada's First Peoples retain many of their ancient traditions.

ARCTIC OCEAN
GREENLAND
(KALAALLIT NUNAAT)
Ellesmere Island
Devon Island
BAFFIN BAY
Davis Strait
Baffin Island
BEAUFORT SEA
Banks Island
Victoria Island
Alaska (U.S.A.)
YUKON TERRITORY
NORTHWEST TERRITORIES
NUNAVUT
CANADA
LABRADOR SEA
HUDSON BAY
NEWFOUNDLAND & LABRADOR
BRITISH COLUMBIA
QUEEN CHARLOTTE ISLANDS
ALBERTA
MANITOBA
QUEBEC
ST.-PIERRE & MIQUELON
Vancouver Island
SASKATCHEWAN
ONTARIO
NEW BRUNSWICK
PRINCE EDWARD ISLAND
NOVA SCOTIA
PACIFIC OCEAN
UNITED STATES OF AMERICA
ATLANTIC OCEAN
0 500 1000 1500 kilometers
0 500 1000 miles
N

DID YOU KNOW?

The leaf on the Canadian flag is that of the maple tree. Canada is famous for its maple syrup, which French Canadians call *sirop d'érable*. It is boiled up from the tree's sticky sap until it is sweet and ready to be poured on pancakes, waffles, or ice cream. Sugar maples grow in the southeast of the country, in Ontario, Quebec, and the Maritimes.

CANADA & GREENLAND

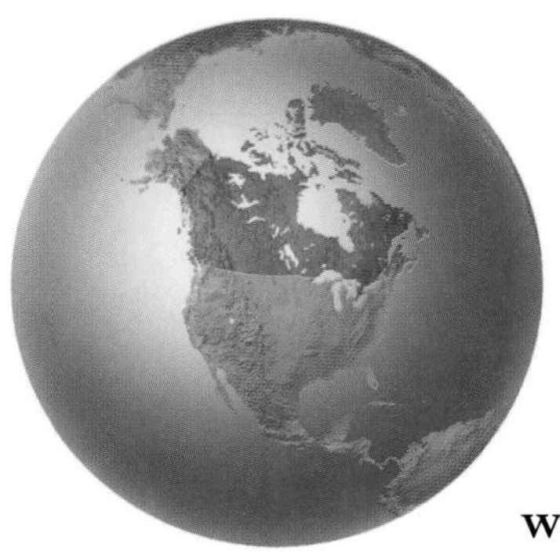

Much of Greenland, the world's biggest island, is an Arctic wilderness. The population lives near the coast, where the climate is milder. Across the Davis Strait lies Canada, the world's second largest country.

The Canadian Arctic is a land of frozen coastlines, ragged islands, and lakes punctured by the great expanse of Hudson Bay. Tundra, mountains, and forests stretch across the north, which is divided into Yukon Territory, Northwest Territories, and Nunavut.

Canada's southern provinces stretch from Vancouver Island in British Columbia to Newfoundland and the "Maritimes" of the Atlantic coast—New Brunswick, Nova Scotia, and Prince Edward Island. In between lie the Rocky Mountains of Alberta and the prairies of Saskatchewan and Manitoba. Ontario, bordering the Great Lakes, is governed from Ottawa (the national capital) and also Toronto (the provincial capital). The St. Lawrence River and Seaway links the Great Lakes with the sea, flowing eastward past Montreal, capital of Quebec province. Canada is a wealthy country, rich in minerals, timber, fish and hydroelectric power for manufacturing. Most of the population lives in the cities of the far south.

CANADIAN PROVINCES & TERRITORIES

ALBERTA

AREA: 638,232 SQ KM (246,421 SQ MI)
POPULATION: 2.97 MILLION
CAPITAL: EDMONTON

BRITISH COLUMBIA

AREA: 829,677 SQ KM (320,338 SQ MI)
POPULATION: 4.02 MILLION
CAPITAL: VICTORIA

MANITOBA

AREA: 547,703 SQ KM (211,468 SQ MI)
POPULATION: 1.14 MILLION
CAPITAL: WINNIPEG

NEW BRUNSWICK

AREA: 71,569 SQ KM (27,633 SQ MI)
POPULATION: 0.76 MILLION
CAPITAL: FREDERICTON

NEWFOUNDLAND & LABRADOR

AREA: 371,634 SQ KM (143,488 SQ MI)
POPULATION: 0.54 MILLION
CAPITAL: ST. JOHN'S

NORTHWEST TERRITORIES

AREA: 1,299,070 SQ KM (501,571 SQ MI)
POPULATION: 41,600
CAPITAL: YELLOWKNIFE

NOVA SCOTIA

AREA: 52,840 SQ KM (20,402 SQ MI)
POPULATION: 0.94 MILLION
CAPITAL: HALIFAX

NUNAVUT

AREA: 1,994,000 SQ KM (769,883 SQ MI)
POPULATION: 27,000
CAPITAL: IQALUIT

ONTARIO

AREA: 916,733 SQ KM (353,951 SQ MI)
POPULATION: 11.5 MILLION
CAPITAL: TORONTO

PRINCE EDWARD ISLAND

AREA: 5,660 SQ KM (2,185 SQ MI)
POPULATION: 138,000
CAPITAL: CHARLOTTETOWN

QUEBEC

AREA: 1,357,811 SQ KM (524,251 SQ MI)
POPULATION: 7.35 MILLION
CAPITAL: QUEBEC

SASKATCHEWAN

AREA: 570,113 SQ KM (220,121 SQ MI)
POPULATION: 1.03 MILLION
CAPITAL: REGINA

YUKON TERRITORY

AREA: 483,450 SQ KM (186,660 SQ MI)
POPULATION: 30,600
CAPITAL: WHITEHORSE

PEOPLES OF THE REGION

Most French-Canadians live in Quebec province, where the chief city is Montreal. Major cities of English-speaking Canada are Toronto and Vancouver. Scattered communites of Inuit live on the coasts of Greenland and in Canada's Nunavut Territory. First Peoples include the Déné group of the sub-Arctic, the Kwakiutl and Haida of British Columbia, and the Ojibwa and Cree of the prairie provinces.

GREENLAND
(KALAALLIT NUNAAT)
ARCTIC OCEAN
BEAUFORT SEA
Ellesmere Island
Devon Island
Banks Island
Victoria Island
BAFFIN BAY
Baffin Island
Davis Strait
Angmagssalik
Godthåb
(Nuuk)
FOXE BASIN
NUNAVUT
Alaska
(U.S.A.)
Dawson
Norman Wells
Great Bear Lake
Fort Norman
YUKON TERRITORY
NORTHWEST TERRITORIES
MACKENZIE MOUNTAINS
Mackenzie
Whitehorse
Yellowknife
Great Slave Lake
Fort Resolution
Fort Smith
Southampton Island
Baker Lake
Hudson Strait
LABRADOR SEA
Nairn
HUDSON BAY
NEWFOUNDLAND
Labrador
Goose Bay
Gander
St. John's
Newfoundland
BRITISH COLUMBIA
Hazelton
Prince Rupert
Prince George
QUEEN CHARLOTTE ISLANDS
Peace
Peace River
SASKATCHEWAN
Churchill
Belcher Islands
CANADA
Edmonton
ALBERTA
MANITOBA
ROCKY MOUNTAINS
Fraser
Vancouver Island
Vancouver
Calgary
Medicine Hat
Prince Albert
Saskatoon
Regina
Lake Winnipeg
Lake Manitoba
Winnipeg
Victoria
PACIFIC OCEAN
JAMES BAY
Fort George
Fort Albany
QUEBEC
ONTARIO
Gulf of St. Lawrence
ST.-PIERRE & MIQUELON
NEW BRUNSWICK
PRINCE EDWARD ISLAND
Charlottetown
Quebec
St. Lawrence River and Seaway
St. John
Halifax
Fredericton
NOVA SCOTIA
Thunder Bay
Lake Superior
Montreal
Ottawa
Lake Michigan
Lake Huron
Toronto
Lake Ontario
Lake Erie
UNITED STATES OF AMERICA
ATLANTIC OCEAN
0
500
1000
1500 kilometers
0
500
1000 miles

DID YOU KNOW?

Canada's Hudson Bay is the largest bay in the world. Its shoreline of 12,268 km (7,623 miles) runs through Nunavut, Manitoba, Ontario, and Quebec. The bay covers an area of about 1,233,000 sq km (476,061 sq miles).

COUNTRIES

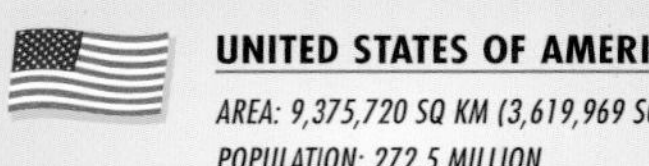

UNITED STATES OF AMERICA

AREA: 9,375,720 SQ KM (3,619,969 SQ MI)
POPULATION: 272.5 MILLION
CAPITAL: WASHINGTON, D.C.

UNITED STATES OF AMERICA

The bald eagle is the national bird of the United States of America.

The United States of America (U.S.A.) is a large country, rich in mineral resources and fertile land. It is a wealthy and very powerful nation. Most United States territory lies between Canada and Mexico and between the Atlantic and Pacific Oceans. However its largest state, Alaska, is an Arctic peninsula on Canada's northwestern border. The state of Hawaii is a group of Pacific islands.

The United States is divided into fifty states, each one represented by a star on the national flag, the "Stars and Stripes." The country has federal government, which means that each state can make its own laws. However, many laws are made nationally, and apply throughout the country. The capital city is Washington, in the federal District of Columbia (D.C.). This is the center of government and home of the president. Each state also has its own capital. The biggest American metropolitan areas are New York, Los Angeles, Chicago, Washington, and San Francisco.

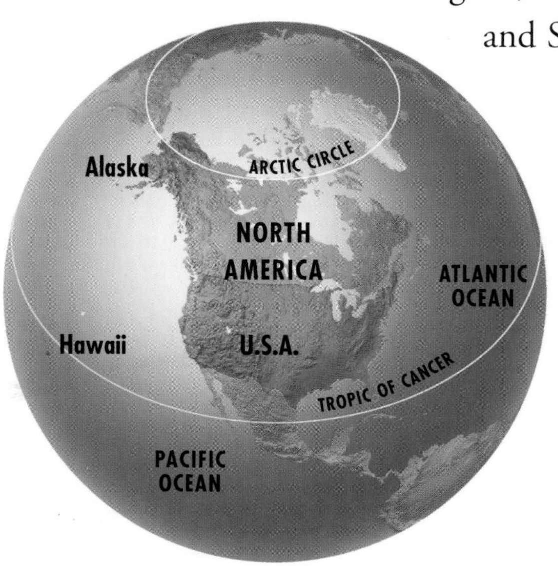
Alaska
ARCTIC CIRCLE
NORTH AMERICA
ATLANTIC OCEAN
Hawaii
U.S.A.
TROPIC OF CANCER
PACIFIC OCEAN

WASHINGTON, D.C.

The Capitol building is the center of federal government in the United States, housing the Senate and the House of Representatives. It towers above the city lights of Washington, D.C., a city of about 600,000 people.

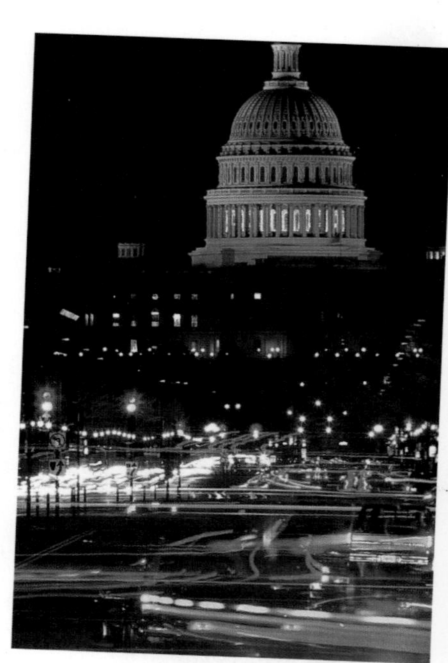

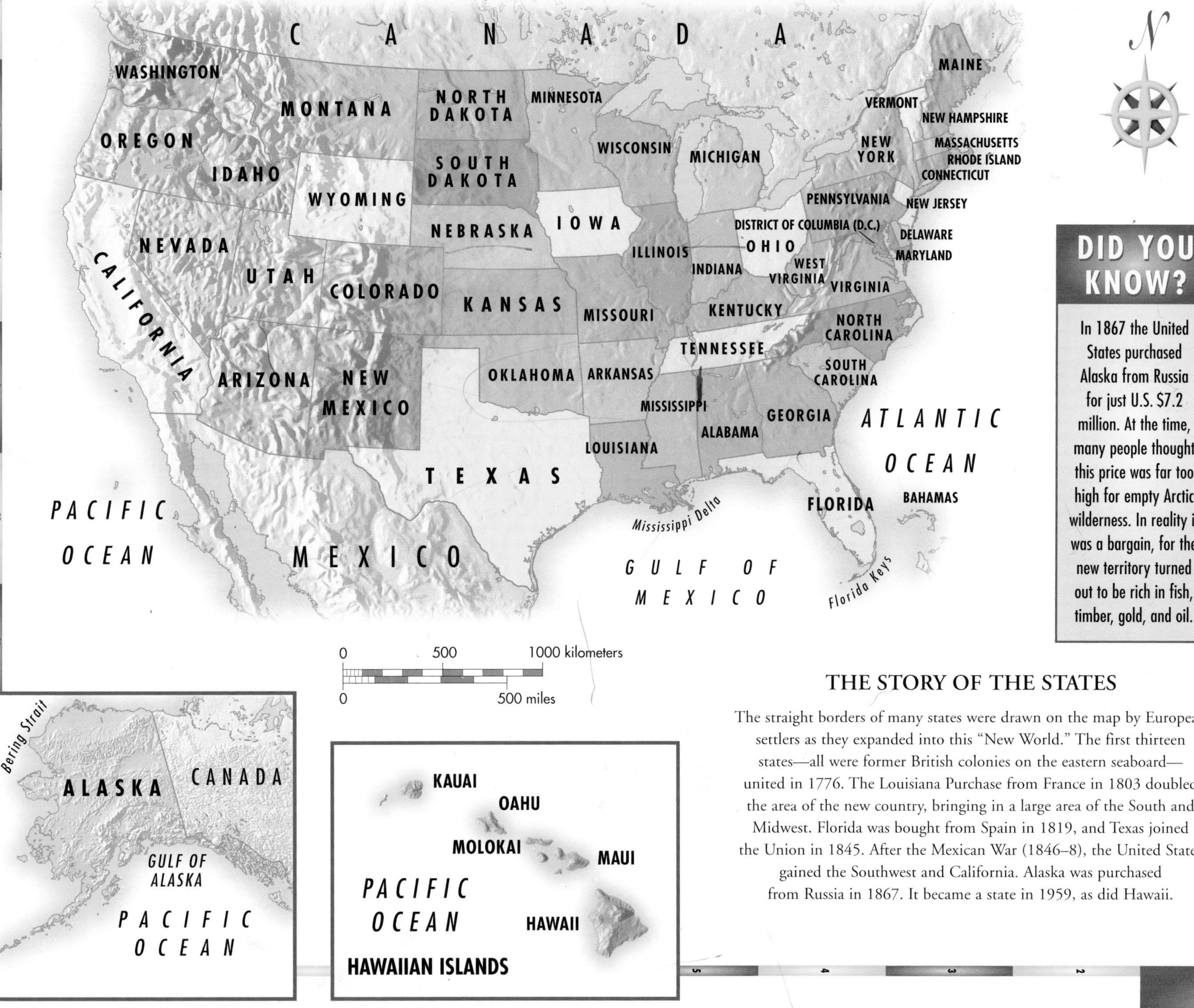
C A N A D A
WASHINGTON
OREGON
IDAHO
MONTANA
WYOMING
NORTH DAKOTA
SOUTH DAKOTA
MINNESOTA
NEBRASKA
IOWA
WISCONSIN
MICHIGAN
NEVADA
UTAH
CALIFORNIA
COLORADO
KANSAS
MISSOURI
ILLINOIS
INDIANA
OHIO
ARIZONA
NEW MEXICO
OKLAHOMA
ARKANSAS
TEXAS
LOUISIANA
MISSISSIPPI
ALABAMA
TENNESSEE
KENTUCKY
GEORGIA
FLORIDA
SOUTH CAROLINA
NORTH CAROLINA
VIRGINIA
WEST VIRGINIA
DISTRICT OF COLUMBIA (D.C.)
PENNSYLVANIA
NEW YORK
VERMONT
NEW HAMPSHIRE
MAINE
MASSACHUSETTS
RHODE ISLAND
CONNECTICUT
NEW JERSEY
DELAWARE
MARYLAND
ATLANTIC OCEAN
BAHAMAS
Florida Keys
GULF OF MEXICO
Mississippi Delta
MEXICO
PACIFIC OCEAN
N
0
500
1000 kilometers
0
500 miles
Bering Strait
ALASKA
CANADA
GULF OF ALASKA
PACIFIC OCEAN
KAUAI
OAHU
MOLOKAI
MAUI
HAWAII
PACIFIC OCEAN
HAWAIIAN ISLANDS

DID YOU KNOW?

In 1867 the United States purchased Alaska from Russia for just U.S. $7.2 million. At the time, many people thought this price was far too high for empty Arctic wilderness. In reality it was a bargain, for the new territory turned out to be rich in fish, timber, gold, and oil.

THE STORY OF THE STATES

The straight borders of many states were drawn on the map by European settlers as they expanded into this "New World." The first thirteen states—all were former British colonies on the eastern seaboard—united in 1776. The Louisiana Purchase from France in 1803 doubled the area of the new country, bringing in a large area of the South and Midwest. Florida was bought from Spain in 1819, and Texas joined the Union in 1845. After the Mexican War (1846–8), the United States gained the Southwest and California. Alaska was purchased from Russia in 1867. It became a state in 1959, as did Hawaii.

CANADA
MAINE
Bangor
Augusta
VERMONT
WHITE MOUNTAINS
GREEN MOUNTAINS
Mt. Washington
Burlington
Portland
Lake Champlain
Montpelier
NEW HAMPSHIRE
Concord
Lake Huron
Lake Ontario
NEW YORK
Boston
Albany
MASSACHUSETTS
Cape Cod
Syracuse
Providence
Nantucket Island
Rochester
Hartford
RHODE ISLAND
Buffalo
Susquehanna
Hudson
CONNECTICUT
Lake Erie
Scranton
Long Island
Erie
New York
PENNSYLVANIA
Trenton
Harrisburg
Philadelphia
NEW JERSEY
Wilmington
Pittsburgh
Dover
ATLANTIC OCEAN
OHIO
Baltimore
Annapolis
DELAWARE
Washington
MARYLAND
WEST VIRGINIA
DISTRICT OF COLUMBIA
Charleston
ALLEGHENY MOUNTAINS
APPALACHIAN MOUNTAINS
VIRGINIA
KENTUCKY
NORTH CAROLINA
N
0 100 200 300 400 500 kilometers
0 100 200 300 400 miles

DID YOU KNOW?

The highest speed ever recorded for wind at the Earth's surface was 371 km/h (231 mph). This was at Mount Washington, New Hampshire, in 1931. The summit towers 1,917 meters (6,288 feet) above forests of birch, sugar maple, and spruce. It is notorious for its storms and heavy winter snowfall.

THE NORTHEAST

The Northeastern states stretch down the eastern seaboard of the United States from the Canadian border to Maryland. The Appalachian Mountains run parallel to the coast, divided by the Hudson River. The range takes in the White and Green Mountains and the Alleghenies.

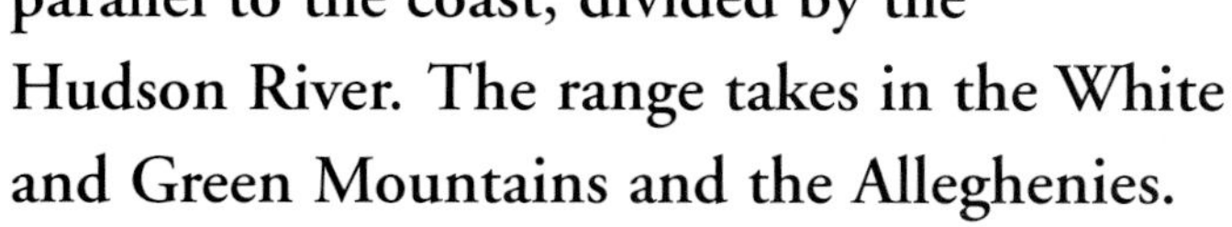

The region includes the temperate woodlands and neat historical towns of New England (Maine, New Hampshire, Vermont, Massachusetts, Rhode Island, and Connecticut) as well as rocky Atlantic shores and foggy estuaries.

Settled by Europeans in the 1600s, the Northeast was the first part of North America to become industrialized. It is now the most densely populated part of the United States, and includes such big cities as Boston, New York, Pittsburgh, Philadelphia, and Baltimore. It is a center of business, finance, communications, art, and theater. Some of America's best-known and oldest universities are in the Northeast—Harvard, Yale, Columbia, and Princeton. Northeastern farmers raise dairy cattle and grow fruit and vegetables. The coast is famous for its lobsters and crabs.

PEOPLES OF THE REGION

When the first European settlers arrived, the region was occupied by many different Native American peoples, including Eastern Algonquian speakers (such as the Eastern Abenaki and the Lenni-Lenape, or Delaware) and Northern Iroquoian speakers (such as the Mohawk, Oneida, Seneca, Cayuga, and Susquehannock). Early European settlers included English, Welsh, Dutch, and Germans. Immigration in the nineteenth century brought large numbers of Irish, Italians, and Jews. Many northeasterners are of African, Hispanic (Latin American), and East Asian descent.

STATES & FEDERAL DISTRICT

CONNECTICUT
AREA: 12,997 SQ KM (5,018 SQ MI)
POPULATION: 3.3 MILLION
CAPITAL: HARTFORD

DELAWARE
AREA: 5,328 SQ KM (2,057 SQ MI)
POPULATION: 0.74 MILLION
CAPITAL: DOVER

DISTRICT OF COLUMBIA (D.C.)
AREA: 179 SQ KM (69 SQ MI)
POPULATION: 7 MILLION
FEDERAL CAPITAL: WASHINGTON D.C.

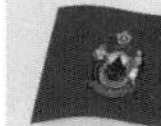

MAINE
AREA: 86,156 SQ KM (33,265 SQ MI)
POPULATION: 1.2 MILLION
CAPITAL: AUGUSTA

MARYLAND
AREA: 27,091 SQ KM (10,460 SQ MI)
POPULATION: 5.1 MILLION
CAPITAL: ANNAPOLIS

MASSACHUSETTS
AREA: 21,456 SQ KM (8,284 SQ MI)
POPULATION: 6.1 MILLION
CAPITAL: BOSTON

NEW HAMPSHIRE
AREA: 24,033 SQ KM (9,279 SQ MI)
POPULATION: 1.2 MILLION
CAPITAL: CONCORD

NEW JERSEY
AREA: 20,168 SQ KM (7,787 SQ MI)
POPULATION: 8.1 MILLION
CAPITAL: TRENTON

NEW YORK
AREA: 128,402 SQ KM (49,576 SQ MI)
POPULATION: 18.2 MILLION
CAPITAL: ALBANY

PENNSYLVANIA
AREA: 117,412 SQ KM (45,333 SQ MI)
POPULATION: 12 MILLION
CAPITAL: HARRISBURG

RHODE ISLAND
AREA: 3,139 SQ KM (1,212 SQ MI)
POPULATION: 0.98 MILLION
CAPITAL: PROVIDENCE

VERMONT
AREA: 24,887 SQ KM (9,609 SQ MI)
POPULATION: 0.59 MILLION
CAPITAL: MONTPELIER

WEST VIRGINIA
AREA: 62,629 SQ KM (24,181 SQ MI)
POPULATION: 1.8 MILLION
CAPITAL: CHARLESTON

OHIO
INDIANA
ILLINOIS
WEST VIRGINIA
WASHINGTON D.C.
DELAWARE
MARYLAND
Chesapeake B
VIRGINIA
Richmond
Norfolk
Frankfort
Lexington
Louisville
Ohio
KENTUCKY
MAMMOTH CAVE NATIONAL PARK
APPALACHIAN MOUNTAINS
BLUE RIDGE MOUNTAINS
Roanoke
Roanoke
MISSOURI
Paducah
Greensboro
Raleigh
Winston-Salem
Cape Hatter
Knoxville
NORTH CAROLINA
Nashville
GREAT SMOKEY MOUNTAINS
Charlotte
TENNESSEE
Wilmington
Chattanooga
Santee
Cape Fear
Greenville
Fort Smith
Memphis
Columbia
SOUTH CAROLINA
ARKANSAS
Tennessee
Savannah
Atlanta
Augusta
Little Rock
Birmingham
Alabama
Charleston
Greenville
Macon
MISSISSIPPI
ALABAMA
Columbus
Savannah
GEORGIA
ATLANTIC OCEAN
Shreveport
Meridian
Montgomery
Jackson
Albany
LOUISIANA
Mississippi
Jacksonville
St. Augustine
Alexandria
Mobile
Pensacola
Tallahassee
Biloxi
Daytona Beach
TEXAS
Baton Rouge
Orlando
Cape Canaveral
New Orleans
Mississippi Delta
Tampa
St. Petersburg
FLORIDA
West Palm Beach
GULF OF MEXICO
Fort Myers
Miami
THE EVERGLADES NATIONAL PARK
Florida Keys
Key West
Straits of Florida
0 100 200 300 400 500 kilometers
0 100 200 300 400 miles
N

DID YOU KNOW?

The longest cave system in the world is in Mammoth Cave National Park in Kentucky. It includes over 480 kilometers (300 miles) of underground caves and passages. Limestone forms stalactites and stalagmites, huge pillars which drip with water in the humid air.

THE SOUTH

The South is bordered by the Atlantic Ocean and the Gulf of Mexico. It runs from Kentucky and Virginia down to the Mississippi delta and the Florida Keys (small islands). The Appalachian ranges form the Blue Ridge and Great Smoky Mountains, reaching their southern limit in Alabama. Crops of the South include cotton and tobacco.

Virginia, the Carolinas, and Georgia have sandy coasts on the Atlantic Ocean. The coastal plains are drained by the Roanoke, Savannah, and Santee Rivers, which rise in the western mountains. West of the Appalachians the land descends to the Mississippi and Ohio Rivers, forming the states of Kentucky and Tennessee.

The sunny peninsula of Florida is dominated by the Everglades wetlands, which attract many tourists. Rockets and space shuttles are launched from Cape Canaveral. The Gulf states (Alabama, Mississippi and Louisiana) have a hot and steamy climate. Their coasts are areas of delta wetlands and bayous (creeks). The old center of New Orleans recalls the city's French past and the early days of jazz. The mighty Mississippi River is contained by high banks called levees. Upstream, it forms the eastern border of Arkansas.

PEOPLES OF THE REGION

Native Americans of the South include the Natchez, Choctaw, Chickasaw, Cherokee, and Seminole peoples. From the 1500s onward, Europeans moved into the region. They imported African slaves to work their tobacco and cotton plantations. Today's southerners include Native Americans, African Americans, and immigrants from Cuba. Those of European origin include Cajuns, descendants of French settlers forced to leave Canada by the British in the 1700s.

STATES

ALABAMA
AREA: 133,916 SQ KM (51,705 SQ MI)
POPULATION: 4.4 MILLION
CAPITAL: MONTGOMERY

ARKANSAS
AREA: 137,754 SQ KM (53,187 SQ MI)
POPULATION: 2.5 MILLION
CAPITAL: LITTLE ROCK

FLORIDA
AREA: 151,940 SQ KM (58,664 SQ MI)
POPULATION: 14.9 MILLION
CAPITAL: TALLAHASSEE

GEORGIA
AREA: 152,577 SQ KM (58,910 SQ MI)
POPULATION: 7.6 MILLION
CAPITAL: ATLANTA

KENTUCKY
AREA: 104,623 SQ KM (40,395 SQ MI)
POPULATION: 3.9 MILLION
CAPITAL: FRANKFORT

LOUISIANA
AREA: 125,674 SQ KM (48,523 SQ MI)
POPULATION: 4.4 MILLION
CAPITAL: BATON ROUGE

MISSISSIPPI
AREA: 123,514 SQ KM (47,689 SQ MI)
POPULATION: 2.8 MILLION
CAPITAL: JACKSON

NORTH CAROLINA
AREA: 136,413 SQ KM (52,669 SQ MI)
POPULATION: 7.5 MILLION
CAPITAL: RALEIGH

SOUTH CAROLINA
AREA: 80,583 SQ KM (31,113 SQ MI)
POPULATION: 3.8 MILLION
CAPITAL: COLUMBIA

TENNESSEE
AREA: 109,153 SQ KM (42,144 SQ MI)
POPULATION: 5.4 MILLION
CAPITAL: NASHVILLE

VIRGINIA
AREA: 105,586 SQ KM (40,767 SQ MI)
POPULATION: 6.8 MILLION
CAPITAL: RICHMOND

THE SOUTHWEST

STATES

ARIZONA

AREA: 295,260 SQ KM (114,000 SQ MI)
POPULATION: 4.7 MILLION
CAPITAL: PHOENIX

NEW MEXICO

AREA: 314,926 SQ KM (121,593 SQ MI)
POPULATION: 1.7 MILLION
CAPITAL: SANTA FE

OKLAHOMA

AREA: 181,186 SQ KM (69,956 SQ MI)
POPULATION: 3.3 MILLION
CAPITAL: OKLAHOMA CITY

TEXAS

AREA: 691,030 SQ KM (266,807 SQ MI)
POPULATION: 19.8 MILLION
CAPITAL: AUSTIN

Texas is the largest state in the Southwest and the second largest in the United States. It is famous for its oilfields and cattle. The Texas coast, on the Gulf of Mexico, breaks up into islands and lagoons. Inland lie coastal plains and grasslands, with canyons and mountains to the west of the Pecos River. The Mexican border runs along the Rio Grande.

Oklahoma lies to the north of Texas, across the Red River. It is a land of plains, rising to the Ouachita Mountains in the east. Crops include cotton, wheat, and sorghum. A long strip of territory, the "Panhandle," extends to the northwest.

New Mexico lies on either side of the Rio Grande. It is a region of plateaus, mountains, and deserts that glisten with white sand dunes. The state is rich in minerals, especially uranium.

Arizona is a land of baking deserts, where the growing of crops such as cotton depends on massive irrigation schemes. Northern Arizona rises to the Colorado plateau, which is cleft by the long, deep gorge of the Grand Canyon. The Colorado River forms Arizona's western border.

THE GRAND CANYON

The Grand Canyon is the world's biggest gorge. It has been carved out of Arizona by the Colorado River. The Grand Canyon is 446 kilometers (277 miles) long. Its width varies between 6 and 24 kilometers (4 and 15 miles). In places it reaches a depth of 1.6 kilometers (1 mile).

PEOPLES OF THE REGION

In 1820 present-day Oklahoma was set aside as Indian Territory, and peoples of the Southeast—Seminole, Choctaw, Creek, Chickasaw, and Cherokee—were re-settled there. Sixty-nine years later part of it was opened to settlers of European descent, who flooded into the territory. Native Americans to the west include the Apache, Mojave, and Hopi. Spanish names such as San Antonio, El Paso and Las Cruces show that Texas, New Mexico, and Arizona were all Mexican lands before they became states.

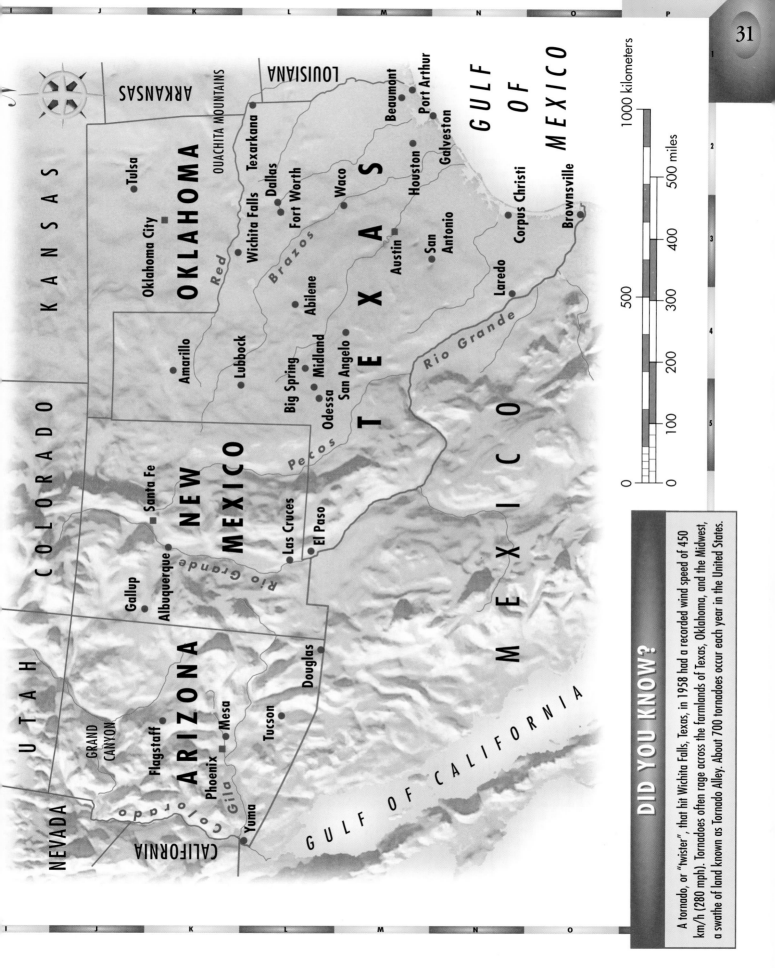

UTAH
NEVADA
COLORADO
KANSAS
GRAND CANYON
CALIFORNIA
Colorado
ARIZONA
Flagstaff
Phoenix
Mesa
Gila
Yuma
Tucson
Douglas
Gallup
Albuquerque
Santa Fe
NEW MEXICO
Rio Grande
Las Cruces
El Paso
Pecos
Amarillo
Lubbock
Big Spring
Midland
Odessa
San Angelo
Abilene
OKLAHOMA
Oklahoma City
Tulsa
ARKANSAS
OUACHITA MOUNTAINS
Red
Wichita Falls
Texarkana
Dallas
Fort Worth
Brazos
LOUISIANA
Waco
TEXAS
Austin
San Antonio
Houston
Beaumont
Port Arthur
Galveston
Laredo
Corpus Christi
Brownsville
GULF OF MEXICO
MEXICO
GULF OF CALIFORNIA
0 500 1000 kilometers
0 100 200 300 400 500 miles

DID YOU KNOW?

A tornado, or "twister", that hit Wichita Falls, Texas, in 1958 had a recorded wind speed of 450 km/h (280 mph). Tornadoes often rage across the farmlands of Texas, Oklahoma, and the Midwest, a swathe of land known as Tornado Alley. About 700 tornadoes occur each year in the United States.

THE MIDWEST & ROCKIES

STATES

COLORADO
AREA: 270,000 SQ KM (104,247 SQ MI)
POPULATION: 3.97 MILLION
CAPITAL: DENVER

IDAHO
AREA: 216,413 SQ KM (83,557 SQ MI)
POPULATION: 1.2 MILLION
CAPITAL: BOISE

ILLINOIS
AREA: 146,076 SQ KM (56,400 SQ MI)
POPULATION: 12 MILLION
CAPITAL: SPRINGFIELD

INDIANA
AREA: 93,994 SQ KM (36,291 SQ MI)
POPULATION: 5.9 MILLION
CAPITAL: INDIANAPOLIS

IOWA
AREA: 145,752 SQ KM (56,275 SQ MI)
POPULATION: 2.9 MILLION
CAPITAL: DES MOINES

KANSAS

KANSAS
AREA: 213,097 SQ KM (82,277 SQ MI)
POPULATION: 2.6 MILLION
CAPITAL: TOPEKA

MICHIGAN
AREA: 151,585 SQ KM (58,527 SQ MI)
POPULATION: 9.8 MILLION
CAPITAL: LANSING

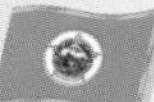

MINNESOTA
AREA: 217,736 SQ KM (84,068 SQ MI)
POPULATION: 4.7 MILLION
CAPITAL: ST. PAUL

MISSOURI
AREA: 180,515 SQ KM (69,697 SQ MI)
POPULATION: 5.4 MILLION
CAPITAL: JEFFERSON CITY

MONTANA

MONTANA
AREA: 380,849 SQ KM (147,046 SQ MI)
POPULATION: 0.88 MILLION
CAPITAL: HELENA

NEBRASKA
AREA: 200,349 SQ KM (77,355 SQ MI)
POPULATION: 1.7 MILLION
CAPITAL: LINCOLN

NORTH DAKOTA
AREA: 183,022 SQ KM (70,665 SQ MI)
POPULATION: 0.63 MILLION
CAPITAL: BISMARCK

OHIO
AREA: 106,765 SQ KM (41,222 SQ MI)
POPULATION: 11.2 MILLION
CAPITAL: COLUMBUS

SOUTH DAKOTA
AREA: 199,730 SQ KM (77,116 SQ MI
POPULATION: 0.73 MILLION
CAPITAL: PIERRE

UTAH
AREA: 219,888 SQ KM (84,899 SQ MI)
POPULATION: 2.1 MILLION
CAPITAL: SALT LAKE CITY

WISCONSIN
1848

WISCONSIN
AREA: 145,439 SQ KM (56,154 SQ MI)
POPULATION: 5.2 MILLION
CAPITAL: MADISON

WYOMING
AREA: 253,597 SQ KM (97,914 SQ MI)
POPULATION: 0.48 MILLION
CAPITAL: CHEYENNE

The lands to the west of the Ohio River and north of the Ozark plateau are known as the Midwest. They are drained by the Missouri River, which joins the southbound Mississippi River above St. Louis. In the far north the Great Lakes all border Canada, except for all-American Lake Michigan. The northeastern states have many large industrial towns.

Vast prairie grasslands stretch westward. Long grasses are native to the wetter east, an area now farmed for corn and wheat. Short grasses are native to the drier Great Plains, the cattle-ranching country at the foot of the mountains.

Twenty mountain ranges make up the backbone of the United States. Together, these ranges are called the Rocky Mountains. The northern section lies in Montana, with many massive peaks included in Glacier National Park. The central section is formed by the Teton range of Wyoming. The southern Rockies tower over Colorado and Utah. To the west, the Rockies descend to the Great Salt Lake and the canyons bordering the Great Basin.

PEOPLES OF THE REGION

Native American peoples of the Great Lakes region included the Winnebago, Illinois, Miami, Sauk, Fox and Kickapoo. The Great Plains were home to hunters of buffalo—Sioux, Blackfeet, Cheyenne, and many other names still remembered from the Indian Wars (1860–90). City names in the Midwest, such as Terre Haute or Des Moines, show that the Missouri basin was explored by the French. People from many different parts of Europe eventually settled the region. Many African Americans live in Chicago, Detroit, Cleveland, and other cities.

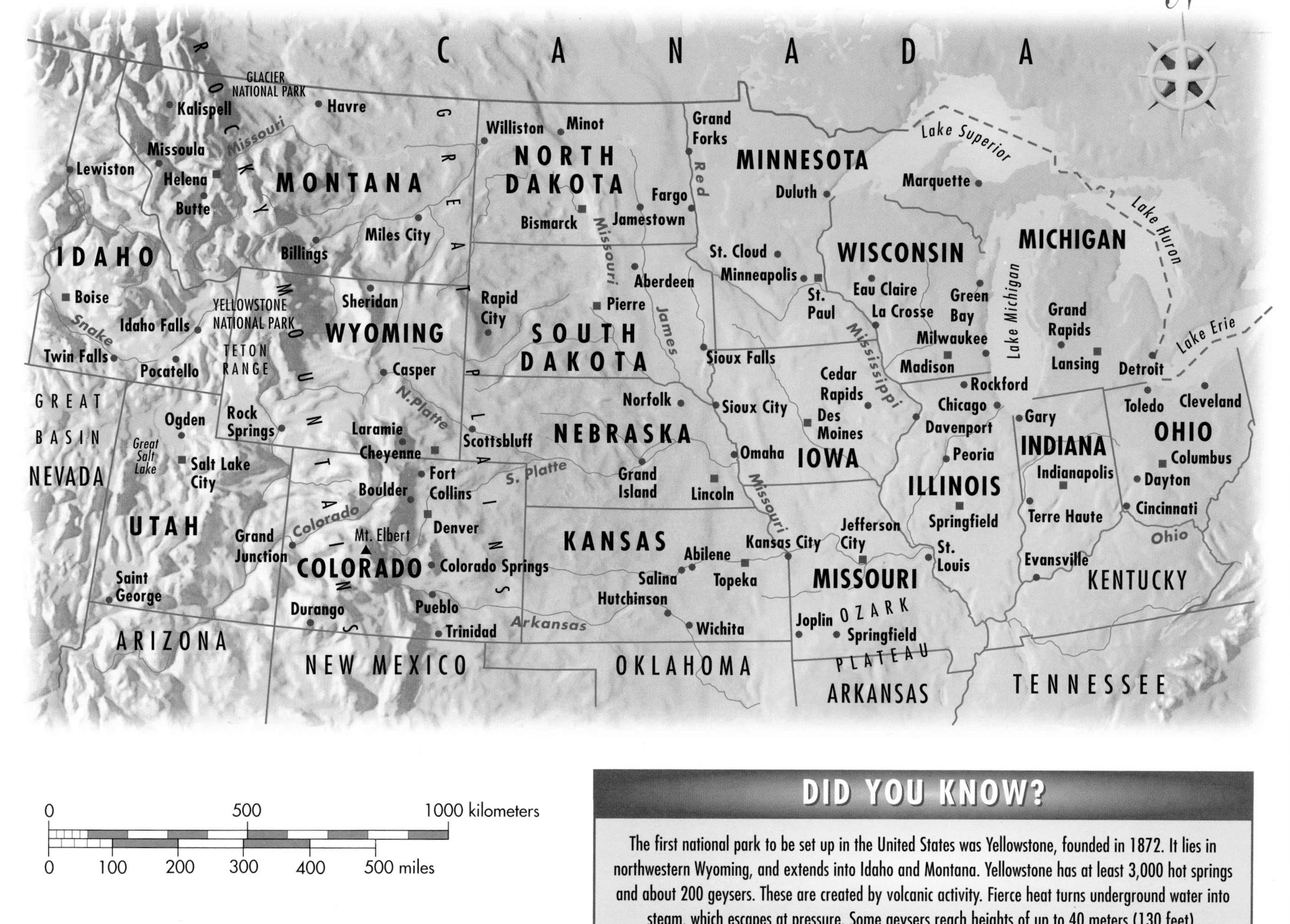
CANADA
GLACIER NATIONAL PARK
Kalispell
Havre
Missoula
Missouri
Lewiston
Helena
Butte
MONTANA
ROCKY MOUNTAINS
GREAT PLAINS
Miles City
Billings
IDAHO
Boise
Snake
Idaho Falls
YELLOWSTONE NATIONAL PARK
Sheridan
WYOMING
TETON RANGE
Twin Falls
Pocatello
Casper
N. Platte
GREAT BASIN
NEVADA
Ogden
Great Salt Lake
Salt Lake City
Rock Springs
Laramie
Cheyenne
Fort Collins
Boulder
Denver
Mt. Elbert
UTAH
Grand Junction
Colorado
COLORADO
Colorado Springs
Pueblo
Trinidad
Durango
Saint George
ARIZONA
NEW MEXICO
Williston
Minot
NORTH DAKOTA
Bismarck
Jamestown
Fargo
Grand Forks
Red
Missouri
Aberdeen
Pierre
James
Rapid City
SOUTH DAKOTA
Scottsbluff
S. Platte
NEBRASKA
Norfolk
Grand Island
Lincoln
Omaha
KANSAS
Abilene
Salina
Hutchinson
Wichita
Topeka
Arkansas
OKLAHOMA
MINNESOTA
Duluth
St. Cloud
Minneapolis
St. Paul
Sioux Falls
Sioux City
IOWA
Cedar Rapids
Des Moines
Mississippi
Kansas City
Jefferson City
MISSOURI
Joplin
Springfield
OZARK PLATEAU
ARKANSAS
WISCONSIN
Eau Claire
La Crosse
Green Bay
Milwaukee
Madison
Marquette
Lake Superior
Lake Michigan
MICHIGAN
Grand Rapids
Lansing
Lake Huron
Detroit
Lake Erie
Rockford
Chicago
Davenport
Peoria
ILLINOIS
Springfield
St. Louis
Gary
INDIANA
Indianapolis
Terre Haute
Evansville
Toledo
Cleveland
OHIO
Columbus
Dayton
Cincinnati
Ohio
KENTUCKY
TENNESSEE
N
0
500
1000 kilometers
0
100
200
300
400
500 miles

DID YOU KNOW?

The first national park to be set up in the United States was Yellowstone, founded in 1872. It lies in northwestern Wyoming, and extends into Idaho and Montana. Yellowstone has at least 3,000 hot springs and about 200 geysers. These are created by volcanic activity. Fierce heat turns underground water into steam, which escapes at pressure. Some geysers reach heights of up to 40 meters (130 feet).

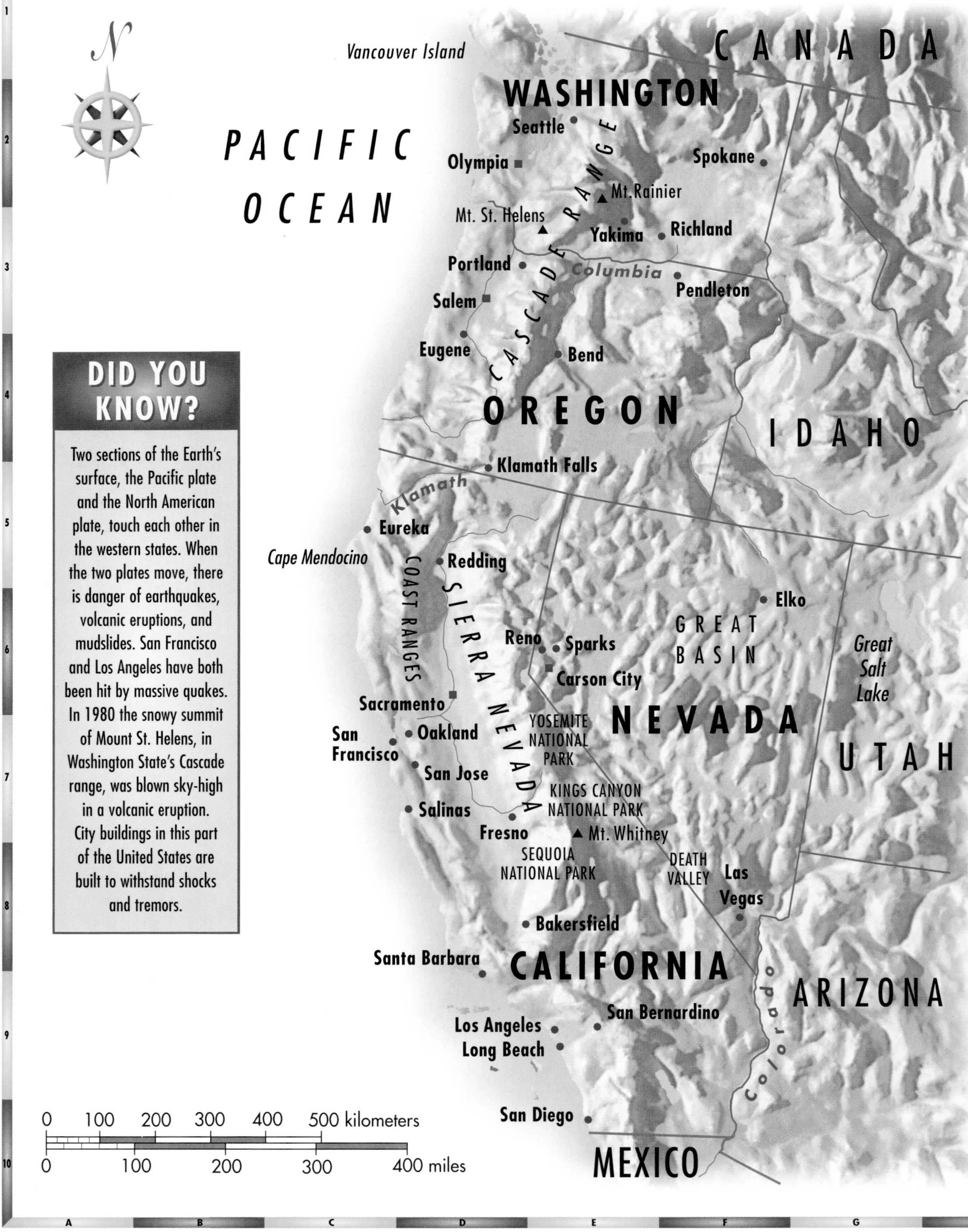
N
Vancouver Island
CANADA
WASHINGTON
PACIFIC OCEAN
Seattle
Olympia
Spokane
CASCADE RANGE
Mt. Rainier
Mt. St. Helens
Yakima
Richland
Portland
Columbia
Pendleton
Salem
Eugene
Bend
OREGON
IDAHO
Klamath Falls
Klamath
Eureka
Cape Mendocino
Redding
COAST RANGES
SIERRA NEVADA
Elko
GREAT BASIN
Great Salt Lake
Reno
Sparks
Carson City
Sacramento
YOSEMITE NATIONAL PARK
NEVADA
San Francisco
Oakland
UTAH
San Jose
KINGS CANYON NATIONAL PARK
Salinas
Fresno
Mt. Whitney
SEQUOIA NATIONAL PARK
DEATH VALLEY
Las Vegas
Bakersfield
Santa Barbara
CALIFORNIA
ARIZONA
Colorado
San Bernardino
Los Angeles
Long Beach
San Diego
MEXICO
0 100 200 300 400 500 kilometers
0 100 200 300 400 miles

DID YOU KNOW?

Two sections of the Earth's surface, the Pacific plate and the North American plate, touch each other in the western states. When the two plates move, there is danger of earthquakes, volcanic eruptions, and mudslides. San Francisco and Los Angeles have both been hit by massive quakes. In 1980 the snowy summit of Mount St. Helens, in Washington State's Cascade range, was blown sky-high in a volcanic eruption. City buildings in this part of the United States are built to withstand shocks and tremors.

THE WEST

STATES

CALIFORNIA
AREA: 411,048 SQ KM (158,706 SQ MI)
POPULATION: 32.7 MILLION
CAPITAL: SACRAMENTO

NEVADA
AREA: 286,353 SQ KM (110,561 SQ MI)
POPULATION: 1.8 MILLION
CAPITAL: CARSON CITY

OREGON
AREA: 251,419 SQ KM (97,073 SQ MI)
POPULATION: 3.3 MILLION
CAPITAL: SALEM

WASHINGTON
AREA: 176,617 SQ KM (68,192 SQ MI)
POPULATION: 5.7 MILLION
CAPITAL: OLYMPIA

The area to the east of the Rockies is called the Great Basin. Nevada lies within this region, a land of plateaus, empty deserts, and eroded rocks. It has rich reserves of minerals, including gold and silver.

The western rim of the Great Basin is bordered by a series of mountain ranges that run parallel to the Pacific coast. They form a barrier to the prevailing ocean winds, which shed heavy rains on west-facing slopes. The Cascade Range runs down the northwestern states of Washington and Oregon. These are lands of cool, foggy, evergreen forests, stretching up to the Canadian border. The chief seaport of the northwest is Seattle.

California extends southward from forests of giant sequoia and redwood trees to warm, sunbaked valleys and deserts bordering the Great Basin. Its mountains form the Coast Ranges and the spectacular Sierra Nevada. San Francisco is a beautiful city, rising steeply from a great bay. California's biggest city—and the second largest city in the United States—is Los Angeles, which sprawls out over southern California. California is famous for wines and citrus fruits, for the film studios of Hollywood, and for the computer technology of "Silicon Valley."

GIANTS OF THE FOREST

In California's national parks, such as Kings Canyon and Sequoia, you can walk with giants. The giant sequoia tree may not be as tall as the coastal redwood, but it is still the most massive living object in the world. It measures up to 25 meters (83 feet) around its base. Its thick, spongy bark protects it against lightning strikes, which often set off forest fires. Sequoias can live to be 2,000 years old.

PEOPLES OF THE REGION

California alone was once home to fifty-three Native American nations. It was conquered by the Spanish as part of Mexico, and joined the United States in 1850. The west was eagerly settled by people from the east even before the two coasts were joined by railroad. The settlement has continued ever since. Today, peoples of the Pacific coast include African Americans, Hispanics, European Americans, Japanese, and Chinese Americans.

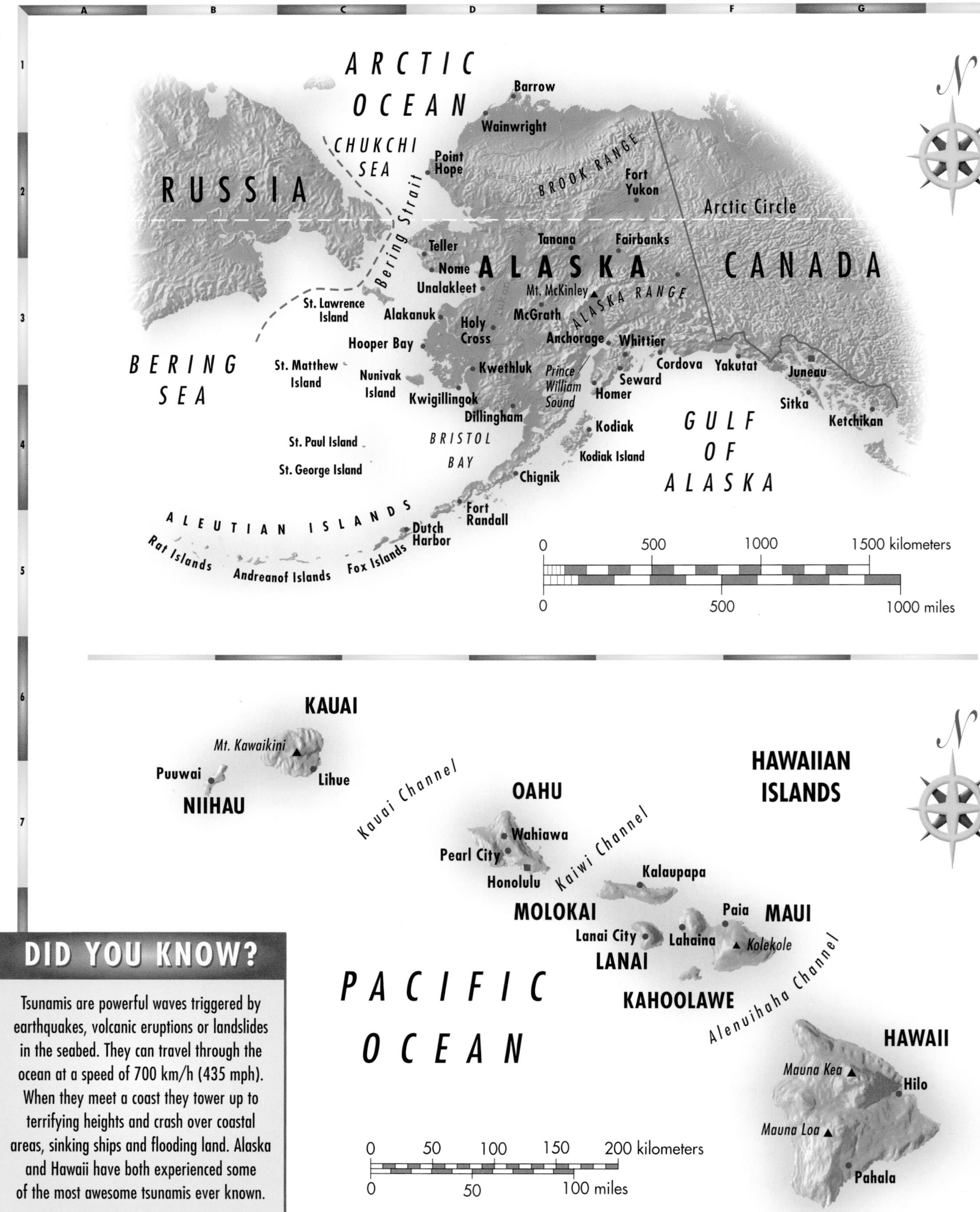
ARCTIC OCEAN
CHUKCHI SEA
RUSSIA
Bering Strait
BROOK RANGE
Arctic Circle
ALASKA
CANADA
ALASKA RANGE
BERING SEA
GULF OF ALASKA
BRISTOL BAY
ALEUTIAN ISLANDS
Rat Islands
Andreanof Islands
Fox Islands
Barrow
Wainwright
Point Hope
Fort Yukon
Teller
Nome
Tanana
Fairbanks
Unalakleet
Mt. McKinley
St. Lawrence Island
Alakanuk
Holy Cross
McGrath
Hooper Bay
Anchorage
Whittier
St. Matthew Island
Nunivak Island
Kwethluk
Prince William Sound
Seward
Cordova
Yakutat
Juneau
Homer
Kwigillingok
Dillingham
Sitka
Ketchikan
Kodiak
Kodiak Island
St. Paul Island
St. George Island
Chignik
Fort Randall
Dutch Harbor
0
500
1000
1500 kilometers
0
500
1000 miles
KAUAI
Mt. Kawaikini
Puuwai
Lihue
NIIHAU
Kauai Channel
OAHU
HAWAIIAN ISLANDS
Wahiawa
Pearl City
Honolulu
Kaiwi Channel
Kalaupapa
MOLOKAI
Paia
MAUI
Lanai City
Lahaina
Kolekole
LANAI
KAHOOLAWE
Alenuihaha Channel
PACIFIC OCEAN
HAWAII
Mauna Kea
Hilo
Mauna Loa
Pahala
0
50
100
150
200 kilometers
0
50
100 miles

DID YOU KNOW?

Tsunamis are powerful waves triggered by earthquakes, volcanic eruptions or landslides in the seabed. They can travel through the ocean at a speed of 700 km/h (435 mph). When they meet a coast they tower up to terrifying heights and crash over coastal areas, sinking ships and flooding land. Alaska and Hawaii have both experienced some of the most awesome tsunamis ever known.

ALASKA & HAWAII

STATES

ALASKA
AREA: 1,530,700 SQ KM (591,003 SQ MI)
POPULATION: 12 MILLION
CAPITAL: JUNEAU

HAWAII
AREA: 16,760 SQ KM (6,471 SQ MI)
POPULATION: 1.4 MILLION
CAPITAL: HONOLULU

Alaska is a land of foggy coasts and icy mountains, while the Hawaiian Islands are tropical and lush. However, these Pacific states have one thing in common. Over the ages, their landscapes have been shattered and shaped by countless volcanic eruptions.

Alaska lies on the Arctic Circle and borders Canada to the east. It is America's biggest state. Alaska is a land of remote wilderness, with mountain slopes, tundra, forests, and deep sea inlets. Mount McKinley, or Denali, is the highest peak in North America, at 6,194 meters (20,321 feet). Alaska's coast breaks up into numerous islands, including the long sweep of the Aleutian archipelago. The state is narrowly separated from Asia by the Bering Strait. Most Alaskans live in the milder south, around Anchorage.

The Hawaiian Islands are the tips of massive, active volcanoes that rise from the floor of the Pacific Ocean. Seven of the eight major islands are inhabited. There are another 114 tiny islands in the chain. The largest island is Hawaii, but the state capital is Honolulu, on Oahu. The islands produce pineapples and sugar-cane. Many tourists are attracted to the islands' beautiful scenery, blue seas and glowing streams of lava.

ARCTIC OIL

The Arctic region of Alaska is rich in oil, which is piped southward across the snowy wilderness. The oil industry has provided routes for migrating caribou to pass under the pipeline. However, oil often presents a danger to the environment. In 1989, the *Exxon Valdez* oil tanker spilled its black, sticky cargo in Prince William Sound, Alaska—coastal waters that are home to all kinds of seabirds, fish and marine mammals.

PEOPLES OF THE REGION

Alaska is home to Inuit and other groups of Native Americans. A closely related people, the Aleuts, inhabit the Aleutian islands. Alaska was settled by Russian fur traders in the 1800s. Today's population mostly comes from the lower 48 states to the south. Native Hawaiians are one of the Polynesian peoples of the Pacific islands. Hawaii has been settled by Americans from the mainland belonging to many different ethnic groups.

CENTRAL AMERICA *with* MEXICO & THE CARIBBEAN

This stone figure at Chichén Itzá, in southern Mexico, was probably carved by the Toltec people about 1,000 years ago.

Central America is the southernmost part of the North American continent, where it joins with South America. To the west lies the Pacific Ocean, to the east are two arms of the Atlantic Ocean: the Gulf of Mexico and the Caribbean Sea. Mexico lies within North America, and extends to Central America, a region of North America. Central America begins at the Isthmus of Tehuantepec in Mexico, and takes in the seven small countries to the south.

Mexico is a land of hot deserts, volcanic peaks, plateaus, and tropical forests. Its capital, Mexico City, is the largest city in the region. It has a population of about 20 million. The seven small Central American nations are Guatemala, Belize, Honduras, El Salvador, Nicaragua, Costa Rica, and Panama. The narrowest part of the land link between North and South America is at the Isthmus of Panama.

The great arc of islands enclosing the Caribbean are divided into three groups, the Bahamas, the Greater Antilles, and the Lesser Antilles. Most of the Caribbean islands are small independent states, but others are dependencies of Britain, France, the Netherlands or the United States of America.

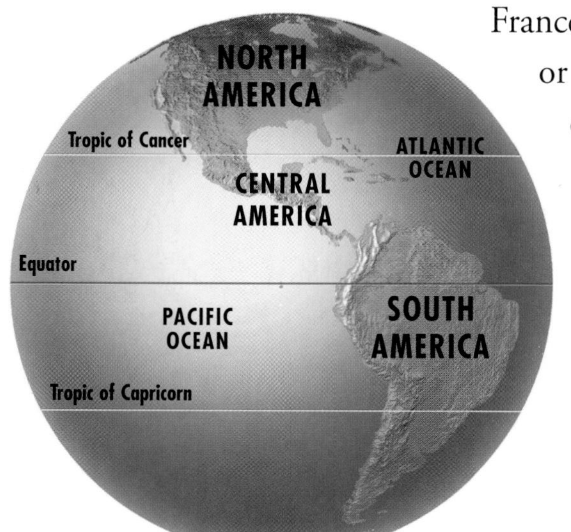
NORTH AMERICA
Tropic of Cancer
ATLANTIC OCEAN
CENTRAL AMERICA
Equator
PACIFIC OCEAN
SOUTH AMERICA
Tropic of Capricorn

THE PANAMA CANAL

It is possible to cross between the Atlantic and Pacific Oceans through the Panama Canal, just 82 kilometers (51 miles) from coast to coast. The first ship passed through the canal in 1914. Before the canal was constructed, ships had to sail all the way around Cape Horn, at the tip of South America. The canal was built by the United States. The United States also governed the zone around it until it was progressively transferred to Panama between 1977 and 1999.

MEXICO & CENTRAL AMERICA

Two mountains chains—the Eastern and Western Sierra Madre—extend down from northern Mexico. In the south of the country, the chains join to form the great mass of the Sierra Madre del Sur. Mountains and highlands also form a rocky spine down much of Central America. Many of these mountains are linked geologically with the mountains of the Caribbean islands. The whole region is a danger zone for severe earthquakes.

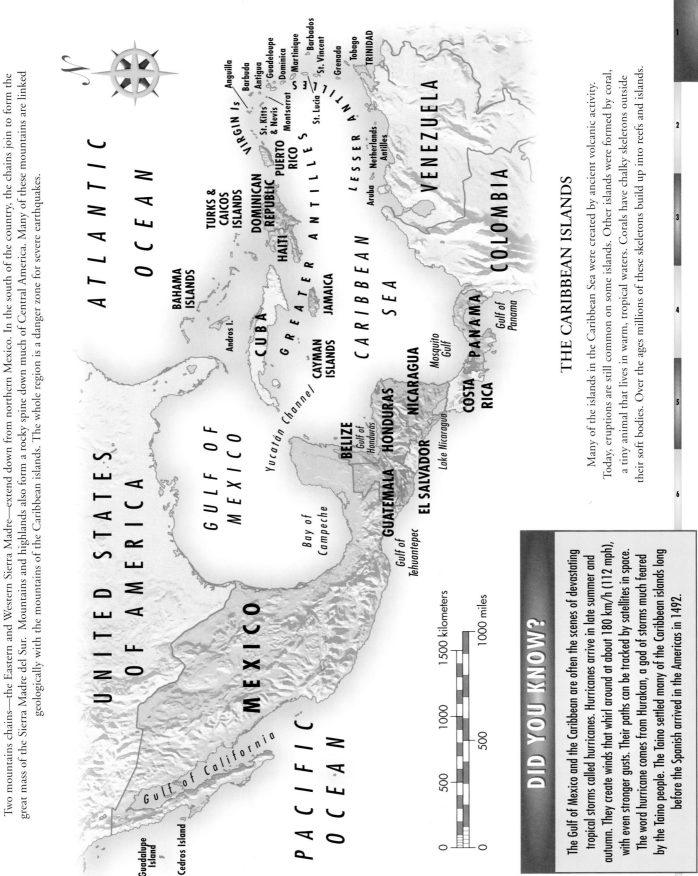

UNITED STATES OF AMERICA
ATLANTIC OCEAN
N
Guadalupe Island
Cedros Island
Gulf of California
MEXICO
GULF OF MEXICO
PACIFIC OCEAN
Bay of Campeche
Yucatán Channel
BAHAMA ISLANDS
Andros I.
TURKS & CAICOS ISLANDS
CUBA
DOMINICAN REPUBLIC
HAITI
PUERTO RICO
VIRGIN Is
Anguilla
Barbuda
Antigua
St. Kitts & Nevis
Montserrat
Guadeloupe
Dominica
Martinique
Barbados
St. Lucia
St. Vincent
Grenada
Tobago
TRINIDAD
GREATER ANTILLES
LESSER ANTILLES
CAYMAN ISLANDS
JAMAICA
CARIBBEAN SEA
Aruba
Netherlands Antilles
BELIZE
Gulf of Honduras
GUATEMALA
HONDURAS
Gulf of Tehuantepec
EL SALVADOR
NICARAGUA
Lake Nicaragua
Mosquito Gulf
COSTA RICA
PANAMA
Gulf of Panama
VENEZUELA
COLOMBIA
0
500
1000
1500 kilometers
0
500
1000 miles

DID YOU KNOW?

The Gulf of Mexico and the Caribbean are often the scenes of devastating tropical storms called hurricanes. Hurricanes arrive in late summer and autumn. They create winds that whirl around at about 180 km/h (112 mph), with even stronger gusts. Their paths can be tracked by satellites in space. The word hurricane comes from Hurakan, a god of storms much feared by the Taino people. The Taino settled many of the Caribbean islands long before the Spanish arrived in the Americas in 1492.

THE CARIBBEAN ISLANDS

Many of the islands in the Caribbean Sea were created by ancient volcanic activity. Today, eruptions are still common on some islands. Other islands were formed by coral, a tiny animal that lives in warm, tropical waters. Corals have chalky skeletons outside their soft bodies. Over the ages millions of these skeletons build up into reefs and islands.

N

DID YOU KNOW?

Mexico City is built on the site of the Aztec capital of Tenochtitlán. Five hundred years ago this city was home to over a quarter of a million people and covered almost 15 square kilometers (5.8 square miles). Built in the center of a lake, Tenochtitlán could be reached by three great causeways. The city included a massive temple, palaces, warehouses, canals, and a bustling market that sold goods from all over the Aztec Empire. Artificial islands of reeds and mud were built on the lake. They were used to grow crops.

UNITED STATES OF AMERICA
MEXICO
PACIFIC OCEAN
GULF OF MEXICO
Tijuana
Mexicali
Ensenada
Guadalupe Island
Cedros Island
Baja California
Gulf of California
Hermosillo
Ciudad Juárez
Chihuahua
WESTERN SIERRA MADRE
EASTERN SIERRA MADRE
Rio Grande
Culiacán
La Paz
Saltillo
Monterrey
Matamoros
Durango
Tampico
Aguascalientes
León
Guadalajara
Ecatepec
Lake de Chapala
Tlalneplanta
Mexico City
Naucalpan
Veracruz
Manzanillo
Puebla
Citlaltépetl
SIERRA MADRE DEL SUR
Oaxaca
Coatzacoalcos
Acapulco
Bay of Campeche
Yucatán Channel
Mérida
Chichén Itzá
Campeche
Yucatán Peninsula
BELIZE
GUATEMALA
Gulf of Tehuantepec

0 500 1000 1500 kilometers
0 500 1000 miles

MEXICO

COUNTRIES

MEXICO

AREA: 1,972,545 SQ KM (761,600 SQ MI)
POPULATION: 99.7 MILLION
CAPITAL: MEXICO CITY

The Río Bravo del Norte, known in America as the Rio Grande, forms part of Mexico's border with the United States of America. The long, thin peninsula of Baja ("lower") California protects Mexico's northwestern coast. The Western and Eastern Sierra Madre ranges and, farther south, the Sierra Madre del Sur range enclose a plateau region that suffers from violent earthquakes and volcanic eruptions.

Much of northern Mexico is covered by hot and dusty desert and scrub. The south, which borders Guatemala and Belize, is lush and tropical.

Mexico was the center of many ancient civilizations, which left behind ruins of cities and temples. The great empire of the Aztecs was conquered by the Spanish between 1519 and 1521. Under Spanish rule, Mexico came to govern large areas that are now part of the United States of America. Mexico became independent in 1821. Today, Mexico is part of the North American Free Trade Agreement (NAFTA), with Canada and the United States of America. Mexico produces cotton, coffee, vegetables, oil, iron, steel, and motor vehicles.

MEXICAN FESTIVALS

Festivals and celebrations are held in every region. Rodeos, called *charreadas*, are held in both town and country. Many festivals mark Catholic holy days, saints' days, and pilgrimages. The most famous is the festival of Our Lady of Guadalupe, held each year on December 12.

At the beginning of November, many Mexicans honor the spirits of their ancestors during the Day of the Dead. Candies are made in the shape of skeletons and skulls. Food is taken to family graves and candles are lit as people pray for the souls of their loved ones.

PEOPLES OF THE REGION

About 30 percent of Mexicans are of Native Mexican, or indigenous, descent. Major groups include the Seri, Yaqui Nahua, Otomi, Tarahumera, Huichol, Huastec, Tzotzil, Tzeltal, and the Maya of the Yucatán peninsula. About 10 percent of Mexicans are of European descent (mostly Spanish), while 60 percent are Mestizos (of mixed origins). Native languages may be heard regionally. The official language is Spanish. It is used throughout the country.

CENTRAL AMERICA & THE CARIBBEAN

COUNTRIES & DEPENDENCIES

BAHAMAS
AREA: 13,950 SQ KM (5,386 SQ MI)
POPULATION: 0.3 MILLION
CAPITAL: NASSAU

BARBADOS
AREA: 430 SQ KM (166 SQ MI)
POPULATION: 0.3 MILLION
CAPITAL: BRIDGETOWN

BELIZE
AREA: 22,966 SQ KM (8,867 SQ MI)
POPULATION: 0.2 MILLION
CAPITAL: BELMOPAN

COSTA RICA
AREA: 50,899 SQ KM (19,652 SQ MI)
POPULATION: 3.6 MILLION
CAPITAL: SAN JOSE

CUBA
AREA: 107,800 SQ KM (41,622 SQ MI)
POPULATION: 11.2 MILLION
CAPITAL: HAVANA

DOMINICAN REPUBLIC
AREA: 48,322 SQ KM (18,657 SQ MI)
POPULATION: 8.3 MILLION
CAPITAL: SANTO DOMINGO

EL SALVADOR
AREA: 21,393 SQ KM (8,260 SQ MI)
POPULATION: 5.9 MILLION
CAPITAL: SAN SALVADOR

GUATEMALA
AREA: 108,889 SQ KM (42,042 SQ MI)
POPULATION: 12.3 MILLION
CAPITAL: GUATEMALA CITY

HAITI
AREA: 27,749 SQ KM (10,714 SQ MI)
POPULATION: 7.8 MILLION
CAPITAL: PORT-AU-PRINCE

HONDURAS
AREA: 112,087 SQ KM (43,277 SQ MI)
POPULATION: 5.9 MILLION
CAPITAL: TEGUCIGALPA

JAMAICA
AREA: 11,580 SQ KM (4,471 SQ MI)
POPULATION: 2.6 MILLION
CAPITAL: KINGSTON

NICARAGUA
AREA: 128,410 SQ KM (49,579 SQ MI)
POPULATION: 5 MILLION
CAPITAL: MANAGUA

PANAMA
AREA: 87,177 SQ KM (33,659 SQ MI)
POPULATION: 2.8 MILLION
CAPITAL: PANAMA CITY

PUERTO RICO
COMMONWEALTH OF THE USA
AREA: 8,897 SQ KM (3,435 SQ MI)
POPULATION: 3.9 MILLION
CAPITAL: SAN JUAN

TRINIDAD & TOBAGO
AREA: 5,128 SQ KM (1,980 SQ MI)
POPULATION: 1.3 MILLION
CAPITAL: PORT OF SPAIN

Central America is a tropical region, but its climate and plant life are largely decided by height above sea level. On lowlands and coastal plains, the climate is hot and humid. On the lower mountainsides it is temperate, or mild. Higher in the mountains, it is quite cool

Central American crops include sugarcane, bananas, coffee, cotton, and corn. The forests of Honduras and Belize produce timber, while shrimp is caught in coastal waters. Guatemala is famous for the handwoven textiles made by native Guatemalan peoples.

The Caribbean climate is warm, but cooled in places by ocean winds or by mountainous altitudes. The Caribbean islands grow sugarcane, bananas, tropical fruits, coffee, and cotton. Trinidad produces oil. The largest island is Cuba, a land of fertile plains and forested mountains. Its most famous exports are rum and cigars. Many Caribbean islands are very small, and increasingly rely on the tourists who come to visit the beaches of white sand and palms.

PEOPLES OF THE REGION

Major indigenous or native groups in Central America include the Maya, the Miskito, and the Cuna. The region was conquered by Spain in the 1500s, and the great majority of people are Mestizos, of mixed native and European descent. Most Caribbean islanders are of African origin, descendants of African slaves brought over on ships.

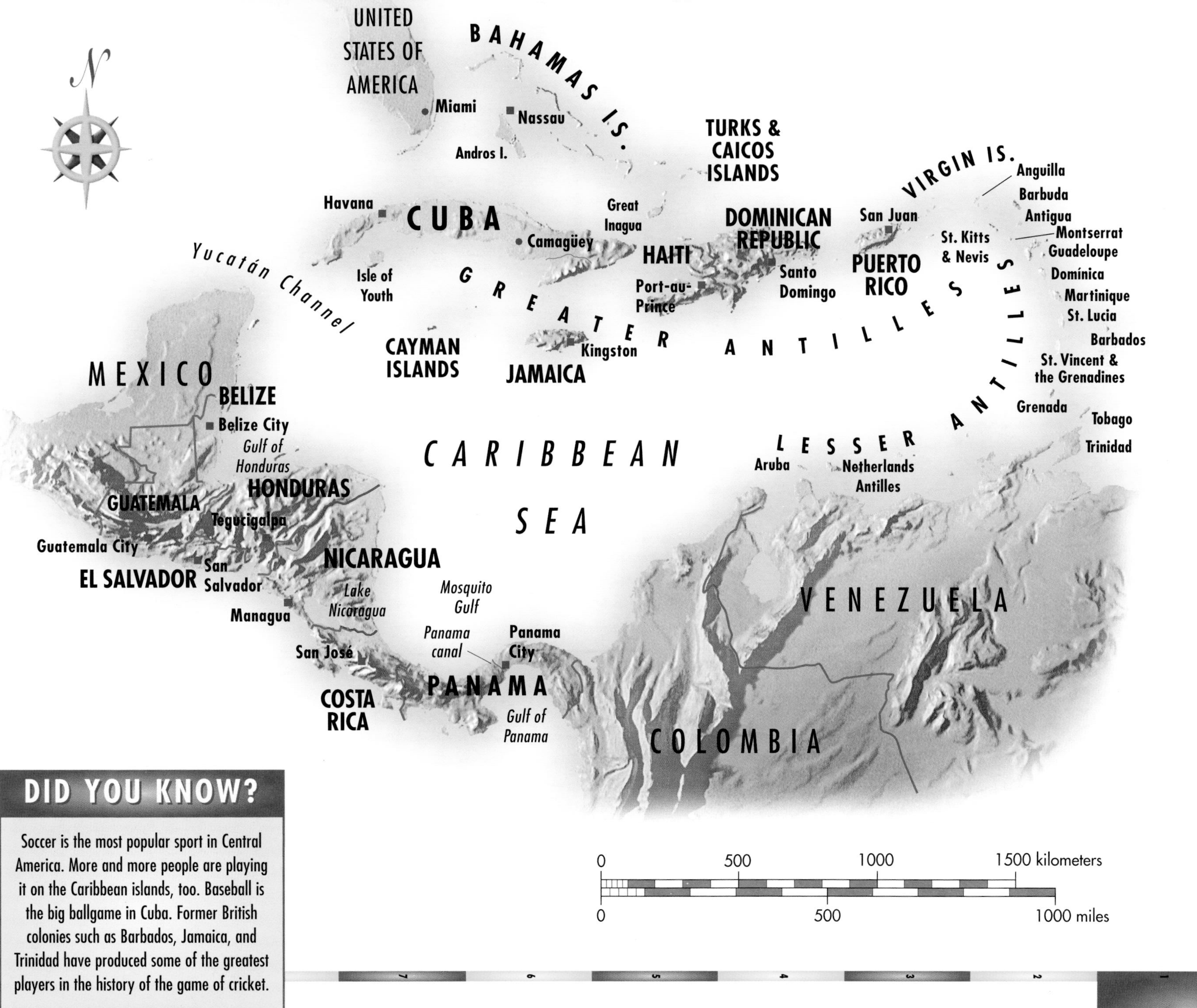
UNITED STATES OF AMERICA
Miami
BAHAMAS IS.
Nassau
Andros I.
TURKS & CAICOS ISLANDS
Havana
CUBA
Camagüey
Great Inagua
Yucatán Channel
Isle of Youth
GREATER ANTILLES
CAYMAN ISLANDS
JAMAICA
Kingston
HAITI
Port-au-Prince
DOMINICAN REPUBLIC
Santo Domingo
PUERTO RICO
San Juan
VIRGIN IS.
Anguilla
Barbuda
Antigua
Montserrat
Guadeloupe
Dominica
Martinique
St. Lucia
Barbados
St. Kitts & Nevis
St. Vincent & the Grenadines
Grenada
Tobago
Trinidad
LESSER ANTILLES
Aruba
Netherlands Antilles
MEXICO
BELIZE
Belize City
Gulf of Honduras
HONDURAS
GUATEMALA
Tegucigalpa
Guatemala City
EL SALVADOR
San Salvador
NICARAGUA
Lake Nicaragua
Managua
San José
COSTA RICA
CARIBBEAN SEA
Mosquito Gulf
Panama canal
Panama City
PANAMA
Gulf of Panama
VENEZUELA
COLOMBIA
N
0 500 1000 1500 kilometers
0 500 1000 miles

DID YOU KNOW?

Soccer is the most popular sport in Central America. More and more people are playing it on the Caribbean islands, too. Baseball is the big ballgame in Cuba. Former British colonies such as Barbados, Jamaica, and Trinidad have produced some of the greatest players in the history of the game of cricket.

SOUTH AMERICA

A narrow strip of land, the Isthmus of Panama, links North America to South America—the world's fourth largest continent. South America stretches from the Caribbean Sea in the northeast to the cold, stormy waters of Cape Horn in the south.

This Inca statue of a parrot eating a cob of corn is one of the many remains left from the Inca empire.

The Andes Mountains run down the continent from north to south (from Colombia to Tierra del Fuego), a distance of about 6,400 kilometers (4,000 miles). They include plateaus, glaciers, volcanoes, and some of the highest peaks in all the Americas.

To the west, the mountains drop to a strip of humid coastal lowlands and dry deserts that border the Pacific Ocean. To the east, they descend to the basin of the Amazon River. Fed by countless streams and rivers, this vast waterway winds through the world's biggest rain forest on its journey eastward to the Atlantic Ocean.

The continent narrows to the south. There are fertile farmlands, rolling grasslands called pampas, and the bleak, windswept valleys of Patagonia in southern Chile and Argentina. Tierra del Fuego, in the far south, is a maze of rocky islands and channels.

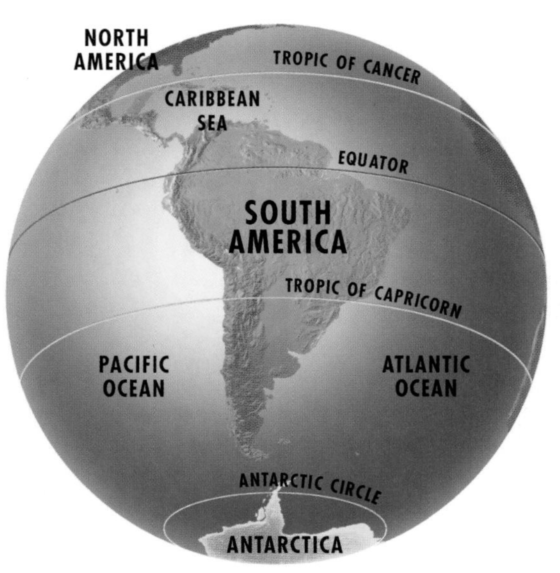
NORTH AMERICA
TROPIC OF CANCER
CARIBBEAN SEA
EQUATOR
SOUTH AMERICA
TROPIC OF CAPRICORN
PACIFIC OCEAN
ATLANTIC OCEAN
ANTARCTIC CIRCLE
ANTARCTICA

MACHU PICCHU

These stone ruins were discovered by American archaeologist Dr. Hiram Bingham in 1911. Set on forested mountain slopes high above the Urubamba River in Peru, Machu Picchu was one of many towns built by the Incas, who ruled a vast South American empire in the 1400s.

CARIBBEAN SEA
Gulf of Venezuela
LESSER ANTILLES
Netherlands Antilles
TRINIDAD & TOBAGO
PANAMA
Gulf of Panama
VENEZUELA
SURINAME
GUYANA
FRENCH GUIANA
COLOMBIA
Marajó Bay
Marajó Island
São Marcos Bay
ECUADOR
Amazon
Fernando de Noronha Island
PACIFIC OCEAN
BRAZIL
PERU
BOLIVIA
PARAGUAY
CHILE
ATLANTIC OCEAN
ARGENTINA
URUGUAY
Blanca Bay
Valdés Peninsula
Gulf of San Jorge
0 500 1000 1500 kilometers
0 500 1000 miles
West Falkland
FALKLAND/MALVINAS ISLANDS
East Falkland
Grande Bay
Strait of Magellan
South Georgia
Isla Grande
Tierra del Fuego
SCOTIA SEA
Cape Horn

THE FIRST SOUTH AMERICANS

Nobody knows when the first humans arrived in South America. Bands of hunters were certainly in the Andes about 13,000 years ago, and maybe much earlier. They were part of the great southward movement of peoples who had originally crossed from Asia into North America. In some places these peoples learned to farm, growing corn, potatoes, squash, and beans. Many great civilizations grew up in the Andes from about 4,500 years ago.

PRESENT-DAY SOUTH AMERICA

Modern South America emerged after Portuguese and Spanish soldiers invaded the continent in the 1500s, greedy for gold, silver, and land. Over the next 400 years, they were followed by African slaves and by settlers from many parts of Europe and Asia. Many native people were killed, or died from diseases brought by the newcomers. Others survived, many marrying Europeans. Spanish and Portuguese rule came to an end in the 1800s. In the 1900s, South America often suffered severe political, economic, and environmental problems. Today it is going through many rapid changes.

SOUTH AMERICA

South America is a beautiful, fascinating, and often confusing continent. It is a land of dense forests, remote mountains, and wide open grasslands. However, more than seven South Americans out of every ten live in towns and cities. It is a continent with great mineral resources. Yet many of its people are desperately poor. Some cities have modern skyscrapers and wealthy suburbs, but they are ringed by shantytowns where people must scavenge the streets to survive.

GENERAL FACTS

HIGHEST POINT
CERRO (Mt.) ACONCAGUA, 6,959 M (22,831 FT), ARGENTINA

LOWEST POINT
VALDÉS PENINSULA, -40 M (-131 FT), ARGENTINA

LONGEST RIVER
AMAZON RIVER, 6,436 KM (3,999 MI), BRAZIL

BIGGEST LAKE
LAKE TITICACA, 8,288 SQ KM (3,200 SQ MI), BOLIVIA-PERU

HIGHEST WATERFALL
SALTO ANGEL (CHERUN-MERU), 979 M (3,212 FT), VENEZUELA

BIGGEST ISLAND
ISLA GRANDE, TIERRA DEL FUEGO, 47,999 SQ KM (18,532 SQ MI), CHILE-ARGENTINA

BIGGEST DESERT
ATACAMA, 80,290 SQ KM (31,000 SQ MI), CHILE

POPULATION OF CONTINENT
331 MILLION (1998)

MOST POPULOUS COUNTRY
BRAZIL, 168 MILLION (1999)

MOST DENSELY POPULATED COUNTRY
COLOMBIA, 34 PER SQ KM (13 PER SQ MI) (1998)

MOST POPULOUS CITY
SÃO PAULO, BRAZIL, 18 MILLION (1998)

POPULATION LIVING IN CITIES
76 PERCENT

INFANT MORTALITY
37 DEATHS PER 1,000 CHILDREN UNDER AGE 1

LIFE EXPECTANCY
MALE 66 YEARS; FEMALE 72 YEARS

WEALTH
GROSS DOMESTIC PRODUCT PER PERSON U.S. $5,374 (1996)

LITERACY RATE
91 PERCENT MALE; 88 PERCENT FEMALE

VEGETATION

The Orinoco and Amazon Rivers and their many tributaries are mostly surrounded by rain forest. The Llanos savanna of Venezuela is made up of grassy plains dotted with trees. It is flooded in the rainy season. The Gran Chaco region, at the center of the continent, is made up of dry scrub and forest. The Pampas, the Argentine grasslands, are largely given over to cattle ranching and crops, while sheep graze the thin grasses of Patagonia. Andes vegetation varies with altitude.

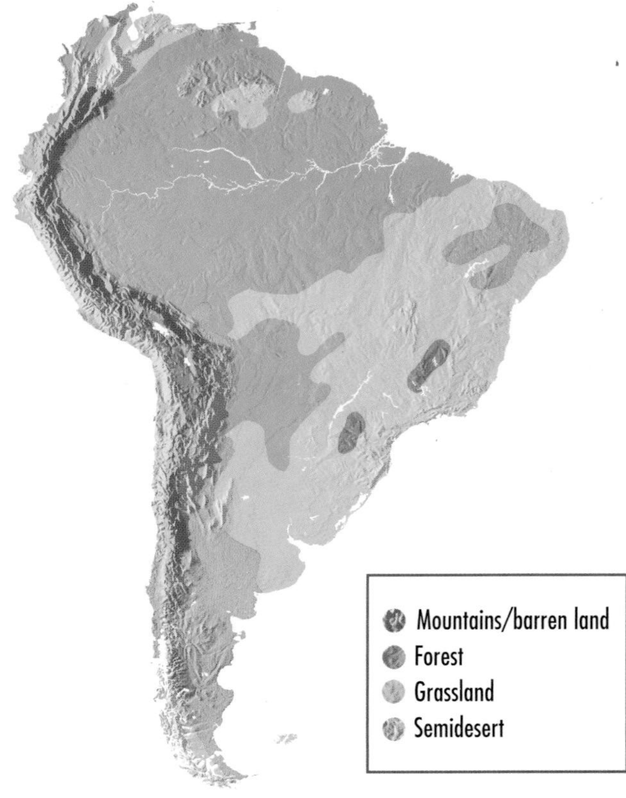
Mountains/barren land
Forest
Grassland
Semidesert

LANGUAGE

Two-thirds of the population of South America speaks Portuguese or Spanish. Portuguese is spoken in Brazil; Spanish in Colombia, Venezuela, Ecuador, Peru, Bolivia, Paraguay, Uruguay, Argentina, and Chile. The native languages of Quechua and Aymara are spoken in Peru, Bolivia, Argentina, and Chile. Guaraní is the native language of Paraguay and parts of Argentina. There are other languages, but all are spoken by less than 500,000 people.

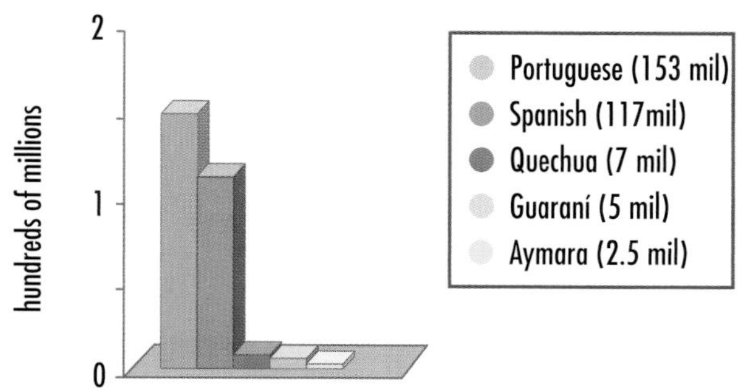
2
1
0
hundreds of millions
Portuguese (153 mil)
Spanish (117mil)
Quechua (7 mil)
Guaraní (5 mil)
Aymara (2.5 mil)

RELIGION

Christianity is widespread throughout South America. Most Christians are Roman Catholics. This form of Christianity was brought to the continent by Spanish and Portuguese missionaries in the 1500s. There are also a number of Protestant churches. In many places the traditional beliefs of the original peoples survive, and have been adapted to Christian rituals. There are small numbers of Jews, Hindus, and Muslims.

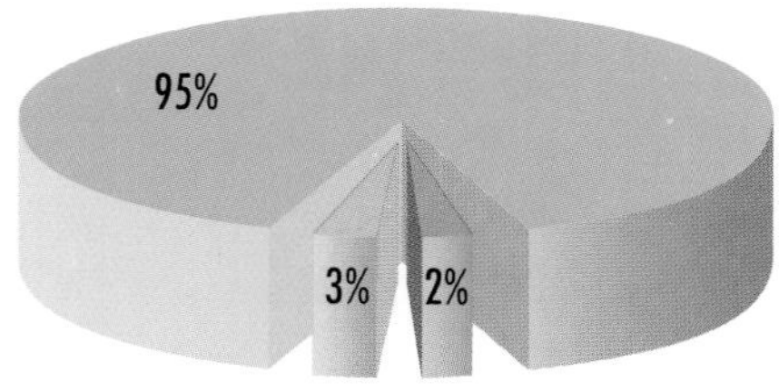
95%
3%
2%

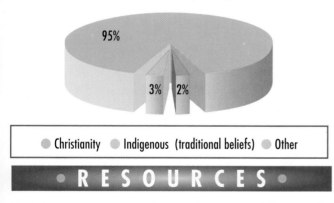

Christianity · Indigenous (traditional beliefs) · Other

CLIMATE

Most of South America lies below the Equator, in the southern hemisphere, so the seasons are reversed compared to the north. When the northern half of the world is enjoying the summer season, the southern half passes through winter. Ecuador, Colombia, and Brazil all lie on the Equator and are mostly hot and humid. However, the mountains and high plateaus of the Andes remain cool. Chile's Atacama Desert is one of the driest places on Earth. In the south, parts of Chile and Argentina are warm enough for growing grapes. In the far south, the continent stretches out toward Antarctica.

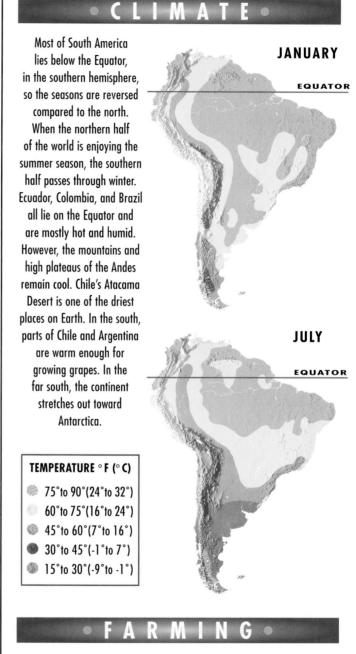

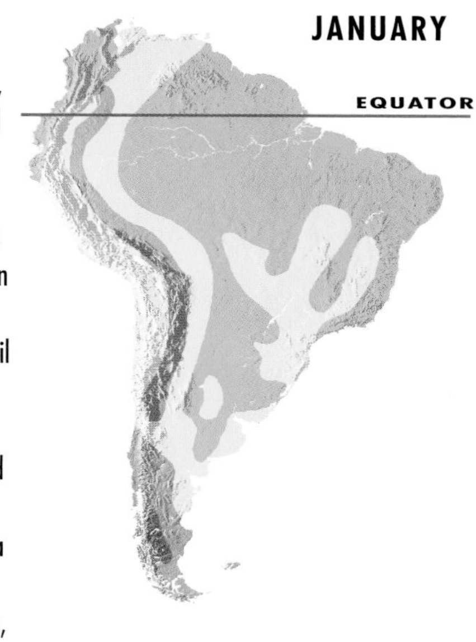
JANUARY
EQUATOR

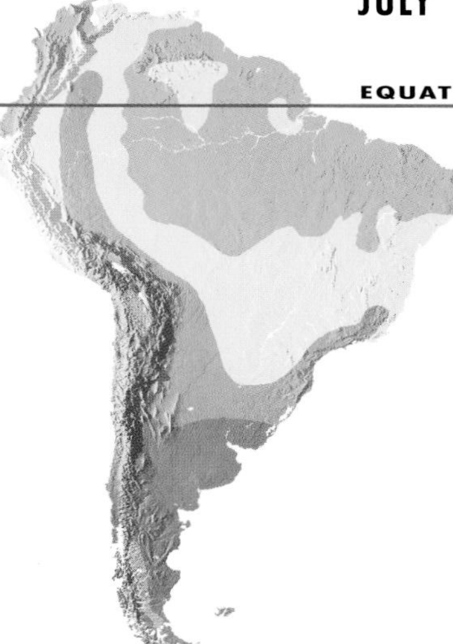
JULY
EQUATOR

TEMPERATURE °F (°C)

- 75° to 90° (24° to 32°)
- 60° to 75° (16° to 24°)
- 45° to 60° (7° to 16°)
- 30° to 45° (-1° to 7°)
- 15° to 30° (-9° to -1°)

RESOURCES

The Andes Mountains are very rich in mineral resources, including emeralds, tin, gold, and silver. Centers of oil production include Venezuela's Lake Maracaibo (an inlet of the Caribbean) and the Atlantic seabed off southern Argentina. Brazil is the second biggest iron ore producer in the world.

COPPER: *Bolivia, Brazil, Chile, Colombia, Guyana, Paraguay, Peru, Venezuela*

IRON: *Argentina, Brazil, Ecuador, Guyana, Paraguay, Venezuela*

OIL: *Argentina, Bolivia, Brazil, Chile, Colombia, Ecuador, Peru, Venezuela*

SILVER: *Argentina, Bolivia, Brazil, Ecuador, Peru, Venezuela*

TIN: *Argentina, Bolivia, Brazil*

FARMING

Potatoes were being grown high in the Andes thousands of years ago. Today, the continent is famous for its coffee, citrus fruits, and wines. Cattle, reared on the Pampas, were the foundation of the beef trade that brought wealth to Argentina.

CATTLE: *Argentina, Brazil, Uruguay*

COFFEE: *Brazil, Colombia, Peru, Venezuela*

CORN: *Argentina, Peru*

POTATO: *Bolivia, Ecuador, Peru*

SUGARCANE: *Brazil, Ecuador, Guyana, Suriname*

SOUTH AMERICA
The Giant Triangle

ALONG THE AMAZON

A small hut provides a home beside the broad, muddy waters of the Amazon. The river is a transport route, a source of fish—and a place to do the washing. For centuries, the river was the only route into the mysterious world of the rain forest.

The dark, dripping rain forests of the Amazon basin are home to countless insects and giant snakes called anacondas. They echo to the roar of howler monkeys. They are also home to a few Native American peoples who still live by hunting with bows and arrows, or by clearing patches of land to grow crops.

On the high, bright plateaus of the Andes, you may see women spinning and weaving by hand. Others lay out potatoes on the ground for drying. Country buses lurch over bumpy roads on their way to the big city.

Many South American cities are lively places, with street markets, cafés, and dance music. The tango is the national dance of Argentina, while people dance the samba in Brazil. Soccer is a passion across the continent. Few national teams in the world can match the proud record of Brazil.

IN THE BOLIVIAN ANDES

South America has four camel-like animals—the llama, the vicuña, the guanaco, and the alpaca. They provide wool for spinning and weaving. Llamas can also be used as pack animals, carrying baggage over mountain passes in the Andes.

HARVESTING GRAPES IN CHILE

Chile's Valle Central has a mild, warm climate, much like that of California or the Mediterranean region of Europe. It is ideal for growing fruit and grapes. Wine has been produced in Chile since the early colonial period. Many of today's vineyards were laid out by French experts in the 1800s. Chilean wines are exported all over the world.

CARNIVAL IN RIO

Wearing glittering costumes, dancers parade through Rio de Janeiro for carnival. Tens of thousands dance the samba in the streets during this five-day festival. Carnival began long ago in Europe. It was a chance for Christians to feast before Lent, a time when eating meat was forbidden. The festival spread around the world, but nowhere is it more spectacular than in Rio de Janeiro.

COWBOYS OF THE PAMPAS

Argentine cowboys are called gauchos. Like North American cowboys, they have passed into folklore and legend. In the 1800s they tended vast herds of cattle on the Pampas. They were famous for their riding skills and their wild way of life. The gaucho tradition lives on today, despite changes in ranching.

BOATS OF REED

The Uru people live on the islands and shores of Lake Titicaca, high on the border between Peru and Bolivia. In an area short of timber, they use bundles of reeds called *totora* to make both fishing boats and houses.

CARIBBEAN SEA

ATLANTIC OCEAN

VENEZUELA
Georgetown
GUYANA
Paramaribo
FRENCH GUIANA
Cayenne
SURINAME
GUIANA HIGHLANDS
COLOMBIA
Branco
Negro
Macapá
Marajó Island
Marajó Bay
Belèm
Japurá
Manaus
Amazon
São Marcos Bay
São Luis
Fortaleza
Fernando Noronha
Tocantins
Xingu
Tapajós
Madeira
Purus
Juruá
Cape São Roque
Araguaia
Parnaíba
CAATINGAS
Recife
BRAZIL
Barragem de Sobradinho
São Francisco
Maceió
Arinos
SIERRA DOS PARECIS
PERU
BOLIVIA
MATO GROSSO PLATEAU
Salvador
Brasília
BRAZILIAN HIGHLANDS
Belo Horizonte
Paraná
Reprêsa Ilha Grande
São Paulo
Cape São Tomé
PARAGUAY
Itaipu Res.
SERRA DO MAR
Santos
Rio de Janeiro
ARGENTINA
ATLANTIC OCEAN
Pôrto Alegre
Patos Lagoon
Lake Mirim
URUGUAY
N

DID YOU KNOW?

The Amazon River basin is the largest in the world. It covers an area of 7,045,000 sq km (2,720,000 sq miles). Crossed by countless tributaries and streams, it may contain as much as one-fifth of all the world's fresh water. The rain forests it supports are being destroyed at an alarming rate, as vast areas are cleared by farmers, loggers, miners, and road-builders.

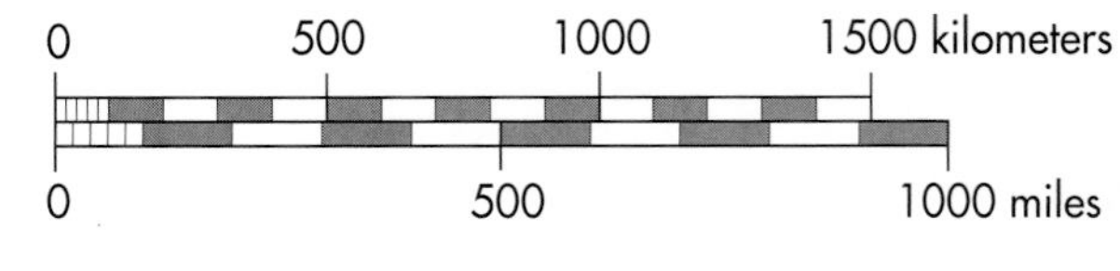
0
500
1000
1500 kilometers
0
500
1000 miles

BRAZIL & THE NORTHEAST

COUNTRIES & DEPENDENCIES

BRAZIL
AREA: 8,506,663 SQ KM (3,284,422 SQ MI)
POPULATION: 168 MILLION
CAPITAL: BRASÍLIA

FRENCH GUIANA
OVERSEAS DEPARTMENT OF FRANCE
AREA: 91,000 SQ KM (35,135 SQ MI)
POPULATION: 0.2 MILLION
CAPITAL: CAYENNE

GUYANA
AREA: 214.970 SQ KM (83,000 SQ MI)
POPULATION: 0.7 MILLION
CAPITAL: GEORGETOWN

SURINAME
AREA: 163,820 SQ KM (63,251 SQ MI)
POPULATION: 0.4 MILLION
CAPITAL: PARAMARIBO

South America's Caribbean coast is hot and humid, rising inland to the forested Guiana Highlands. Three small countries occupy the coast. Guyana is a former British colony, Suriname is a former Dutch colony, and French Guiana—a former colony—is now an overseas department of France. The region has reserves of gold, bauxite, and oil and grows sugarcane, bananas, rice, and peppers.

Brazil, once ruled by Portugal, is the giant of South America. The rain forest of the Amazon River basin takes up one-third of the whole country. Much of the rest is hill country, with large areas of dry scrub. Nine out of ten Brazilians live on the Atlantic coast, where most industry is located. In 1961, the country's capital was moved inland from Rio de Janeiro to a new city, named Brasília. Brazil is the world's biggest grower of soy beans and sugarcane. It is rich in iron, gold and silver, and manufactures steel.

COFFEE BEANS

No other country in the world produces as much coffee as Brazil. About two million tons a year are grown there. Coffee was originally planted in the rich, red soil of São Paulo state. It was later introduced to large areas of the south. Much of it is grown on large plantations called *fazendas*. For many years the Brazilian economy depended on this single crop, but today many other plants are grown as well.

PEOPLES OF THE REGION

The northeast of South America is home to a rich mixture of peoples and cultures. Small groups of Native Americans live throughout the region. Some still follow a traditional way of life. Many have suffered from persecution and poverty. People of African origin are found throughout the region, and the Caribbean coast is home to people of South and East Asian origin. Many Brazilians are of European descent, including ethnic Portuguese, Italians, and Germans. The great majority are people of mixed descent.

DID YOU KNOW?

The Andes Mountains are the product of a massive collision between two sections of the Earth's crust, the Nazca Plate and the South American Plate. The great pressure between them has crumpled up rocks as if they were paper. The process is still going on, which is why the region is often shaken by earthquakes and subject to mudslides and volcanic eruptions.

0
500
1000
1500 kilometers
0
500
1000 miles
CARIBBEAN SEA
Gulf of Venezuela
Netherlands Antilles
TRINIDAD & TOBAGO
Barranquilla
Maracaibo
Caracas
Lake Maracaibo
LLANOS
PANAMA
Gulf of Panama
Orinoco
Orinoco Delta
VENEZUELA
Medellín
Salto Angel
GUYANA
PACIFIC OCEAN
Bogotá
SURINAM
Cali
Huila
Orinoco
COLOMBIA
ECUADOR
Quito
Chimborazo
Guayaquil
Putumayo
Marañón
Punta Aguja
ANDES MOUNTAINS
BRAZIL
Nevado Huascarán
PERU
Lima
Lake Titicaca
BOLIVIA
La Paz
Lake Poopó
Sucre
CHILE
PARAGUAY
Galápagos Islands (ECUADOR)
PACIFIC OCEAN
ISLA PINTA (Abingdon Is.)
ISLA MARCHENA (Bindloe Is.)
ISLA GENOVESA (Tower Is.)
ISLA ISABELA (Albemarle Is.)
ISLA SAN SALVADOR (Santiago Is.)
ISLA FERNANDINA (Narborough Is.)
ISLA SANTA CRUZ (Indefatigable Is.)
Santa Rosa
Bellavista
Puerto Ayora
Santo Tomás
Puerto Villamil
ISLA SAN CRISTÓBAL (Chatham Is.)
ISLA SANTA MARÍA (Charles Is.)
0 50 kilometers
0 40 miles

NORTHERN ANDES

COUNTRIES
BOLIVIA AREA: 1,098,579 SQ KM (424,161 SQ MI) POPULATION: 8 MILLION CAPITALS: SUCRE, LA PAZ
COLOMBIA AREA: 1,138,915 SQ KM (439,735 SQ MI) POPULATION: 38.6 MILLION CAPITAL: BOGOTA
ECUADOR AREA: 283,561 SQ KM (109,483 SQ MI) POPULATION: 12.2 MILLION CAPITAL: QUITO
PERU AREA: 1,285,215 SQ KM (496,222 SQ MI) POPULATION: 26.1 MILLION CAPITAL: LIMA
VENEZUELA AREA: 912,045 SQ KM (352,140 SQ MI) POPULATION: 23.3 MILLION CAPITAL: CARACAS

The Andes make up the world's longest mountain range. In places, they split into two or three parallel chains. Their northeastern limit lies in Venezuela.

Venezuela's Caribbean coastline is broken up into islands, lagoons, and deltas. The north of the country is the Llanos savanna region, while the Orinoco River crosses the center. Colombia has coasts bordering both the Caribbean Sea and the Pacific Ocean. Most Colombian cities are on the coast, or in the cool foothills of the Andes.

The Andes continue southward through Ecuador, Peru, and Bolivia. Here, the coastal regions are hot and sticky, but temperatures drop as the land rises to the plateaus and peaks of the Andes. In the far west lie the fringes of the rain forest. The Pacific Ocean provides a rich source of fish. Bananas and sugarcane can be grown on the Pacific coast, while highland crops include potatoes and a grain named quinoa.

MINERAL WEALTH

To the Incas, gold was the "sweat of the Sun," and silver the "tears of the Moon." It was the mineral wealth of the Andes that first lured Spanish adventurers to the region, forever changing the continent. The Andes are still rich in tin, copper, emeralds, silver, and gold. Working conditions in some mines are very harsh. Many poor people pan mountain streams for gold in the slim hope of making their fortune.

PEOPLES OF THE REGION

The population of the Northern Andes includes a large number of Native American peoples. Many speak their own languages, such as Quechua or Aymara. The European settlers in the region were mostly Spanish, and the majority of people today are of mixed descent but speak Spanish. While some city dwellers are quite wealthy, many of the farmers living in the mountains are very poor.

PERU
BOLIVIA
BRAZIL
Arica
ATACAMA DESERT
Antofagasta
ANDES MOUNTAINS
GRAN CHACO
PARAGUAY
Paraná
Asunción
PACIFIC OCEAN
Mar Chiquito
Paraná
ARGENTINA
CHILE
Cerro Aconcagua
Rosario
URUGUAY
Buenos Aires
Montevideo
La Plata
PLATE RIVER
Salado
Santiago
CENTRAL VALLEY
PAMPAS
ATLANTIC OCEAN
Cape San Antonio
Bahia Blanca
Negro
Blanca Bay
Valdés Peninsula
Chubut
Chiloé Island
Gulf of San Jorge
LOS CHONOS ARCHIPELAGO
PATAGONIA
FALKLAND ISLANDS/ ISLAS MALVINAS
REINA ADELAIDE ARCHIPELAGO
Grande Bay
West Falkland
Stanley
East Falkland
Strait of Magellan
Punta Arenas
Ushuaia
Tierra del Fuego
ISLA GRANDE
Cape Horn
0 500 1000 1500 kilometers
0 500 1000 miles
N

DID YOU KNOW

The southernmost town in the world is called Ushuaia. It is a fishing port and naval base, with a population of about 40,000 people, in the Tierra del Fuego province of Argentina. Ushuaia lies on the Beagle Channel. The channel is named after the ship of the great naturalist Charles Darwin, who visited these southern lands in the 1830s.

SOUTHERN LANDS

COUNTRIES & DEPENDENCIES

ARGENTINA
AREA: 2,776,884 SQ KM (1,072,155 SQ MI)
POPULATION: 36.1 MILLION
CAPITAL: BUENOS AIRES

CHILE
AREA: 756,946 SQ KM (292,257 SQ MI)
POPULATION: 14.8 MILLION
CAPITAL: SANTIAGO

FALKLAND (MALVINAS) ISLANDS
BRITISH DEPENDENCY
AREA: 12,175 SQ KM (4,700 SQ MI)
POPULATION: 2,000
CAPITAL: STANLEY

PARAGUAY
AREA: 406,750 SQ KM (157,046 SQ MI)
POPULATION: 5.2 MILLION
CAPITAL: ASUNCIÓN

URUGUAY
AREA: 176,221 SQ KM (68,039 SQ MI)
POPULATION: 3.2 MILLION
CAPITAL: MONTEVIDEO

The Andes Mountains run southward to the very tip of the continent, where glaciers grind their way down from high, snowy peaks to deep sea inlets. The Andes form the eastern border of Chile, a long, narrow country on the Pacific coast.

Chile's north coast is a harsh area, where farming is made possible only by irrigation. However, the north is rich in nitrates and copper. In the Atacama Desert, a coastal desert, rain is almost unknown. Most of Chile's population lives in the mild, green Valle Central, where most farming and industry takes place. The far south is a remote wilderness of ice and rocky islands.

Paraguay lies in central South America, between the hot Gran Chaco region and the Paraná River. Most Paraguyans live on the eastern grasslands. Uruguay lies to the north of the Plate River estuary. Cattle are raised in both countries.

Argentina is a large country lying to the east of the southern Andes. There is farming in the northeast and central regions. In places these regions are warm enough for vineyards. Cattle are raised on the Pampas grasslands and sheep in the remote valleys of Patagonia.

PEOPLES OF THE REGION

Surviving Native American groups include the Araucanian peoples, such as the Mapuche of Chile, and the Guaraní of Paraguay, Uruguay, and northern Argentina. The whole of this region was colonized by Spain, but today's population is a melting pot of peoples and cultures. It includes Italians, Germans, Slavs, Basques, Jews, Welsh, Hungarians, Poles, Russians, Lebanese, Syrians, Japanese, and Koreans. People of English descent live on the Falkland Islands, a British dependency in the South Atlantic Ocean that is also claimed by Argentina.

DRINKING HOT MATÉ

A drink like tea is made from the leaves of the Paraguay holly. It is called yerba maté and is very popular in Argentina and Paraguay. Traditionally, maté is drunk through a metal straw from a gourd or a gourd-shaped flask. It may be sweetened with sugar and flavored with herbs. The gauchos, the cowboys of the Pampas, like it brewed bitter and strong.

AFRICA

Africa is the second largest continent in the world. To the north it is bordered by the Mediterranean Sea. To the east lie the sweltering coasts of the Red Sea and the Horn of Africa (with Somalia at its point), and the coral islands and reefs of the Indian Ocean. The bulging coastline of West Africa sweeps out into the breakers of the Atlantic Ocean, forming the Gulf of Guinea (from Liberia to Gabon). The continent's southernmost point is Cape Agulhas, in South Africa.

The Nile, the world's longest river, flows northward from Central Africa through the swamps of southern Sudan and the deserts of Egypt. The mighty Congo drains a vast area of rain forest before flowing into the Atlantic. Africa has lakes as big as seas. Its huge deserts include the Sahara, Kalahari, and Namib. Africa has many mountain chains, from the Atlas Mountains in Morocco and Algeria to the volcanoes of Tanzania and the Democratic Republic of Congo and the Drakensberg Mountains in South Africa. The summits of Mount Kilimanjaro and Mount Kenya are always covered with snow, even though they are on the Equator.

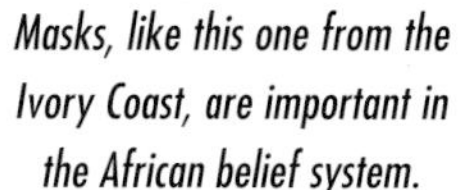

Masks, like this one from the Ivory Coast, are important in the African belief system.

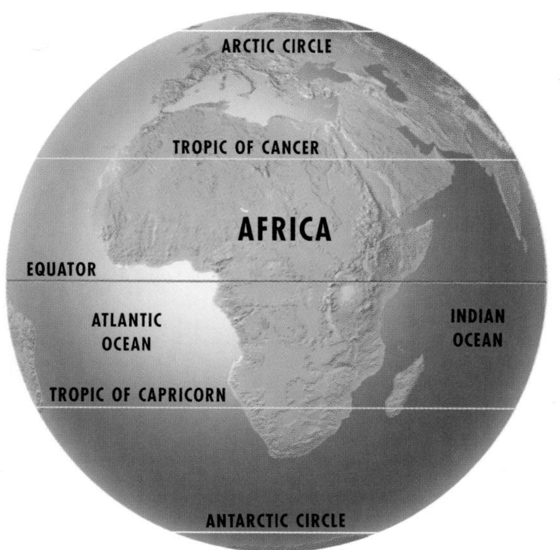
ARCTIC CIRCLE
TROPIC OF CANCER
AFRICA
EQUATOR
ATLANTIC OCEAN
INDIAN OCEAN
TROPIC OF CAPRICORN
ANTARCTIC CIRCLE

AN ANCIENT LAND

Africa has a very long history. A great civilization grew up in Egypt, on the banks of the Nile River, beginning about 5,000 years ago. The Egyptians built impressive buildings for their pharoahs, like the Great Pyramids and the temple at Abu Simbel (right). Later, powerful kingdoms and empires developed in Africa's other regions. The forests and deserts of Africa kept people from drawing good maps of the continent before the 1800s.

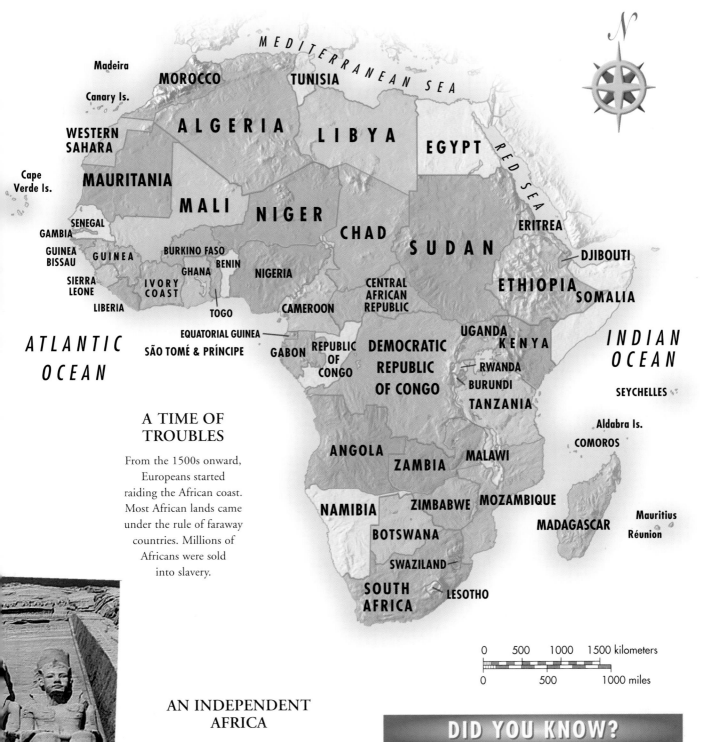

MEDITERRANEAN SEA
Madeira
Canary Is.
MOROCCO
TUNISIA
ALGERIA
LIBYA
EGYPT
RED SEA
WESTERN SAHARA
Cape Verde Is.
MAURITANIA
MALI
NIGER
CHAD
SUDAN
ERITREA
DJIBOUTI
SENEGAL
GAMBIA
GUINEA BISSAU
GUINEA
BURKINO FASO
BENIN
GHANA
NIGERIA
SIERRA LEONE
IVORY COAST
LIBERIA
TOGO
CAMEROON
CENTRAL AFRICAN REPUBLIC
ETHIOPIA
SOMALIA
EQUATORIAL GUINEA
SÃO TOMÉ & PRÍNCIPE
GABON
REPUBLIC OF CONGO
DEMOCRATIC REPUBLIC OF CONGO
UGANDA
KENYA
RWANDA
BURUNDI
TANZANIA
ATLANTIC OCEAN
INDIAN OCEAN
SEYCHELLES
Aldabra Is.
COMOROS
ANGOLA
ZAMBIA
MALAWI
NAMIBIA
ZIMBABWE
MOZAMBIQUE
MADAGASCAR
Mauritius
Réunion
BOTSWANA
SWAZILAND
SOUTH AFRICA
LESOTHO
0 500 1000 1500 kilometers
0 500 1000 miles

A TIME OF TROUBLES

From the 1500s onward, Europeans started raiding the African coast. Most African lands came under the rule of faraway countries. Millions of Africans were sold into slavery.

AN INDEPENDENT AFRICA

In the 1900s, the African lands began to govern themselves once again. Some took new names, or names based on earlier African empires. Today, almost the whole African mainland is independent.

DID YOU KNOW?

Fossil remains discovered in Ethiopia, Kenya, Tanzania, and South Africa suggest that the ancestors of all the human beings on Earth came from Africa. They were probably ape-like creatures who evolved, or developed, over 5 million years ago. Modern human beings began to develop about 200,000 years ago.

AFRICA

Africa is a vast continent, three times the size of Europe. Its population is not much larger than Europe's, but it is growing faster than that of any other continent. Africa already faces severe problems in health care and education, for many of its countries are desperately poor. Some African lands have problems of drought, others have political unrest or large international debts to repay. However, the continent has rich resources, too. One of these is its young people, who want to build a new future.

• GENERAL FACTS •

HIGHEST POINT
MT. KILIMANJARO, 5,895 M (19,340 FT), TANZANIA

LOWEST POINT
LAC ASSAL, -153 M (-502 FT), DJIBOUTI

LONGEST RIVER
NILE RIVER, 6,671 KM (4,145 MI), SUDAN-EGYPT

BIGGEST LAKE
LAKE VICTORIA, 68,100 SQ KM (26,293 SQ MI), KENYA-UGANDA-TANZANIA

HIGHEST WATERFALL
TUGELA FALLS, 614 M (2,014 FT), SOUTH AFRICA

BIGGEST ISLAND
MADAGASCAR, 587,000 SQ KM (226,641 SQ MI), INDIAN OCEAN

BIGGEST DESERT
SAHARA, 9,065,000 SQ KM (3,500,000 SQ MI), MOROCCO-ALGERIA-TUNISIA-LIBYA-EGYPT-SUDAN-WESTERN SAHARA-MAURITANIA-MALI-NIGER-CHAD

POPULATION OF CONTINENT
771 MILLION (1999)

MOST POPULOUS COUNTRY
NIGERIA, 113.8 MILLION (1999)

MOST DENSELY POPULATED COUNTRY
MAURITIUS, 593 PER SQ KM (1,229 PER SQ MI) (1998)

MOST POPULOUS CITY
CAIRO, EGYPT, 9.9 MILLION (1996)

POPULATION LIVING IN CITIES
30 PERCENT

INFANT MORTALITY
88 DEATHS PER 1,000 CHILDREN UNDER AGE 1

LIFE EXPECTANCY
MALE 51 YEARS; FEMALE 54 YEARS

WEALTH
GROSS DOMESTIC PRODUCT PER PERSON U.S. $2,115 (1996)

LITERACY RATE
MALE 65 PERCENT; FEMALE 42 PERCENT

• VEGETATION •

Olive groves and orange trees thrive on the North African coast, but little can grow in the dry Sahara region. What's more, the desert is spreading into the grasslands to the south. A belt of dense rain forest surrounds the Congo River, giving way in the east and south to savanna grasslands. Southern Africa takes in deserts, high-level grassland known as veld, and the orchards and vineyards of the Cape region.

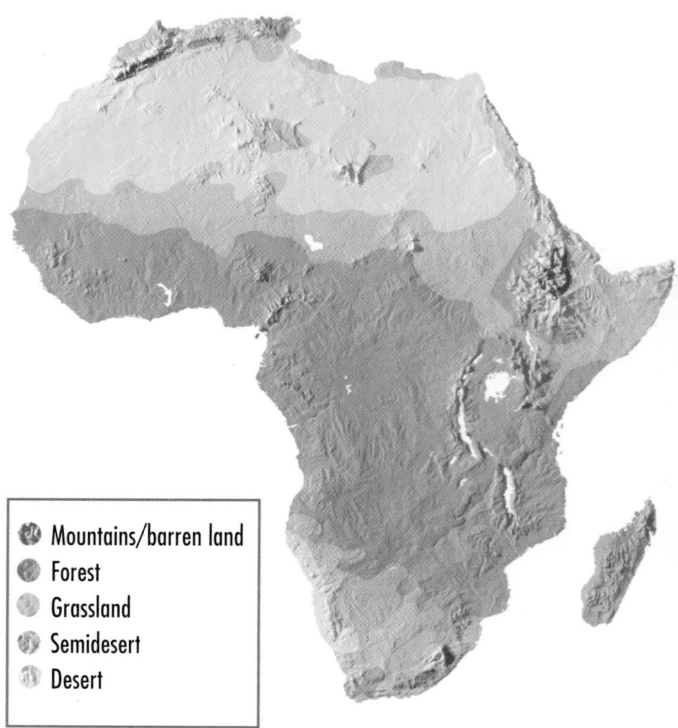
Mountains/barren land
Forest
Grassland
Semidesert
Desert

LANGUAGE

Perhaps as many as 2,000 languages may be heard in Africa, belonging to five main language groups. The most widespread group is made up of Bantu, or Niger-Congo, languages. The old colonial languages of English and French are still widely used. Kiswahili is understood over a very wide area, with 25 million people using it as a second language.

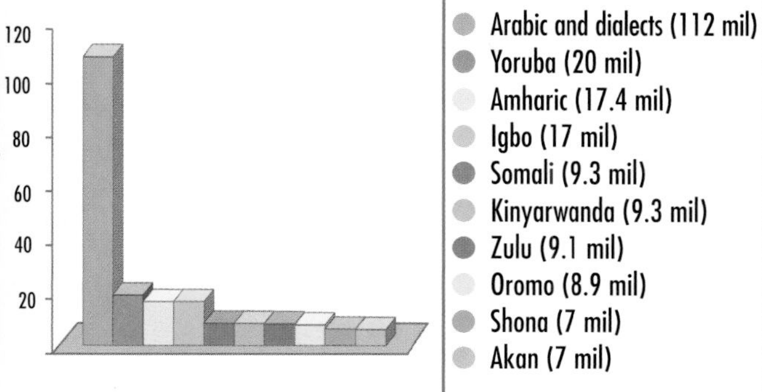
120
100
80
60
40
20
Arabic and dialects (112 mil)
Yoruba (20 mil)
Amharic (17.4 mil)
Igbo (17 mil)
Somali (9.3 mil)
Kinyarwanda (9.3 mil)
Zulu (9.1 mil)
Oromo (8.9 mil)
Shona (7 mil)
Akan (7 mil)

RELIGION

African religious traditions are based on a belief in a life force present in all things, in magic, healing, and honoring one's ancestors. Ethiopia has been Christian for nearly 1,700 years and European missionaries introduced Christianity to Central and Southern Africa in the 1800s. Islam is widespread in North Africa, across the Sahel, and on the East African coast.

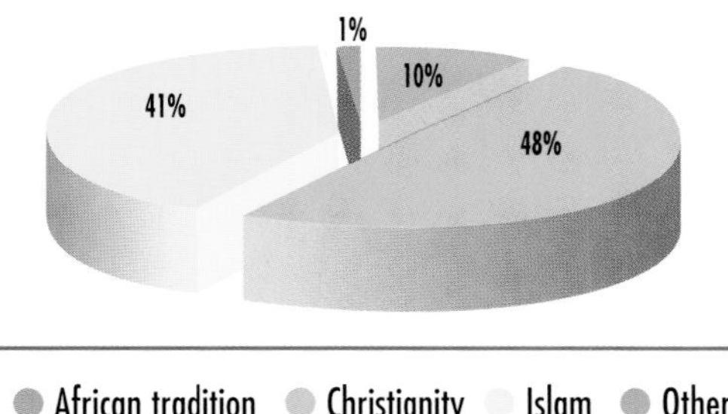
1%
10%
41%
48%
African tradition
Christianity
Islam
Other

RESOURCES

Many parts of Africa are rich in minerals, in tropical forests, and in rivers that can generate hydroelectric power. However, many resources are still not developed because of economic or political problems.

COPPER: *Democratic Republic of Congo, Zambia*

DIAMONDS: *Angola, Botswana, Democratic Republic of Congo, Sierra Leone, South Africa*

GOLD: *Ghana, South Africa, Tanzania, Zimbabwe*

OIL: *Algeria, Libya, Nigeria*

PHOSPHATES: *Algeria, Mauritania, Morocco*

CLIMATE

Africa as a whole has a warm climate, except where there are high mountains. The Sahara is one of the hottest, driest places on Earth, while the region around the Equator is very warm and humid, with heavy rains. The savanna grasslands have a tropical climate and drought is common.

EQUATOR

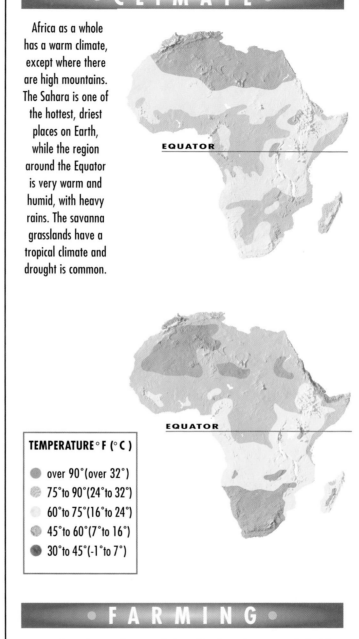

EQUATOR
TEMPERATURE °F (°C)
over 90° (over 32°)
75° to 90° (24° to 32°)
60° to 75° (16° to 24°)
45° to 60° (7° to 16°)
30° to 45° (-1° to 7°)

FARMING

Many African farmers have small plots of land, producing enough food for themselves and for local markets. Others work on large farms to produce cash crops such as vegetables, coffee, peanuts, and fruit for export.

CATTLE: *Botswana, Ethiopia, Kenya, Madagascar*

COCOA: *Cameroon, Ghana, Malawi*

COFFEE: *Ethiopia, Kenya, Tanzania*

CORN: *Egypt, Kenya, Malawi, Nigeria, South Africa, Tanzania, Zimbabwe*

MILLET: *Burkina Faso, Cameroon, Chad, Egypt, Ethiopia, Ghana, Kenya, Mali, Niger, Nigeria, Sudan*

AFRICA:
A Land of Contrast

Much of the African landscape may seem ancient and unchanging. A lion roars as night falls over the savanna. Camels grumble and grunt as they start a long journey across the Sahara Desert. Dugout canoes drift down the muddy waters of the Congo River. Women work in the fields, hoeing the red soil. Thatched grass huts sit on lush green mountainsides under blue skies and towering white clouds.

However, Africa is changing rapidly. Roads are being cut through the forests. Rivers are being dammed for electricity and irrigation. In big cities such as Nairobi or Dakar there are gleaming high-rise offices and hotels. At street level, all is hustle and bustle. Passengers carrying bundles of goods climb onto brightly painted trucks and buses, while loudspeakers pump out African pop songs.

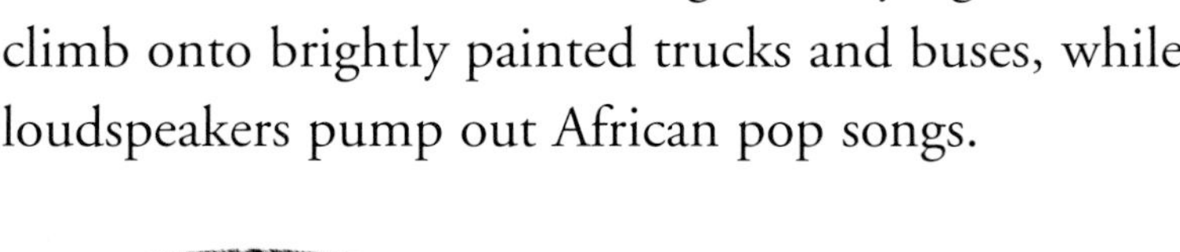

WORLD COMPETITORS

The Cameroon national soccer team lines up for photos before beating Zimbabwe in a World Cup qualifier in 1997. Soccer is Africa's most popular sport. From Cairo to Zanzibar, Lagos to Yaoundé, youngsters practice kicking soccer balls and dream of playing in the big time. Other sports are popular in Africa, too. Kenya and Ethiopia are renowned for long-distance running, and South Africa for rugby and cricket.

AFRICAN WILDLIFE

A pride of lions basks in the sunshine, sleepy after a night of hunting. Africa is one of the last great havens for wildlife in the world, but as cities grow and new roads are built, there is less and less space for wild creatures, except in reserves and national parks.

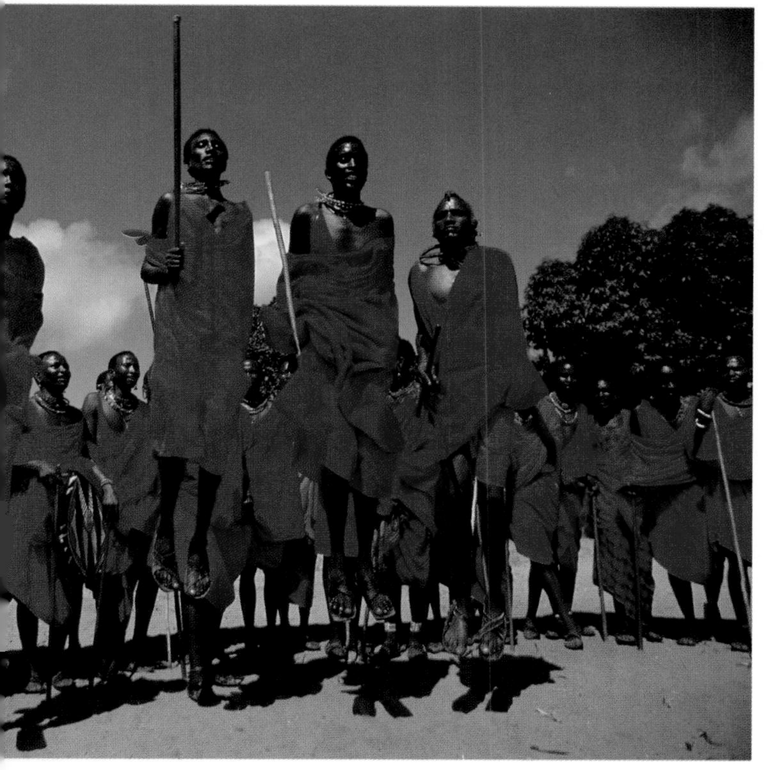

THE MASAI

Masai warriors perform a dance, leaping high into the air. The Masai live on both sides of the Kenya–Tanzania border. Unlike many African peoples, they still wear traditional dress. The women wear large beaded collars and hooped earrings. The young men wear scarlet cloaks or checked blankets and carry spears.

THE GREAT RIFT VALLEY

The Great Rift Valley is a deep crack in the Earth's surface, which runs down the length of East Africa, from the Red Sea southward through Ethiopia, Kenya right, Tanzania, Malawi, and Mozambique. It is marked by volcanoes and craters. In many places it has flooded, forming a long chain of lakes.

THE DESERT

The Sahara is the biggest desert in the world, a vast area of rock and shifting sands. The highest temperature ever known was recorded in the Libyan part of the desert. There are two large deserts in the south of the continent, too—the Kalahari and the Namib.

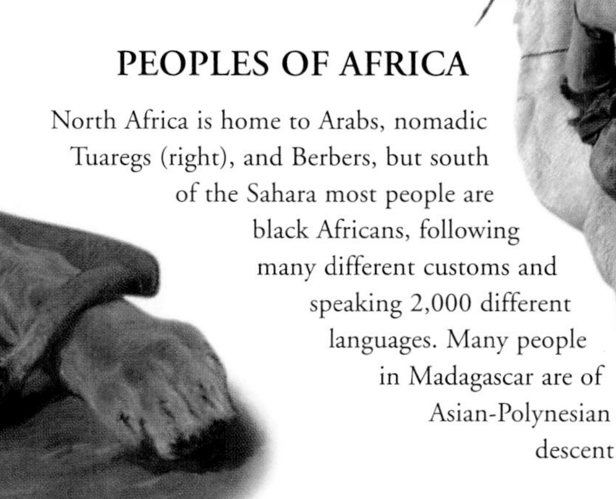

PEOPLES OF AFRICA

North Africa is home to Arabs, nomadic Tuaregs (right), and Berbers, but south of the Sahara most people are black Africans, following many different customs and speaking 2,000 different languages. Many people in Madagascar are of Asian-Polynesian descent.

NORTH AFRICA

North Africa lies just 13 kilometers (8 miles) from Europe across the Strait of Gibraltar. It is separated from Asia by the Red Sea and the Suez Canal. Most North Africans live along its Mediterranean coast, where there is farmland and large whitewashed cities, many with mazes of small streets and busy markets. Calls to prayer are broadcast from mosques, for most of the people are Muslims.

To the west, the Atlas Mountains run across Morocco and Algeria. To the south lie the empty, burning sands and rocks of the Sahara Desert. Here, farming is impossible, but there are rich reserves of oil and phosphates. Some peoples survive in the desert, herding camels and moving from one oasis, or water source, to another. Farther south lie the thin pastures of the dry Sahel region, where people struggle to raise cattle.

In Sudan, Africa's largest country, and Ethiopia are lands of desert, swamp, and mountains. Both have suffered from drought and many years of war and political unrest.

COUNTRIES

ALGERIA
AREA: 2,378,907 SQ KM (918,496 SQ MI)
POPULATION: 30.8 MILLION
CAPITAL: ALGIERS

CHAD
AREA: 1,284,000 SQ KM (495,752 SQ MI)
POPULATION: 7.7 MILLION
CAPITAL: NDJAMENA

DJIBOUTI
AREA: 23,000 SQ KM (8,880 SQ MI)
POPULATION: 0.6 MILLION
CAPITAL: DJIBOUTI

EGYPT
AREA: 1,002,071 SQ KM (386,900 SQ MI)
POPULATION: 66.9 MILLION
CAPITAL: CAIRO

ERITREA
AREA: 117,599 SQ KM (45,405 SQ MI)
POPULATION: 4 MILLION
CAPITAL: ASMARA

ETHIOPIA
AREA: 1,221,897 SQ KM (471,774 SQ MI)
POPULATION: 59.7 MILLION
CAPITAL: ADDIS ABABA

LIBYA
AREA: 1,759,540 SQ KM (679,358 SQ MI)
POPULATION: 5 MILLION
CAPITAL: TRIPOLI

MALI
AREA: 1,239,709 SQ KM (478,652 SQ MI)
POPULATION: 11 MILLION
CAPITAL: BAMAKO

MAURITANIA
AREA: 1,030,801 SQ KM (397,992 SQ MI)
POPULATION: 2.6 MILLION
CAPITAL: NOUAKCHOTT

MOROCCO
(EXCLUDING WESTERN SAHARA)
AREA: 446,550 SQ KM (172,413 SQ MI)
POPULATION: 28.2 MILLION
CAPITAL: RABAT

NIGER
AREA: 1,188,999 SQ KM (459,173 SQ MI)
POPULATION: 10 MILLION
CAPITAL: NIAMEY

SUDAN
AREA: 2,505,825 SQ KM (967,500 SQ MI)
POPULATION: 28.9 MILLION
CAPITAL: KHARTOUM

TUNISIA
AREA: 164,150 SQ KM (63,378 SQ MI)
POPULATION: 9.5 MILLION
CAPITAL: TUNIS

WESTERN SAHARA
DISPUTED TERRITORY/ MOROCCO
AREA: 266,001 SQ KM (102,703 SQ MI)
POPULATION: 0.2 MILLION
CAPITAL: LAÂYOUNE

CAIRO, EGYPT

Egypt is a mostly desert country, with the Nile River as its lifeline. It is the most populous country in North Africa, producing cotton, textiles, and dates. Its capital, Cairo, has the largest population of any city in Africa.

PEOPLES OF THE REGION

The Berbers have always lived in the northwest part of the region. Arabs occupied most of the north beginning about 1,350 years ago. Both are Muslim. South of the Sahara are many different black African peoples, some of whom are Christian.

DID YOU KNOW?

Ancient rock paintings show that in 6000 B.C. the Sahara Desert was lush and green, and filled with wild animals. By 2500 B.C. major climate changes and overgrazing by cattle and goats had turned the land to desert, causing people to migrate southward.

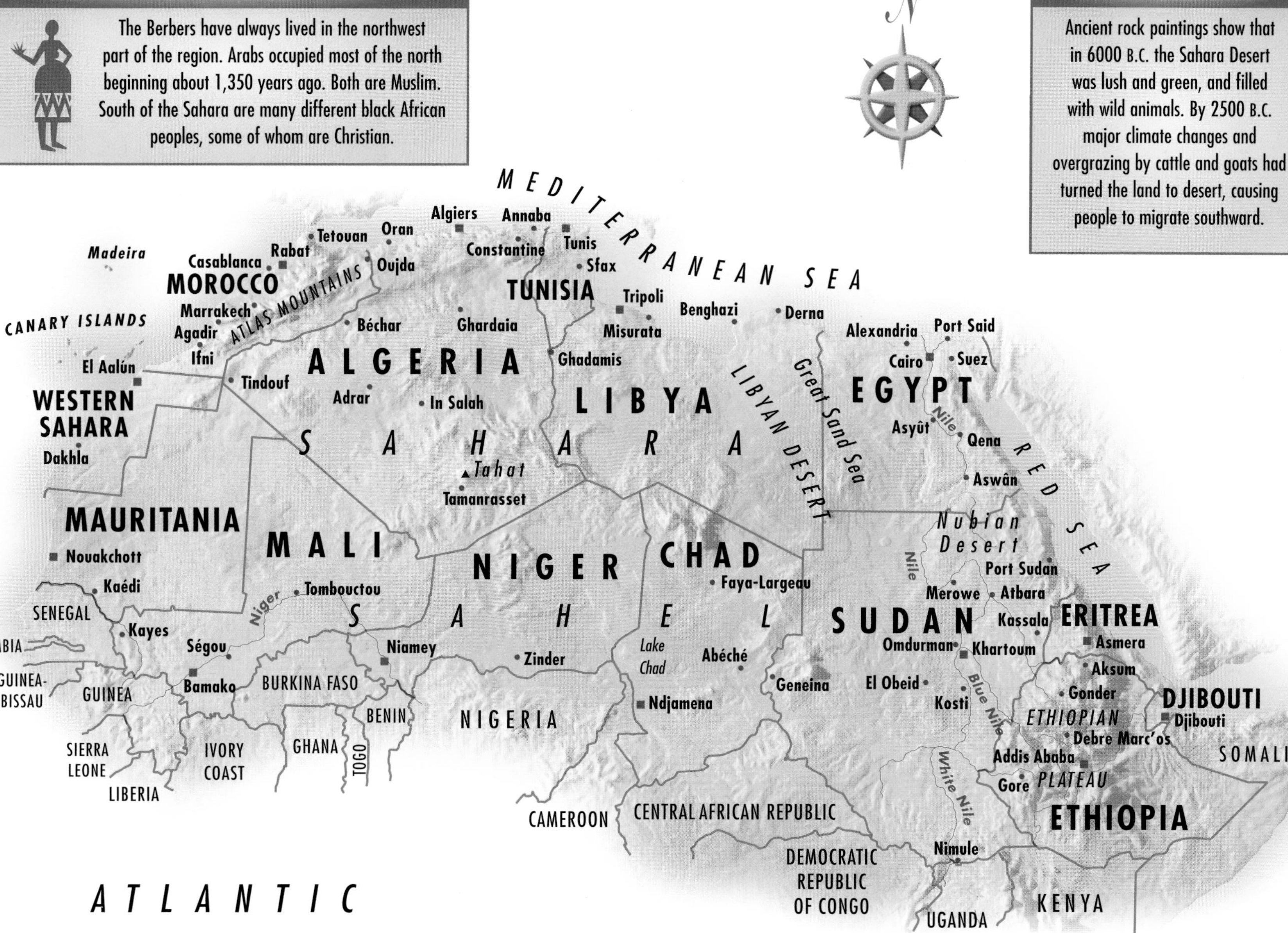
N
MEDITERRANEAN SEA
Madeira
CANARY ISLANDS
MOROCCO
Casablanca
Rabat
Tetouan
Oran
Oujda
Algiers
Annaba
Constantine
Tunis
Sfax
TUNISIA
Tripoli
Misurata
Benghazi
Derna
Alexandria
Port Said
Cairo
Suez
EGYPT
Marrakech
Agadir
Ifni
ATLAS MOUNTAINS
Béchar
Ghardaia
Ghadamis
El Aalún
Tindouf
ALGERIA
Adrar
In Salah
LIBYA
LIBYAN DESERT
Great Sand Sea
Asyût
Nile
Qena
Aswân
RED SEA
WESTERN SAHARA
Dakhla
SAHARA
Tahat
Tamanrasset
MAURITANIA
Nouakchott
Kaédi
MALI
NIGER
CHAD
Nubian Desert
Port Sudan
Merowe
Atbara
Faya-Largeau
Tombouctou
Niger
SENEGAL
Kayes
SAHEL
SUDAN
Kassala
ERITREA
Asmera
Omdurman
Khartoum
Aksum
Gonder
GAMBIA
Ségou
Niamey
Zinder
Lake Chad
Abéché
Geneina
El Obeid
Kosti
Blue Nile
DJIBOUTI
Djibouti
GUINEA-BISSAU
GUINEA
Bamako
BURKINA FASO
BENIN
NIGERIA
Ndjamena
ETHIOPIAN PLATEAU
Debre Marc'os
Addis Ababa
Gore
SIERRA LEONE
LIBERIA
IVORY COAST
GHANA
TOGO
White Nile
SOMALIA
ETHIOPIA
CAMEROON
CENTRAL AFRICAN REPUBLIC
DEMOCRATIC REPUBLIC OF CONGO
Nimule
UGANDA
KENYA
ATLANTIC OCEAN
0
500
1000
1500 kilometers
0
500
1000 miles

SAHARA
MAURITANIA
MALI
NIGER
SAHEL
Sénégal
Dakar
SENEGAL
Gambia
GAMBIA
Banjul
Bissau
GUINEA-BISSAU
GUINEA
Niger
BURKINA FASO
Ouagadougou
Lake Chad
CHAD
Conakry
Kankan
Freetown
SIERRA LEONE
IVORY COAST
Man
Bouaké
Monrovia
LIBERIA
Yamoussoukro
Abidjan
Greenville
Volta
Tamale
GHANA
TOGO
BENIN
Kumasi
Accra
Lomé
Porto-Novo
Kano
Zaria
Kaduna
Maiduguri
Abuja
Benue
Yola
Garoua
Niger
Ibadan
NIGERIA
Lagos
Onitsha
Benin City
Port Harcourt
CAMEROON
Yaoundé
Malabo
Douala
EQUATORIAL GUINEA
GABON
REPUBLIC OF CONGO
Gulf of Guinea
ATLANTIC OCEAN
N

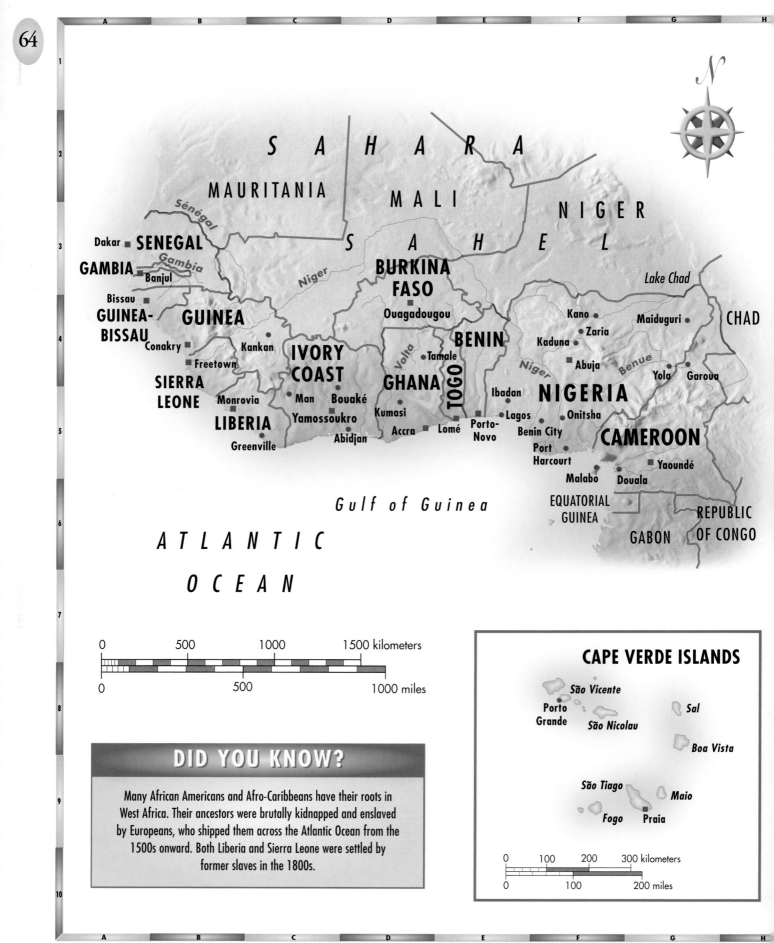

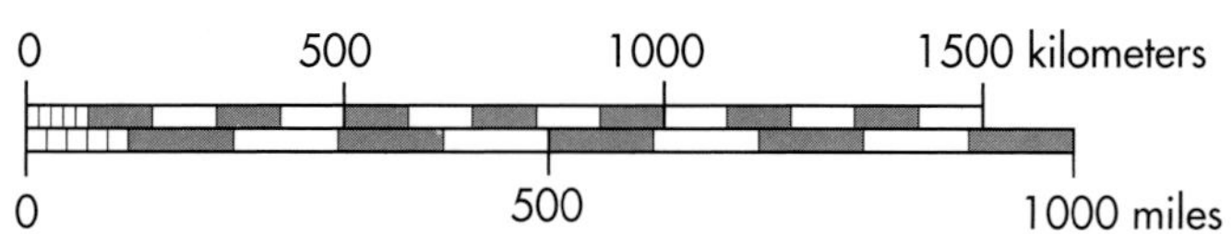
0
500
1000
1500 kilometers
0
500
1000 miles

DID YOU KNOW?

Many African Americans and Afro-Caribbeans have their roots in West Africa. Their ancestors were brutally kidnapped and enslaved by Europeans, who shipped them across the Atlantic Ocean from the 1500s onward. Both Liberia and Sierra Leone were settled by former slaves in the 1800s.

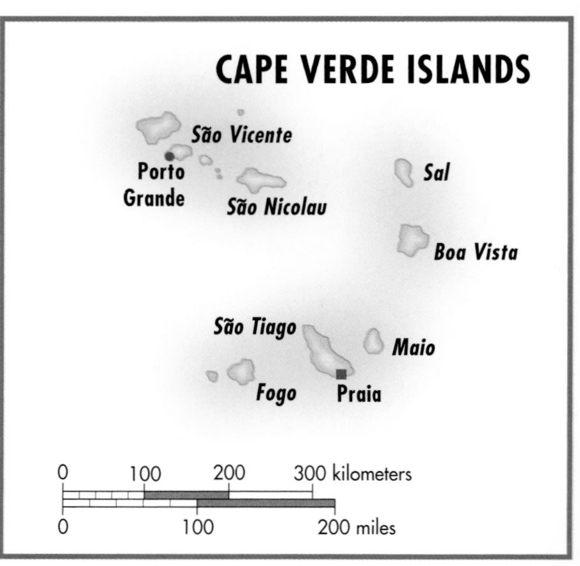
CAPE VERDE ISLANDS
São Vicente
Porto Grande
São Nicolau
Sal
Boa Vista
São Tiago
Maio
Fogo
Praia
0
100
200
300 kilometers
0
100
200 miles

WEST AFRICA

West Africa lies between the Sahel region, which fringes the southern Sahara, and the Atlantic Ocean. The region's southern coast forms the Gulf of Guinea. The Cape Verde Islands are a far western outpost, lying 645 kilometers (401 miles) off Senegal.

The northern part of the region is dry and dusty, with a winter wind called the harmattan that blows in sand from the desert. The central belt is made up of savanna grasslands and plateaus, with some fertile farmland to the south. The coastal region, with its forests and lagoons, is warm and extremely humid. Much of it is suitable for growing cocoa, rubber, palms, and cotton. Southern Cameroon runs into the great rain forests of Central Africa. Two great waterways—the Volta and the Niger—spill across West Africa.

West Africa has reserves of oil, gold, and diamonds. It has many large, modern cities, such as Dakar, Abidjan, Accra, and Lagos. More people live in Nigeria than in any other African country.

PEOPLES OF THE REGION

Islam was brought to the northern part of the region by traders crossing the Sahara over 1,000 years ago. Most of the population in the southern part of West Africa is Christian or follows African spiritual traditions. Major ethnic groups of West Africa include the Wolof, Mende, Fulani, Hausa, Igbo, and Yoruba. Most West African languages are part of the Niger-Congo group. French and English are widely spoken and taught.

COUNTRIES

BENIN
AREA: 112,620 SQ KM (43,483 SQ MI)
POPULATION: 6.2 MILLION
CAPITAL: PORTO-NOVO

BURKINA FASO
AREA: 274,201 SQ KM (105,869 SQ MI)
POPULATION: 11.6 MILLION
CAPITAL: OUAGOUDOUGOU

CAMEROON
AREA: 475,500 SQ KM (183,591 SQ MI)
POPULATION: 15.5 MILLION
CAPITAL: YAOUNDÉ

CAPE VERDE
AREA: 4,035 SQ KM (1,558 SQ MI)
POPULATION: 0.4 MILLION
CAPITAL: PRAIA

GAMBIA
AREA: 10,368 SQ KM (4,003 SQ MI)
POPULATION: 1.3 MILLION
CAPITAL: BANJUL

GHANA
AREA: 238,539 SQ KM (92,100 SQ MI)
POPULATION: 19.7 MILLION
CAPITAL: ACCRA

GUINEA
AREA: 245,855 SQ KM (94,925 SQ MI)
POPULATION: 7.5 MILLION
CAPITAL: CONAKRY

GUINEA BISSAU
AREA: 36,125 SQ KM (13,948 SQ MI)
POPULATION: 1.2 MILLION
CAPITAL: BISSAU

IVORY COAST
AREA: 322,465 SQ KM (124,504 SQ MI)
POPULATION: 15.8 MILLION
CAPITAL: YAMOSSOUKRO

LIBERIA
AREA: 111,370 SQ KM (43,000 SQ MI)
POPULATION: 2.9 MILLION
CAPITAL: MONROVIA

NIGERIA
AREA: 923,850 SQ KM (356,698 SQ MI)
POPULATION: 113.8 MILLION
CAPITAL: ABUJA

SENEGAL
AREA: 197,161 SQ KM (76,124 SQ MI)
POPULATION: 9.2 MILLION
CAPITAL: DAKAR

SIERRA LEONE
AREA: 71,740 SQ KM (27,699 SQ MI)
POPULATION: 5.3 MILLION
CAPITAL: FREETOWN

TOGO
AREA: 56,599 SQ KM (21,853 SQ MI)
POPULATION: 4.5 MILLION
CAPITAL: LOMÉ

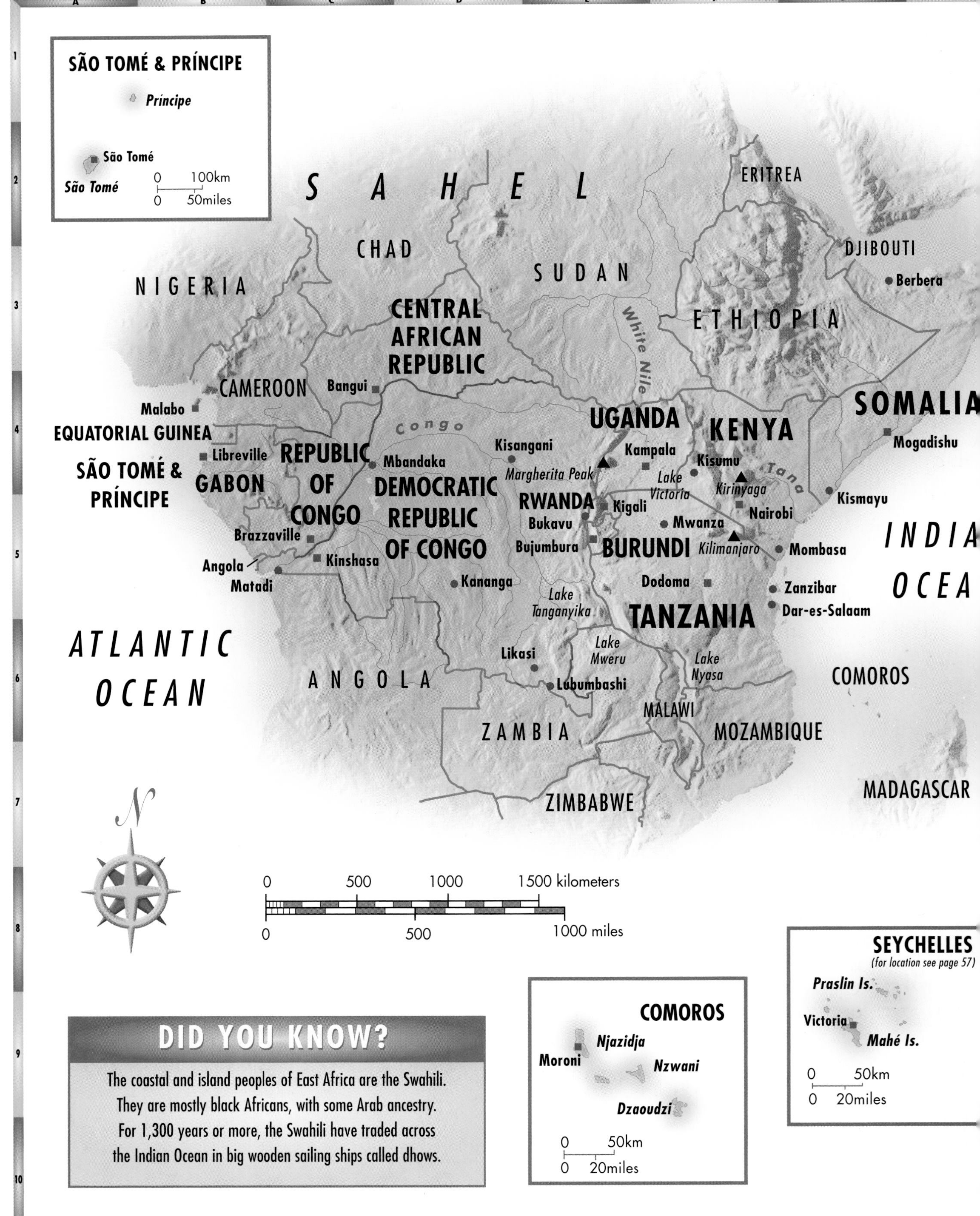
SÃO TOMÉ & PRÍNCIPE
Príncipe
São Tomé
São Tomé
0 100km
0 50miles
S A H E L
CHAD
SUDAN
ERITREA
DJIBOUTI
Berbera
NIGERIA
CENTRAL AFRICAN REPUBLIC
White Nile
ETHIOPIA
CAMEROON
Bangui
Malabo
EQUATORIAL GUINEA
UGANDA
KENYA
SOMALIA
Mogadishu
Congo
Libreville
REPUBLIC OF CONGO
Mbandaka
Kisangani
Kampala
Kisumu
SÃO TOMÉ & PRÍNCIPE
GABON
DEMOCRATIC REPUBLIC OF CONGO
Margherita Peak
Lake Victoria
Tana
Kirinyaga
Kismayu
RWANDA
Kigali
Nairobi
Bukavu
Mwanza
Brazzaville
Bujumbura
BURUNDI
Kilimanjaro
Mombasa
INDIA
Angola
Kinshasa
Matadi
Kananga
Dodoma
Zanzibar
OCEA
Lake Tanganyika
TANZANIA
Dar-es-Salaam
ATLANTIC OCEAN
Likasi
Lake Mweru
Lake Nyasa
ANGOLA
Lubumbashi
COMOROS
MALAWI
ZAMBIA
MOZAMBIQUE
ZIMBABWE
MADAGASCAR
N
0 500 1000 1500 kilometers
0 500 1000 miles
SEYCHELLES
(for location see page 57)
Praslin Is.
Victoria
Mahé Is.
0 50km
0 20miles
COMOROS
Njazidja
Moroni
Nzwani
Dzaoudzi
0 50km
0 20miles

DID YOU KNOW?

The coastal and island peoples of East Africa are the Swahili. They are mostly black Africans, with some Arab ancestry. For 1,300 years or more, the Swahili have traded across the Indian Ocean in big wooden sailing ships called dhows.

CENTRAL & EASTERN AFRICA

Central Africa lies on both sides of the Equator. It is bordered to the north by the Sahel region and to the south by savanna. It extends westward to the Atlantic Ocean and eastward as far as the Great Rift Valley (which runs from far north of Ethiopia to south of Tanzania). Much of this region is taken up by the basin of the Congo River, which is covered by the largest rain forest in Africa.

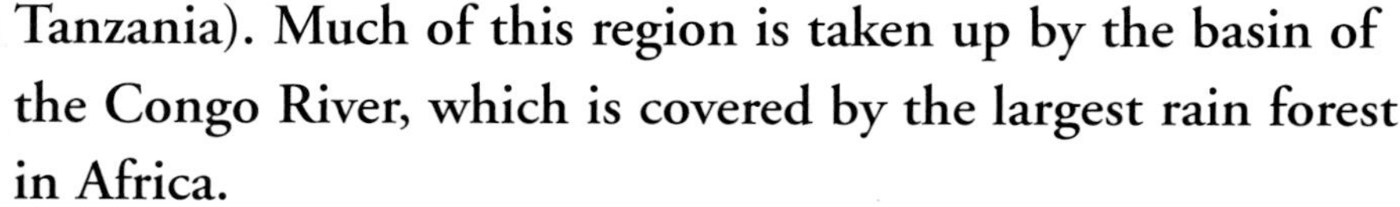

The Democratic Republic of Congo has rich mineral reserves, but the region as a whole is poor and has suffered greatly from war and strife. Many areas are far from sea ports, and their roads are often washed away in the rainy season.

East Africa stretches from the volcanoes and lakes of the Great Rift Valley to the shores and islands of the Indian Ocean. Its northern borders include the hot, sandy deserts of Kenya and Somalia. However, most of the area is taken up by farmland, open savanna—the home of lions, giraffes, and elephants—or by highlands and mountains. Farming, cattle-herding, and fishing are important ways of earning a living, and tourism is a major industry.

RIVER TRANSPORT

In the thick forests of the Congo River basin, roads are few and far between. The great river, and the streams that flow into it, provide the best way of getting around. Crowded riverboats carry passengers up and downstream. Most journeys between villages are made in canoes hollowed from tree trunks .

COUNTRIES

BURUNDI

AREA: 27,835 SQ KM (10,747 SQ MI)
POPULATION: 5.7 MILLION
CAPITAL: BUJUMBURA

CENTRAL AFRICAN REPUBLIC

AREA: 624,975 SQ KM (241,302 SQ MI)
POPULATION: 3.4 MILLION
CAPITAL: BANGUI

COMOROS

AREA: 2,235 SQ KM (863 SQ MI)
POPULATION: 0.6 MILLION
CAPITAL: MORONI

DEMOCRATIC REPUBLIC OF CONGO

AREA: 2,345,410 SQ KM (905,563 SQ MI)
POPULATION: 50.5 MILLION
CAPITAL: KINSHASA

EQUATORIAL GUINEA

AREA: 28,050 SQ KM (10,830 SQ MI)
POPULATION: 0.4 MILLION
CAPITAL: MALABO

GABON

AREA: 265,001 SQ KM (102,317 SQ MI)
POPULATION: 1.2 MILLION
CAPITAL: LIBREVILLE

KENYA

AREA: 582,645 SQ KM (224,959 SQ MI)
POPULATION: 28.8 MILLION
CAPITAL: NAIROBI

REPUBLIC OF CONGO

AREA: 342,000 SQ KM (132,046 SQ MI)
POPULATION: 2.7 MILLION
CAPITAL: BRAZZAVILLE

RWANDA

AREA: 26,338 SQ KM (10,169 SQ MI)
POPULATION: 8.2 MILLION
CAPITAL: KIGALI

SÃO TOMÉ & PRÍNCIPE

AREA: 964 SQ KM (372 SQ MI)
POPULATION: 0.2 MILLION
CAPITAL: SÃO TOMÉ

SEYCHELLES

AREA: 404 SQ KM (156 SQ MI)
POPULATION: 0.1 MILLION
CAPITAL: VICTORIA

SOMALIA

AREA: 637,539 SQ KM (246,154 SQ MI)
POPULATION: 7.1 MILLION
CAPITAL: MOGADISHU

TANZANIA

AREA: 945,091 SQ KM (364,900 SQ MI)
POPULATION: 31.3 MILLION
CAPITAL: DODOMA

UGANDA

AREA: 236,037 SQ KM (91,134 SQ MI)
POPULATION: 22.8 MILLION
CAPITAL: KAMPALA

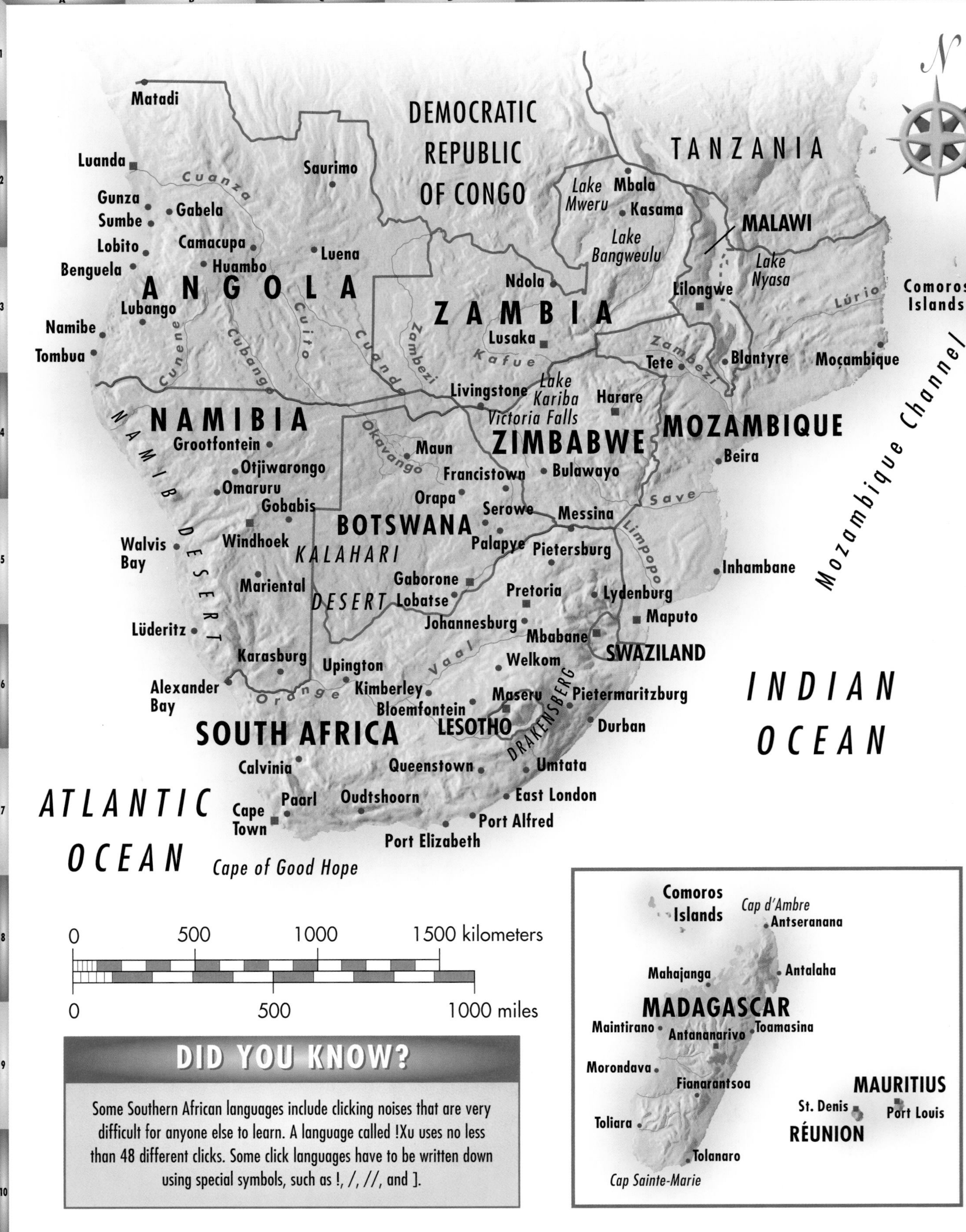
DEMOCRATIC REPUBLIC OF CONGO
TANZANIA
MALAWI
ANGOLA
ZAMBIA
NAMIBIA
ZIMBABWE
MOZAMBIQUE
BOTSWANA
SWAZILAND
LESOTHO
SOUTH AFRICA
Matadi
Luanda
Saurimo
Gunza
Gabela
Sumbe
Lobito
Camacupa
Luena
Benguela
Huambo
Lubango
Namibe
Tombua
Cuanza
Cuito
Cunene
Cubango
Cuando
Zambezi
Kafue
Lake Mweru
Mbala
Kasama
Lake Bangweulu
Ndola
Lilongwe
Lake Nyasa
Lúrio
Comoros Islands
Lusaka
Tete
Blantyre
Moçambique
Mozambique Channel
Livingstone
Lake Kariba
Victoria Falls
Harare
NAMIB DESERT
Grootfontein
Otjiwarongo
Omaruru
Okavango
Maun
Francistown
Bulawayo
Beira
Orapa
Gobabis
Serowe
Messina
Save
Windhoek
Walvis Bay
KALAHARI DESERT
Palapye
Pietersburg
Limpopo
Inhambane
Mariental
Gaborone
Lobatse
Pretoria
Lydenburg
Maputo
Johannesburg
Mbabane
Lüderitz
Karasburg
Upington
Vaal
Welkom
Alexander Bay
Orange
Kimberley
Maseru
Pietermaritzburg
DRAKENSBERG
Bloemfontein
Durban
INDIAN OCEAN
Calvinia
Queenstown
Umtata
East London
ATLANTIC OCEAN
Paarl
Oudtshoorn
Cape Town
Port Alfred
Port Elizabeth
Cape of Good Hope
0
500
1000
1500 kilometers
0
500
1000 miles
Comoros Islands
Cap d'Ambre
Antseranana
Antalaha
Mahajanga
MADAGASCAR
Maintirano
Antananarivo
Toamasina
Morondava
Fianarantsoa
MAURITIUS
St. Denis
Port Louis
Toliara
RÉUNION
Tolanaro
Cap Sainte-Marie

DID YOU KNOW?

Some Southern African languages include clicking noises that are very difficult for anyone else to learn. A language called !Xu uses no less than 48 different clicks. Some click languages have to be written down using special symbols, such as !, /, //, and].

SOUTHERN AFRICA

Southern Africa narrows to form a wedge of land below the Congo basin and Tanzania. Its west coast is bordered by the Atlantic Ocean, its east coast by the Indian Ocean. Across the Mozambique Channel is the large island of Madagascar.

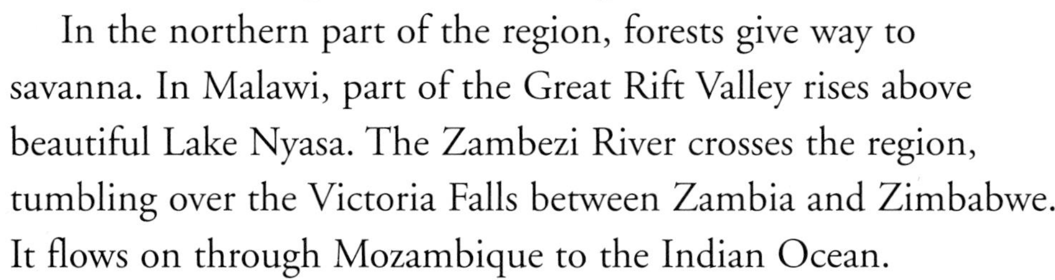

In the northern part of the region, forests give way to savanna. In Malawi, part of the Great Rift Valley rises above beautiful Lake Nyasa. The Zambezi River crosses the region, tumbling over the Victoria Falls between Zambia and Zimbabwe. It flows on through Mozambique to the Indian Ocean.

The Okavango River never reaches the ocean. It flows into shallow pools and swamps in Botswana. To the south, the dry, dusty Kalahari Desert straddles the Botswana-Namibia border. Another desert lies along the Namibian coast. South Africa is a country of mountains, veld (grasslands), and, around the Cape of Good Hope, fertile farmland.

Southern Africa has rich mineral resources, cattle ranching country, and large areas of farmland given over to cash crops for export. South Africa is the wealthiest country in all of Africa, but even there many people suffer from poverty.

ISLAND WILDLIFE

Madagascar is the fourth largest island in the world. Cut off from the African mainland, all sorts of animals developed there that are seen nowhere else on Earth. These include many species of lemur, long-tailed relatives of the monkey. Human settlement has destroyed 90 percent of Madagascar's natural forest, so the survival of many of these beautiful creatures is threatened.

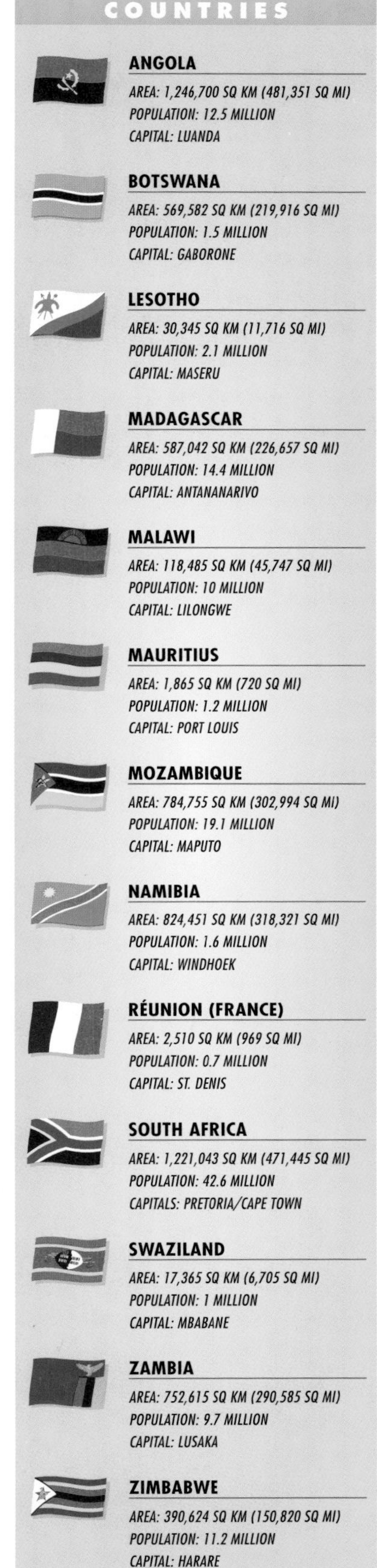

COUNTRIES

ANGOLA
AREA: 1,246,700 SQ KM (481,351 SQ MI)
POPULATION: 12.5 MILLION
CAPITAL: LUANDA

BOTSWANA
AREA: 569,582 SQ KM (219,916 SQ MI)
POPULATION: 1.5 MILLION
CAPITAL: GABORONE

LESOTHO
AREA: 30,345 SQ KM (11,716 SQ MI)
POPULATION: 2.1 MILLION
CAPITAL: MASERU

MADAGASCAR
AREA: 587,042 SQ KM (226,657 SQ MI)
POPULATION: 14.4 MILLION
CAPITAL: ANTANANARIVO

MALAWI
AREA: 118,485 SQ KM (45,747 SQ MI)
POPULATION: 10 MILLION
CAPITAL: LILONGWE

MAURITIUS
AREA: 1,865 SQ KM (720 SQ MI)
POPULATION: 1.2 MILLION
CAPITAL: PORT LOUIS

MOZAMBIQUE
AREA: 784,755 SQ KM (302,994 SQ MI)
POPULATION: 19.1 MILLION
CAPITAL: MAPUTO

NAMIBIA
AREA: 824,451 SQ KM (318,321 SQ MI)
POPULATION: 1.6 MILLION
CAPITAL: WINDHOEK

RÉUNION (FRANCE)
AREA: 2,510 SQ KM (969 SQ MI)
POPULATION: 0.7 MILLION
CAPITAL: ST. DENIS

SOUTH AFRICA
AREA: 1,221,043 SQ KM (471,445 SQ MI)
POPULATION: 42.6 MILLION
CAPITALS: PRETORIA/CAPE TOWN

SWAZILAND
AREA: 17,365 SQ KM (6,705 SQ MI)
POPULATION: 1 MILLION
CAPITAL: MBABANE

ZAMBIA
AREA: 752,615 SQ KM (290,585 SQ MI)
POPULATION: 9.7 MILLION
CAPITAL: LUSAKA

ZIMBABWE
AREA: 390,624 SQ KM (150,820 SQ MI)
POPULATION: 11.2 MILLION
CAPITAL: HARARE

The Eiffel Tower in Paris is one of the most distinctive monuments in Europe.

EUROPE

Eurasia is one great landmass. It is divided into two continents, Europe and Asia. Europe is bordered in the east by the Ural Mountains and the Caspian Sea. To the south lie the Caucasus ranges, the Black Sea, and the Mediterranean Sea. Europe's western coastline faces the stormy North Atlantic Ocean, which sweeps into the North Sea and the Baltic Sea.

The far north has an Arctic climate and is fringed by pack ice. Frozen plains of the tundra give way to forests of spruce and birch. Central and Eastern Europe lie on a great plain, with warm summers and very cold winters. The northwest has a mild climate, thanks to the North Atlantic drift, a warm ocean current. Winds from the sea shed rain over western areas. The snowy Pyrenees, Alps, and Carpathians form high mountain barriers from west to east. The lands to the south have hot summers and mild winters, with vineyards and olive groves.

NORTH AMERICA
ARCTIC CIRCLE
ATLANTIC OCEAN
EUROPE
ASIA
TROPIC OF CANCER
AFRICA

WAR & PEACE

An Albanian girl flees from violence in Kosovo, an area north of Macedonia that was the scene of fighting in 1999. Europe is a patchwork of small nations and peoples, with a long history of fighting and conquest. The European Union (EU) has tried to end ancient rivalries within Europe by economic and political cooperation. Set up in 1957, the EU now has 15 member states.

EUROPE: OLD & NEW

Two thousand years ago, much of Europe was united under the rule of the Romans, whose empire stretched from Spain to the Black Sea. Since then, Europe has seen empires rise and fall. Nations have joined together and split apart many times. Since 1989, the map of Europe has changed all over again. The Soviet Union became the Russian Federation, and new countries that used to be part of the Soviet Union formed around its western and southern borders, from Estonia to Georgia. Yugoslavia broke up into five nations, and Czechoslovakia into two. Germany was reunited as a single country.

DID YOU KNOW?

Most European languages are related to others, but one of them doesn't fit into the jigsaw puzzle. Basque, or Euskara, spoken in northern Spain and southwestern France, has no connections with other languages spoken on Earth. It must have been one of the earliest European languages.

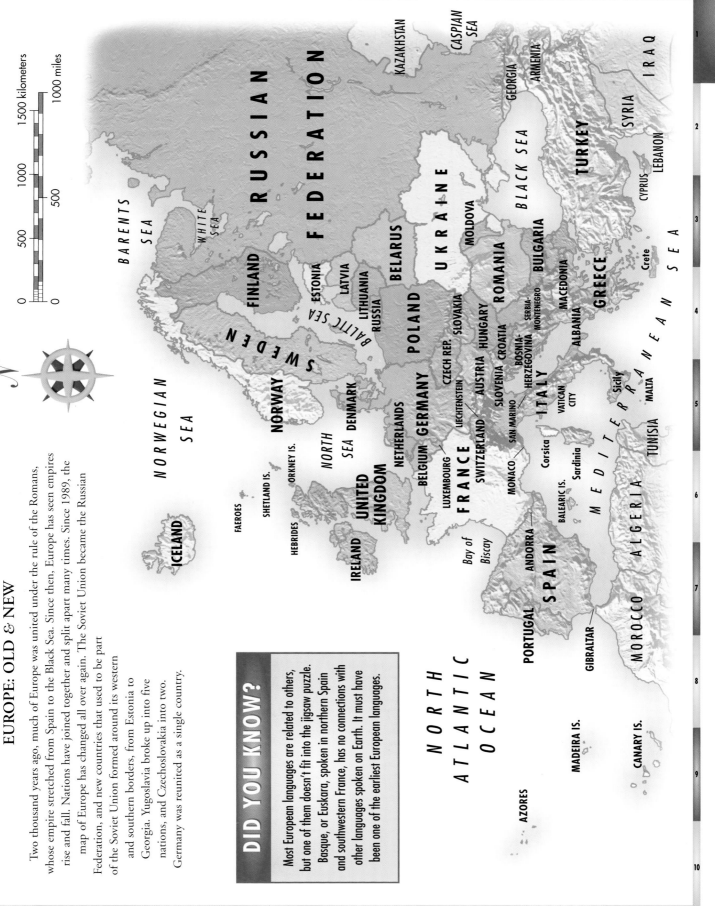

N
0 500 1000 1500 kilometers
0 500 1000 miles
BARENTS SEA
NORWEGIAN SEA
ICELAND
WHITE SEA
FAEROES
SHETLAND IS.
HEBRIDES
ORKNEY IS.
NORWAY
SWEDEN
FINLAND
RUSSIAN FEDERATION
ESTONIA
LATVIA
LITHUANIA
RUSSIA
BALTIC SEA
NORTH SEA
DENMARK
IRELAND
UNITED KINGDOM
NETHERLANDS
BELGIUM
GERMANY
POLAND
BELARUS
UKRAINE
KAZAKHSTAN
CASPIAN SEA
NORTH ATLANTIC OCEAN
LUXEMBOURG
CZECH REP.
SLOVAKIA
Bay of Biscay
FRANCE
LIECHTENSTEIN
SWITZERLAND
AUSTRIA
HUNGARY
MOLDOVA
SLOVENIA
CROATIA
ROMANIA
MONACO
SAN MARINO
BOSNIA-HERZEGOVINA
SERBIA-MONTENEGRO
BULGARIA
BLACK SEA
GEORGIA
ARMENIA
AZORES
PORTUGAL
ANDORRA
SPAIN
Corsica
ITALY
BALEARIC IS.
VATICAN CITY
MACEDONIA
MADEIRA IS.
Sardinia
ALBANIA
TURKEY
GIBRALTAR
MEDITERRANEAN SEA
GREECE
Sicily
SYRIA
CANARY IS.
MOROCCO
ALGERIA
TUNISIA
MALTA
Crete
CYPRUS
LEBANON
IRAQ

EUROPE

Many Europeans live in large towns and cities. The continent is criss-crossed by motorways and railways. The seas have some of the world's busiest shipping routes. The European countryside has been farmed for thousands of years and there are many ancient ruins, castles, cathedrals, and old villages. There are few remaining areas of wilderness. Europeans have a high standard of living. The wealthiest countries are in the west of the continent.

• GENERAL FACTS •

HIGHEST POINT
MOUNT ELBRUS, 5,642 M (18,510 FT), RUSSIAN FEDERATION

LOWEST POINT
VOLGA DELTA, CASPIAN SEA,-28 M (- 92 FT), RUSSIAN FEDERATION

LONGEST RIVER
VOLGA RIVER, 3,688 KM (2,292 MI), RUSSIAN FEDERATION

BIGGEST LAKE
LAKE LADOGA, 18,390 SQ KM (7,100 SQ MI), RUSSIAN FEDERATION

HIGHEST WATERFALL
UTIGÅRD, JOSTEDAL GLACIER, 800 M (2,625 FT), NORWAY

BIGGEST ISLAND
GREAT BRITAIN, 229,885 SQ KM (88,759 SQ MI), UNITED KINGDOM

POPULATION OF CONTINENT
728 MILLION (1999)

MOST POPULOUS COUNTRY
RUSSIAN FEDERATION (INCL. ASIA), 147 MILLION (1999)

MOST DENSELY POPULATED COUNTRY
MONACO, 140,723 PER SQ KM (54,333 PER SQ MI) (1999)

MOST POPULOUS CITY
MOSCOW, RUSSIAN FEDERATION, 9 MILLION (1999)

POPULATION LIVING IN CITIES
73 PERCENT

INFANT MORTALITY
9 DEATHS PER 1,000 CHILDREN UNDER AGE 1

LIFE EXPECTANCY
MALE 69 YEARS; FEMALE 78 YEARS

WEALTH
GROSS DOMESTIC PRODUCT PER PERSON U.S. $13,338 (1997)

LITERACY RATE
97 PERCENT MALE; 97 PERCENT FEMALE

• VEGETATION •

Tundra borders the Arctic Ocean. There is a broad belt of taiga (northern forest) lying to the south. Temperate woodlands once covered much of western Europe. These have mostly been felled in the last 1,000 years, and have been replaced by farmland, pasture or managed forests. In mountain regions the vegetation depends on altitude, with wooded valleys rising to high Alpine pastures and bare rock. Southern Europe has dry scrub, or maquis. Parts of Spain are so dry that they are turning into desert.

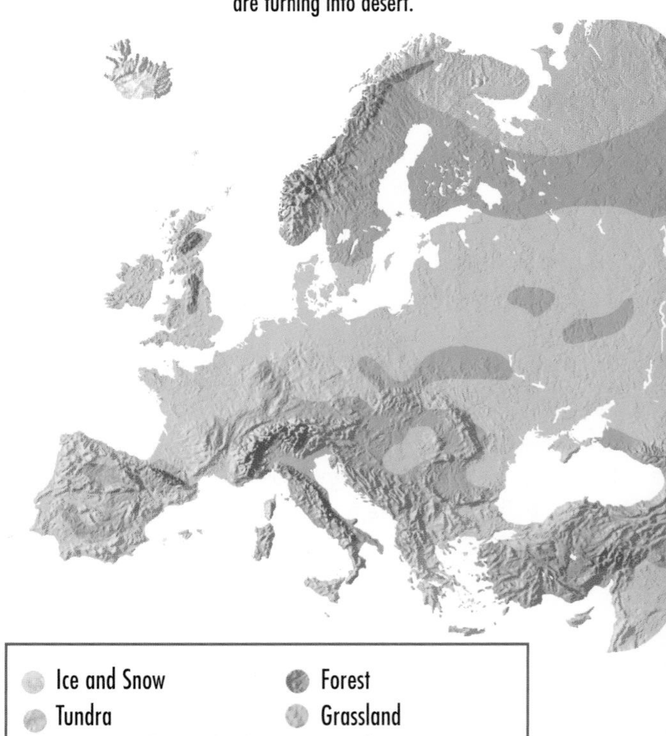
Ice and Snow
Tundra
Mountains/barren land
Forest
Grassland
Semidesert

LANGUAGE

Russian is the dominant language in the Russian Federation, Ukraine and Belarus, although other regional languages are spoken. German is not only spoken in Germany, but also in Austria, Poland, the Russian Federation and Switzerland. The small population of Switzerland is split between German-speakers, Italian-speakers, French-speakers, and Romansh-speakers.

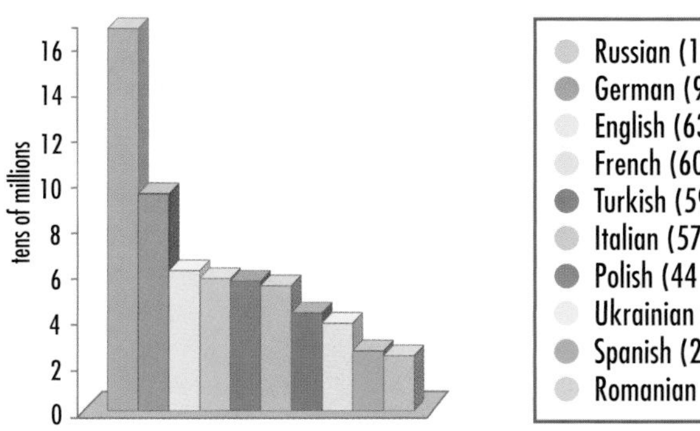
tens of millions
16
14
12
10
8
6
4
2
0
Russian (170 mil)
German (98 mil)
English (63 mil)
French (60 mil)
Turkish (59 mil)
Italian (57 mil)
Polish (44 mil)
Ukrainian (41mil)
Spanish (28 mil)
Romanian (26 mil)

RELIGION

Christianity is the chief religion of Europe. There are three main branches: the Roman Catholic tradition, the Eastern tradition, and the Protestant tradition. Europe's Jewish population has suffered from persecution in Germany, Central, and Eastern Europe. Islam is based in southeast Europe and is also the religion of many immigrants, alongside Hinduism and Sikhism.

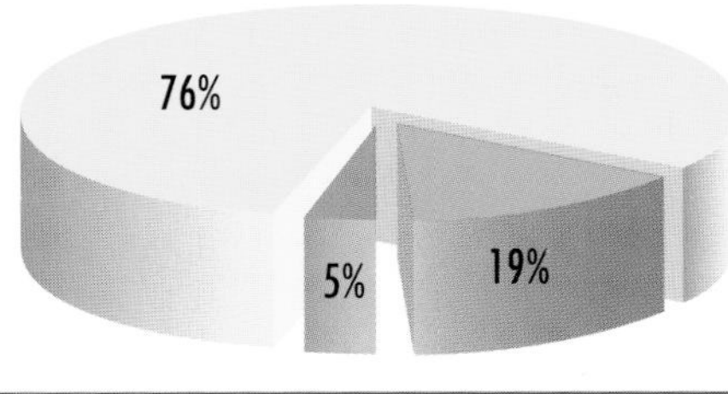
76%
5%
19%
Christianity
Non-religious
Islam, Judaism and others

CLIMATE

Europe has an Arctic climate in the far north. The great plain occupying Central and Eastern Europe has a continental climate, marked by cold winters and sunny summers. The greatest rainfall is in the northwest, brought by ocean winds. The temperate zone includes most of western Europe. The climate gets warmer as it nears the Mediterranean region. Spain, Italy, and Greece have high summer temperatures.

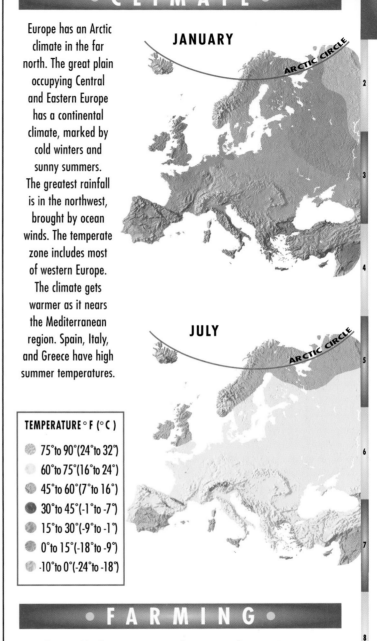

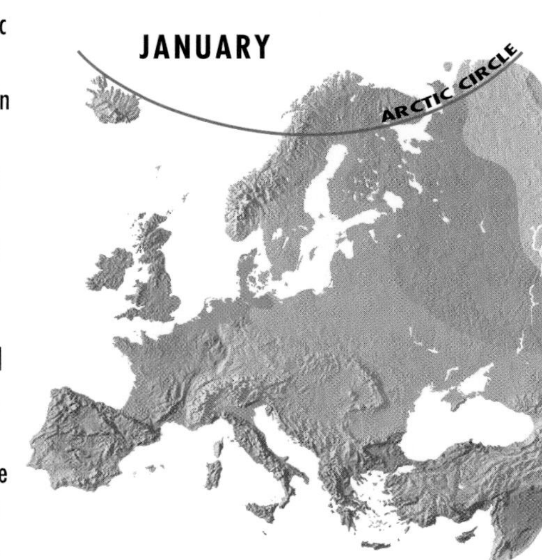
JANUARY
ARCTIC CIRCLE

JULY
ARCTIC CIRCLE

TEMPERATURE °F (°C)

- 75° to 90° (24° to 32°)
- 60° to 75° (16° to 24°)
- 45° to 60° (7° to 16°)
- 30° to 45° (-1° to -7°)
- 15° to 30° (-9° to -1°)
- 0° to 15° (-18° to -9°)
- -10° to 0° (-24° to -18°)

RESOURCES

Northwestern Europe has rich mineral resources, such as iron ore and coal. It became the world's first industrial region, in the 1700s and 1800s. However mining and heavy industry are now in decline in these areas. They are being replaced by service industries.

COAL: *Germany, Poland, Romania, Russian Federation, U.K., Ukraine*

COPPER: *Bulgaria, Finland, Norway, Poland, Portugal, Spain, Sweden*

IRON: *Austria, France, Russian Federation, Sweden, Ukraine*

OIL: *Norway, Russian Federation, U.K.*

TIMBER: *Finland, Norway, Russian Federation, Sweden*

FARMING

Wheat and barley are grown over large areas of Europe. So are root crops, such as potatoes and sugar beet. Dairy farming is important in the northwest, which also produces apples and pears. The south produces citrus fruits, sunflower seeds and olives.

CITRUS FRUITS: *Greece, Italy, Portugal, Spain*

DAIRY PRODUCE: *Denmark, France, Ireland, Switzerland, U.K.*

POTATOES: *Greece, Ireland, Poland, Russian Federation, Ukraine, U.K.*

VINEYARDS: *Bulgaria, France, Germany, Greece, Hungary, Italy, Portugal, Spain*

WHEAT: *France, Germany, Russian Federation, Ukraine, U.K.*

EUROPE: *Tradition & Change*

BESIDE THE SEA

Blue waters lap a sunny shore on the island of Cephalonia in Greece. The warm climate along the coasts of the Mediterranean Sea and the Black Sea attracts many tourists from the colder lands of the north.

Europe is a small continent, but it is a land of many different peoples and cultures. Even within one small country, you may hear different languages, experience different manners and customs and see different styles of building or methods of farming.

In the last 500 years, European people have settled in many other parts of the world. In the last 50 years, people from other parts of the world, including Africa, Asia and the Caribbean islands, have in turn settled in Europe. This is a continent of history and tradition, but it is also going through great changes—in national borders, in types of government and in the growth of the European Union.

CONTINENT OF CULTURE

The Kirov Ballet Company is one of the many long-established European ballet companies. During the last 500 years, Europe has been at the center of world developments in dance, classical music, opera, painting, sculpture, and literature. European cities have many famous theaters, galleries, and museums.

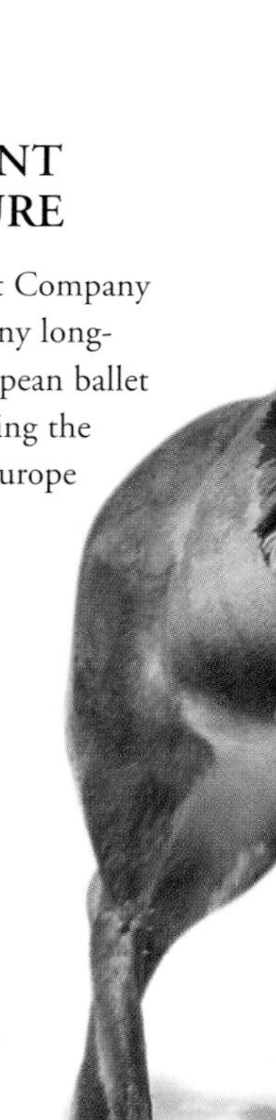

THE SAAMI

The Saami people live in Lapland, a region which spreads from Arctic Scandinavia into the Russian Federation. They have always been reindeer herders, but many now work in forestry or other industries.

LA TERRASSE
BRASSERIE

BRIGHT LIGHTS, BIG CITIES

In the warmer parts of Europe, city life centers on street cafés, bars, and restaurants, or an evening stroll through parks and squares. There is a chance to exchange gossip, argue about politics, or just enjoy good food, coffee or a glass of wine.

OLD WORLD CHARM

An English country garden surrounds a fine old half-timbered house, once lived in by William Shakespeare's wife, Anne Hathaway. Its roof is made of thatch. Europe still has many villages that date back 500 years or more. Traditional building styles vary greatly from one region to another.

POLITICS & PROTEST

A woman carries a portrait of V.I. Lenin, communist leader of Russia's October Revolution in 1917. Just as most world religions had their origins in Asia, so most world political and economic systems— from democracy to socialism and fascism—were first tried out in Europe.

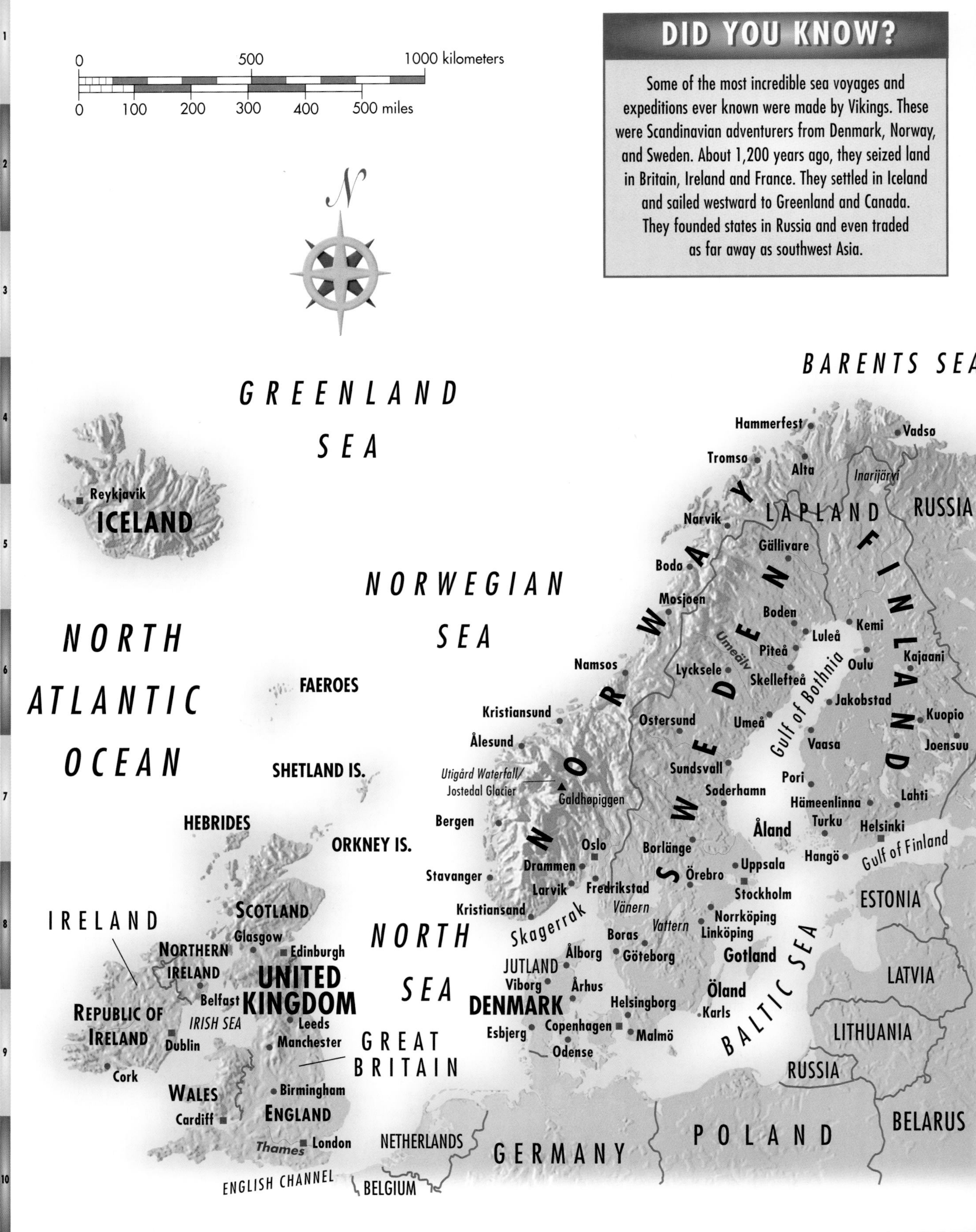
0
500
1000 kilometers
0
100
200
300
400
500 miles
N
GREENLAND SEA
BARENTS SEA
NORWEGIAN SEA
NORTH ATLANTIC OCEAN
NORTH SEA
Reykjavik
ICELAND
FAEROES
SHETLAND IS.
ORKNEY IS.
HEBRIDES
IRELAND
SCOTLAND
Glasgow
Edinburgh
NORTHERN IRELAND
Belfast
UNITED KINGDOM
REPUBLIC OF IRELAND
Dublin
IRISH SEA
Cork
Leeds
Manchester
GREAT BRITAIN
WALES
Cardiff
Birmingham
ENGLAND
Thames
London
ENGLISH CHANNEL
NETHERLANDS
BELGIUM
GERMANY
POLAND
BELARUS
RUSSIA
LITHUANIA
LATVIA
ESTONIA
Hammerfest
Vadso
Tromso
Alta
Inarijärvi
Narvik
LAPLAND
RUSSIA
Gällivare
Boda
NORWAY
SWEDEN
FINLAND
Mosjoen
Boden
Kemi
Luleå
Umeälv
Piteå
Oulu
Kajaani
Lycksele
Skellefteå
Gulf of Bothnia
Namsos
Jakobstad
Kristiansund
Ostersund
Umeå
Kuopio
Ålesund
Vaasa
Joensuu
Sundsvall
Pori
Utigård Waterfall/
Jostedal Glacier
Galdhøpiggen
Soderhamn
Hämeenlinna
Lahti
Bergen
Turku
Helsinki
Åland
Oslo
Borlänge
Hangö
Gulf of Finland
Drammen
Uppsala
Stavanger
Örebro
Larvik
Fredrikstad
Stockholm
Kristiansand
Vänern
Skagerrak
Norrköping
Vattern
Linköping
Boras
Ålborg
Göteborg
Gotland
JUTLAND
Viborg
Århus
Öland
DENMARK
Helsingborg
Karls
BALTIC SEA
Esbjerg
Copenhagen
Malmö
Odense

DID YOU KNOW?

Some of the most incredible sea voyages and expeditions ever known were made by Vikings. These were Scandinavian adventurers from Denmark, Norway, and Sweden. About 1,200 years ago, they seized land in Britain, Ireland and France. They settled in Iceland and sailed westward to Greenland and Canada. They founded states in Russia and even traded as far away as southwest Asia.

NORTHERN EUROPE

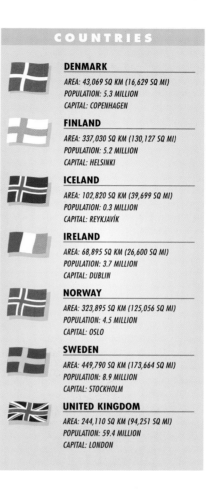

Europe's northwest coast forms a continental shelf, a ledge of low-lying land that has been flooded by the Atlantic Ocean. This has formed the North Sea and the Baltic Sea, valuable for their offshore oilfields and fisheries.

The British Isles rise from the shelf. They are kept green by rain-bearing ocean winds. The largest island is Great Britain and the second biggest is Ireland. The British Isles are occupied by two nations. English is the most commonly spoken language. The United Kingdom is a union of three small countries, England, Scotland, and Wales, and the province of Northern Ireland. The Republic of Ireland takes up the rest of Ireland. The British Isles have rolling farmlands and plains, bleak moors, low mountains, and many large cities. London, on the Thames River, is a center of world finance and banking.

The flat, windy farmland of Denmark takes in the peninsula of Jutland and the islands nearby. Across the strait of Skagerrak, the long Scandinavian peninsula stretches north to the Arctic. Farmland gives way to lakes and forests. Mountains rise from sea inlets called fjords. Europe's far north includes Norway, Sweden, and Finland. Far away in the North Atlantic lies the volcanic island of Iceland.

COUNTRIES

DENMARK
AREA: 43,069 SQ KM (16,629 SQ MI)
POPULATION: 5.3 MILLION
CAPITAL: COPENHAGEN

FINLAND
AREA: 337,030 SQ KM (130,127 SQ MI)
POPULATION: 5.2 MILLION
CAPITAL: HELSINKI

ICELAND
AREA: 102,820 SQ KM (39,699 SQ MI)
POPULATION: 0.3 MILLION
CAPITAL: REYKJAVÍK

IRELAND
AREA: 68,895 SQ KM (26,600 SQ MI)
POPULATION: 3.7 MILLION
CAPITAL: DUBLIN

NORWAY
AREA: 323,895 SQ KM (125,056 SQ MI)
POPULATION: 4.5 MILLION
CAPITAL: OSLO

SWEDEN
AREA: 449,790 SQ KM (173,664 SQ MI)
POPULATION: 8.9 MILLION
CAPITAL: STOCKHOLM

UNITED KINGDOM
AREA: 244,110 SQ KM (94,251 SQ MI)
POPULATION: 59.4 MILLION
CAPITAL: LONDON

PEOPLES OF THE REGION

Three chief ethnic groups occupy north-western Europe. Finno-Ugric peoples include the Finns and the Saami people of Lapland. Germanic peoples include the Danes, Swedes, Norwegians, Icelanders, and the English. Their languages are all closely related. English has become the most widely-used language in the world. Celtic peoples include the Scots, Welsh, and Irish. More recent arrivals include people of Asian and African descent.

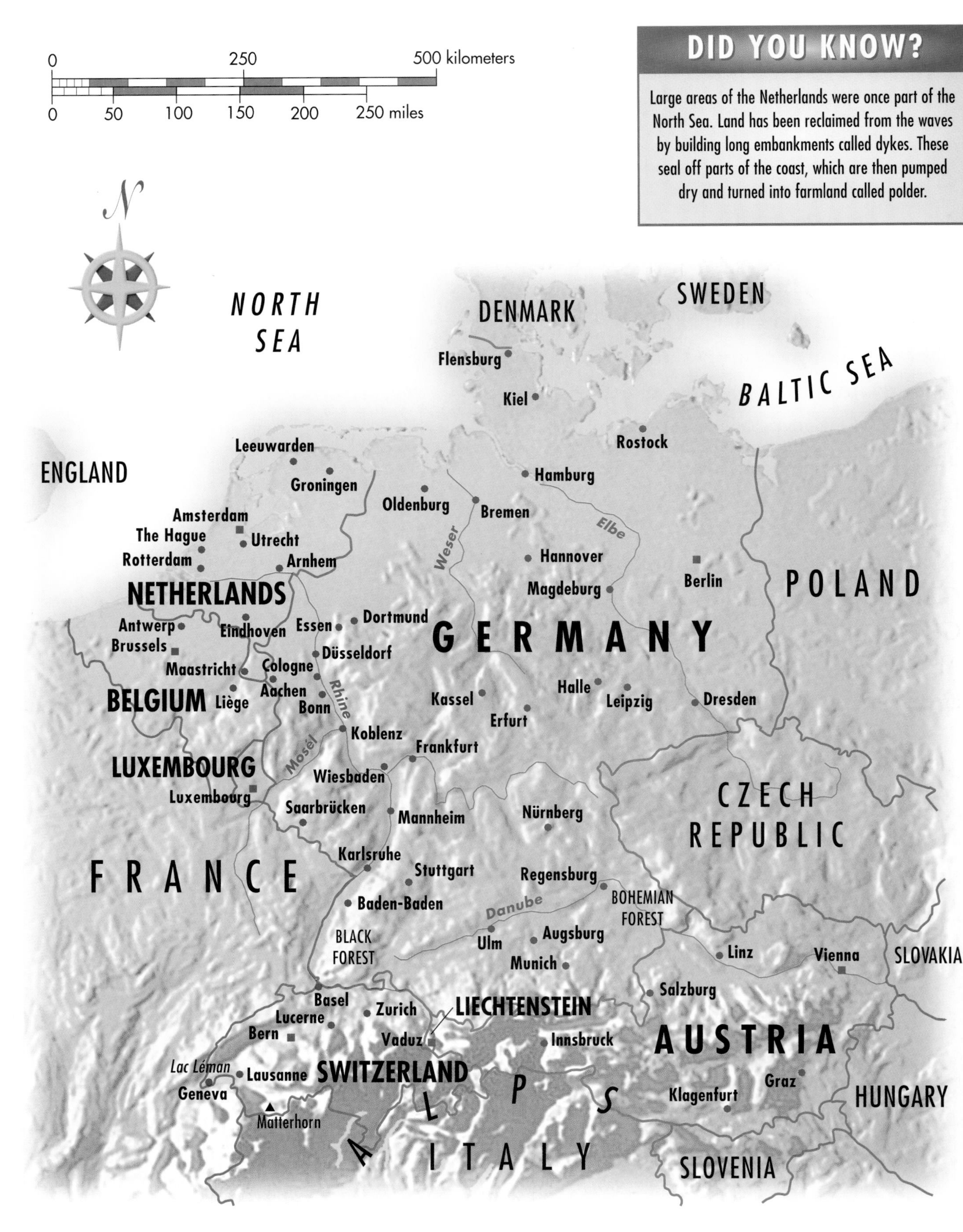
0
250
500 kilometers
0
50
100
150
200
250 miles
N
NORTH SEA
DENMARK
SWEDEN
BALTIC SEA
ENGLAND
Flensburg
Kiel
Rostock
Leeuwarden
Groningen
Hamburg
Oldenburg
Bremen
Amsterdam
The Hague
Utrecht
Rotterdam
Arnhem
Elbe
Weser
Hannover
Magdeburg
Berlin
POLAND
NETHERLANDS
Antwerp
Eindhoven
Essen
Dortmund
Brussels
Düsseldorf
GERMANY
Maastricht
Cologne
Aachen
Liège
Bonn
Rhine
BELGIUM
Kassel
Halle
Leipzig
Erfurt
Dresden
Koblenz
Frankfurt
Mosel
LUXEMBOURG
Wiesbaden
Luxembourg
Saarbrücken
Mannheim
Nürnberg
CZECH REPUBLIC
Karlsruhe
Stuttgart
Regensburg
FRANCE
Baden-Baden
Danube
BOHEMIAN FOREST
BLACK FOREST
Ulm
Augsburg
Munich
Linz
Vienna
SLOVAKIA
Salzburg
Basel
Zurich
LIECHTENSTEIN
Lucerne
Bern
Vaduz
Innsbruck
AUSTRIA
Lac Léman
Lausanne
SWITZERLAND
Geneva
Matterhorn
ALPS
Graz
Klagenfurt
HUNGARY
ITALY
SLOVENIA

DID YOU KNOW?

Large areas of the Netherlands were once part of the North Sea. Land has been reclaimed from the waves by building long embankments called dykes. These seal off parts of the coast, which are then pumped dry and turned into farmland called polder.

LOWLANDS TO ALPS

Flat lands and dunes border the southern shores of the North Sea and the Baltic. The low-lying coast of the Netherlands has to be protected from storms and floods by sea barriers and embankments. A broad plain extends from northeastern Germany far into central and eastern Europe.

COUNTRIES

AUSTRIA
AREA: 83,855 SQ KM (32,376 SQ MI)
POPULATION: 8.1 MILLION
CAPITAL: VIENNA

BELGIUM
AREA: 30,520 SQ KM (11,784 SQ MI)
POPULATION: 10.2 MILLION
CAPITAL: BRUSSELS

GERMANY
AREA: 356,734 SQ KM (137,740 SQ MI)
POPULATION: 82 MILLION
CAPITAL: BERLIN

LIECHTENSTEIN
AREA: 160 SQ KM (62 SQ MI)
POPULATION: 0.03 MILLION
CAPITAL: VADUZ

LUXEMBOURG
AREA: 2,585 SQ KM (998 SQ MI)
POPULATION: 0.4 MILLION
CAPITAL: LUXEMBOURG

NETHERLANDS
AREA: 41,525 SQ KM (16,033 SQ MI)
POPULATION: 15.8 MILLION
CAPITAL: AMSTERDAM

SWITZERLAND
AREA: 41,285 SQ KM (15,940 SQ MI)
POPULATION: 7.1 MILLION
CAPITAL: BERN

In southern Belgium, Luxembourg, and central Germany, the land rises to hills and river valleys. Southern Germany, Switzerland, Liechtenstein, and Austria have the Alps, the highest mountain range in western Europe. They are fringed by the Black Forest and the Bohemian Forest.

The northwestern climate is mild and moist. The northeast has warm summers but cold winters. In the Alps, summer sunshine melts heavy winter snows.

The Netherlands and Switzerland produce dairy products and are famous for their cheeses. Beer, cold meats, and sausages are specialities of Belgium and Germany. Wines are produced in Germany along the valleys of the Rhine and Mosel Rivers. Manufactures include Dutch (Netherlands) electrical goods, German cars, and Swiss watches and precision instruments. Major financial centers are Zurich, Switzerland, and Frankfurt, Germany. Many European Union (EU) institutions are based in Brussels and Luxembourg. Geneva, Switzerland, is a center for various United Nations bodies and the International Red Cross.

PEOPLES OF THE REGION

Germanic peoples occupy most of the region. They include the Germans, the Dutch, the Friesians of northern Germany and the Netherlands, and the Flemings of Belgium. Each of these have their own language. The German language is spoken in Germany, in Austria, Liechtenstein and Switzerland. Italic (Latin-based) languages include French (spoken by the French, the Walloons of Belgium, and in southwest Switzerland), Italian, and Romansh (in the Swiss Alps).

DID YOU KNOW?

The walls of caves at Lascaux in France and Altamira in Spain are covered in fantastic red and black paintings of animals, including bulls, boars, and galloping bison. They were painted by a prehistoric people known as the Cro-Magnons, who lived in Europe between 40,000 and 10,000 years ago.

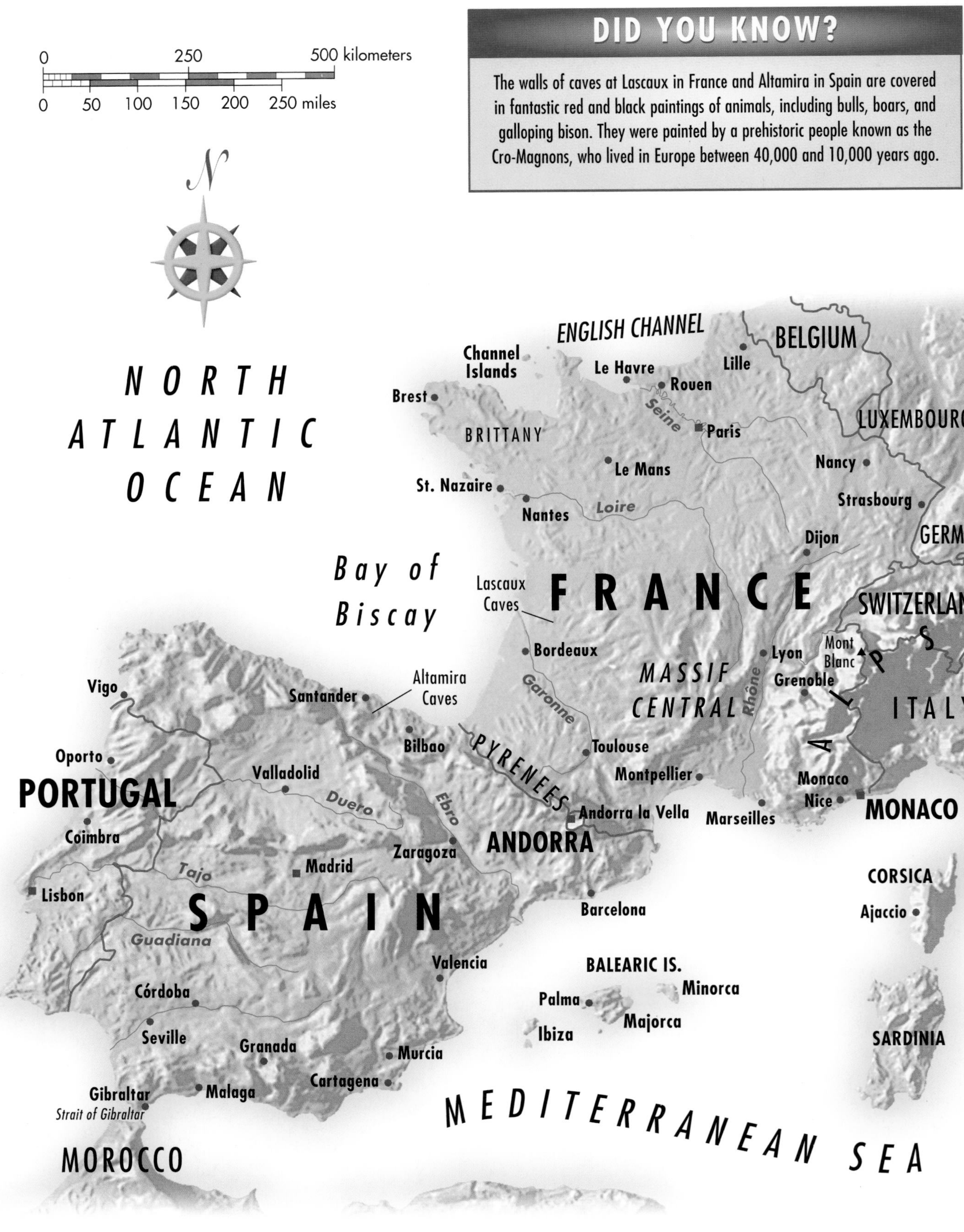
0
250
500 kilometers
0
50
100
150
200
250 miles
N
NORTH ATLANTIC OCEAN
ENGLISH CHANNEL
Channel Islands
Brest
Le Havre
Rouen
Lille
BELGIUM
Seine
Paris
LUXEMBOURG
BRITTANY
Le Mans
Nancy
St. Nazaire
Nantes
Loire
Strasbourg
Dijon
GERMA
Bay of Biscay
Lascaux Caves
FRANCE
SWITZERLAND
Bordeaux
Lyon
Mont Blanc
MASSIF CENTRAL
Rhône
Grenoble
ALPS
ITALY
Garonne
Altamira Caves
Vigo
Santander
Bilbao
PYRENEES
Toulouse
Oporto
Montpellier
Monaco
Valladolid
PORTUGAL
Duero
Ebro
Andorra la Vella
Marseilles
Nice
MONACO
Coimbra
ANDORRA
Zaragoza
Tajo
Madrid
CORSICA
Lisbon
SPAIN
Barcelona
Ajaccio
Guadiana
Valencia
BALEARIC IS.
Minorca
Córdoba
Palma
Majorca
Seville
Ibiza
Granada
Murcia
SARDINIA
Cartagena
Gibraltar
Malaga
Strait of Gibraltar
MEDITERRANEAN SEA
MOROCCO

FRANCE & IBERIA

COUNTRIES

ANDORRA
AREA: 482 SQ KM (186 SQ MI)
POPULATION: 0.1 MILLION
CAPITALL: ANDORRA LA VELLA

FRANCE
AREA: 551,458 SQ KM (212,918 SQ MI)
POPULATION: 59.1 MILLION
CAPITAL: PARIS

MONACO
AREA: 1.6 SQ KM (0.6 SQ MI)
POPULATION: 0.03 MILLION
CAPITAL: MONACO

PORTUGAL
AREA: 91,630 SQ KM (35,378 SQ MI)
POPULATION: 10 MILLION
CAPITAL: LISBON

SPAIN
AREA: 504,742 SQ KM (194,881 SQ MI)
POPULATION: 39.4 MILLION
CAPITAL: MADRID

GIBRALTAR
BRITISH OVERSEAS TERRITORY
AREA: 6.5 SQ KM (2.5 SQ MI)
POPULATION: 0.03 MILLION
CAPITAL: GIBRALTAR

France is bordered by hills and mountains in the east, with the Alps reaching 4,810 meters (15,781 feet) at Mont Blanc. The fertile plains and chalk cliffs of the north border the English Channel. Below the rocky headlands of Brittany, the west coast borders the Bay of Biscay.

Southern France lies on the Mediterranean and surrounds the little state of Monaco. South-central France is dominated by the highlands of the Massif Central and the valley of the Rhône River. France has a mild climate, cool in the north, and warm in the south. Its capital, Paris, is a fine, historical city on the Seine River.

Across the high mountain barrier of the Pyrenees, the Iberian peninsula juts out into the Atlantic Ocean. The peninsula is occupied by Spain, Portugal, the tiny mountain state of Andorra, and the British territory of Gibraltar. Gibraltar is just 13 kilometers (8 miles) from North Africa. The Spanish capital, Madrid, lies in the center of a baking plateau, called the Meseta. This is fringed by mountains to the north and south, and drained by rivers that flow westward into Portugal. France and the Iberian peninsula produce wines, fruit, and motor vehicles. The entire region has a thriving tourist industry.

PEOPLES OF THE REGION

French, Spanish, and Portuguese are the chief languages of the region. You may also hear minority languages such as Catalan, Basque, Galician, Corsican, or Breton. Regional cultures are especially strong in Spain. The Spanish and Portuguese were the first modern Europeans to build up large overseas empires, in the 1500s. Far more people now speak their languages in the Americas than in their European homeland.

N

DID YOU KNOW?

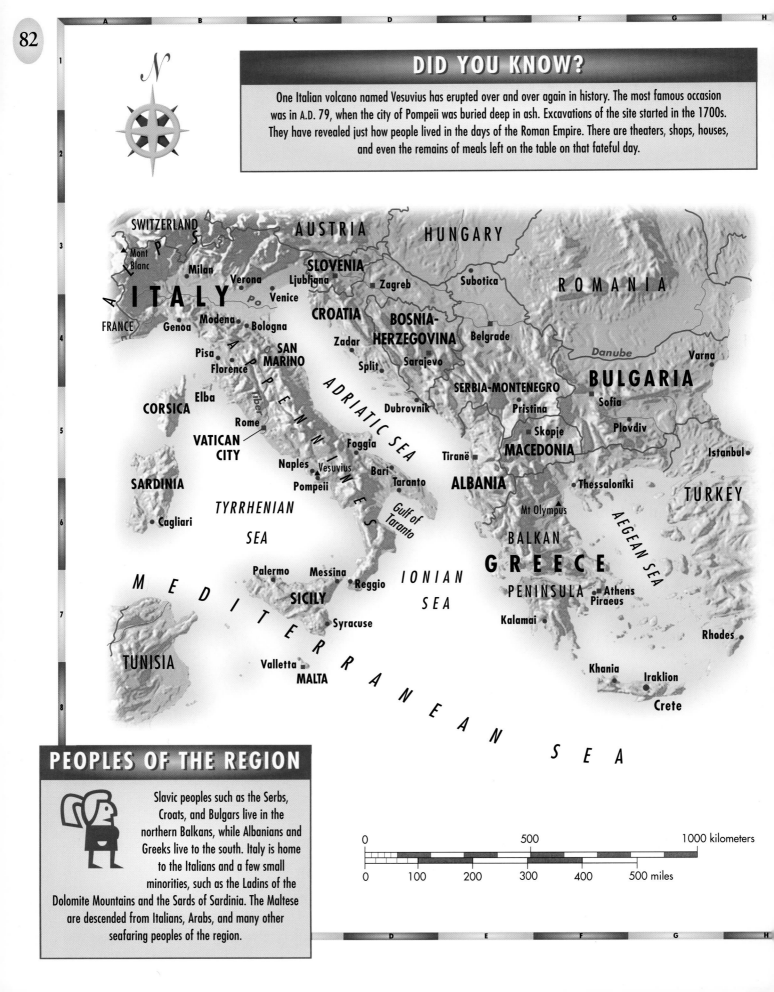

One Italian volcano named Vesuvius has erupted over and over again in history. The most famous occasion was in A.D. 79, when the city of Pompeii was buried deep in ash. Excavations of the site started in the 1700s. They have revealed just how people lived in the days of the Roman Empire. There are theaters, shops, houses, and even the remains of meals left on the table on that fateful day.

SWITZERLAND
AUSTRIA
HUNGARY
ALPS
Mont Blanc
Milan
Verona
SLOVENIA
Ljubljana
Zagreb
Subotica
ROMANIA
ITALY
Po
Venice
FRANCE
Genoa
Modena
Bologna
CROATIA
BOSNIA-HERZEGOVINA
Belgrade
Zadar
Danube
Varna
Pisa
Florence
SAN MARINO
APPENNINES
Split
Sarajevo
ADRIATIC SEA
SERBIA-MONTENEGRO
BULGARIA
Sofia
CORSICA
Elba
Tiber
Dubrovnik
Pristina
Rome
Skopje
Plovdiv
VATICAN CITY
Foggia
Tiranë
MACEDONIA
Istanbul
Naples
Vesuvius
Bari
SARDINIA
Pompeii
Taranto
ALBANIA
Thessaloniki
TURKEY
TYRRHENIAN SEA
Gulf of Taranto
Mt Olympus
Cagliari
AEGEAN SEA
BALKAN PENINSULA
GREECE
Palermo
Messina
Reggio
IONIAN SEA
Athens
Piraeus
SICILY
Kalamai
Syracuse
Rhodes
TUNISIA
Valletta
MALTA
Khania
Iraklion
Crete
MEDITERRANEAN SEA

PEOPLES OF THE REGION

Slavic peoples such as the Serbs, Croats, and Bulgars live in the northern Balkans, while Albanians and Greeks live to the south. Italy is home to the Italians and a few small minorities, such as the Ladins of the Dolomite Mountains and the Sards of Sardinia. The Maltese are descended from Italians, Arabs, and many other seafaring peoples of the region.

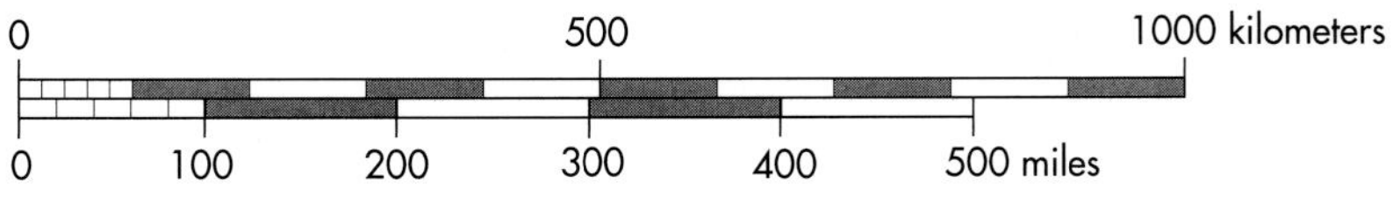
0
500
1000 kilometers
0
100
200
300
400
500 miles

ITALY & THE BALKANS

Boot-shaped Italy cuts into the eastern Mediterranean to form the Tyrrhenian Sea and the Adriatic Sea. Farther east the great wedge of the Balkan peninsula separates the Ionian Sea and Aegean Sea.

These lands are hot and dry, although the northern Balkan countries have cold, snowy winters. The south of the region is a danger zone for volcanoes and earthquakes.

The Alps tower along Italy's northern border, overlooking still, blue lakes. Fertile plains drain into the Po River. To the south the land rises again to form the long chain of the Apennine Mountains. Rich farmland runs down the coasts, but the far south is dry and dusty. Italy is the world's biggest wine producer. Most Italian industry is based in the northern cities. Sardinia and Sicily are Italy's largest offshore islands. Malta is an independent island nation lying nearer Africa.

The small countries of the Balkan peninsula have seen war and strife since the breakup of the Yugoslav federation (from Slovenia through Macedonia) in 1991–92. Albania is one of the poorest countries in Europe. To the north and east are Bulgaria and the small part of Turkey that is in Europe. The historic city of Istanbul is partly in Europe and partly in Asia. The Balkans end at Greece, where a long chain of islands is strung across the deep blue sea.

SUN & CIVILIZATION

Italy, Greece, and Croatia all have the sunshine and beaches that tourists from northern Europe love. Visitors from all over the world come to marvel at the ruins of ancient Greece and Rome, which were Europe's first great civilizations. They also enjoy the beautiful palaces, churches, and paintings that were produced in the ages that followed.

COUNTRIES

ALBANIA
AREA: 28,750 SQ KM (11,100 SQ MI)
POPULATION: 3.5 MILLION
CAPITAL: TIRANA

BOSNIA-HERZEGOVINA
AREA: 51,750 SQ KM (19,980 SQ MI)
POPULATION: 3.8 MILLION
CAPITAL: SARAJEVO

BULGARIA
AREA: 110,910 SQ KM (42,822 SQ MI)
POPULATION: 8.2 MILLION
CAPITAL: SOFIA

CROATIA
AREA: 56,540 SQ KM (21,830 SQ MI)
POPULATION: 4.6 MILLION
CAPITAL: ZAGREB

GREECE
AREA: 131,985 SQ KM (50.959 SQ MI)
POPULATION: 10.5 MILLION
CAPITAL: ATHENS

ITALY
AREA: 301,245 SQ KM (116,311 SQ MI)
POPULATION: 57.7 MILLION
CAPITAL: ROME

MACEDONIA
AREA: 25,715 SQ KM (9,929 SQ MI)
POPULATION: 2 MILLION
CAPITAL: SKOPJE

MALTA
AREA: 316 SQ KM (122 SQ MI)
POPULATION: 0.4 MILLION
CAPITAL: VALLETTA

SAN MARINO
AREA: 61 SQ KM (24 SQ MI)
POPULATION: 0.03 MILLION
CAPITAL: SAN MARINO

SERBIA-MONTENEGRO
AREA: 102,170 SQ KM (39,435 SQ MI)
POPULATION: 10.6 MILLION
CAPITAL: BELGRADE

SLOVENIA
AREA: 20,250 SQ KM (7,818 SQ MI)
POPULATION: 2.0 MILLION
CAPITAL: LJUBLJANA

TURKEY
EUROPEAN AND ASIAN TURKEY
AREA: 780,574 SQ KM (301,380 SQ MI)
POPULATION: 65.9 MILLION
CAPITAL: ANKARA

VATICAN CITY
AREA: 0.44 SQ KM (0.17 SQ MI)
POPULATION: 1,000
CAPITAL: VATICAN CITY

DID YOU KNOW?

The Transylvania region of Romania is for ever linked with the legend of the vampire Dracula, the villain of many horror films. Dracula is thought to be based upon two historical figures—Vlad Dracul (Vlad the Devil) and his son, Vlad Tepes (Vlad the Impaler), fierce princes who ruled the region in the 1400s. During his reign Vlad Tepes had 40,000 people executed by being impaled on stakes.

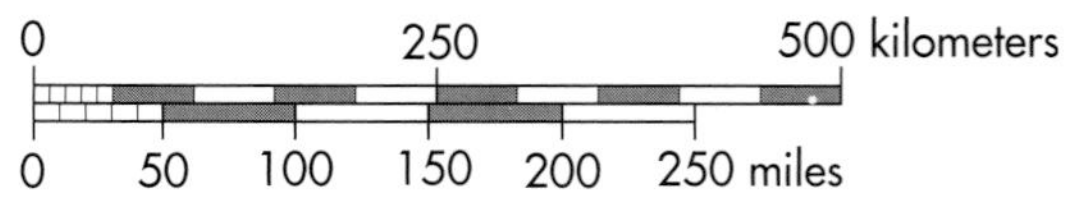
0
250
500 kilometers
0
50
100
150
200
250 miles

CENTRAL EUROPE

Central Europe lies between the Baltic Sea and the Balkan peninsula. Great kingdoms grew up here during the Middle Ages. Over many years national borders have changed again and again, as powerful neighbors such as Austria, Germany, Sweden, and Russia have tried to control the region. Today, Russia governs only a small pocket of territory south of Lithuania. The rest of Central Europe is made up of independent states.

Estonia, Latvia, and Lithuania are small countries on the Baltic coast. Northern Poland occupies the great plain that stretches across Central and Eastern Europe. This is a land of lakes and forests, with snowy winters. Southern Poland rises to highlands, and the high ranges of the Sudety and Carpathian Mountains. Beyond lie the twins at the heart of Central Europe, the Czech Republic and Slovakia. Here also are the fertile plains of Hungary and the mountains and forests of Romania.

Central Europe is drained by great rivers—the Vistula, Oder, and Elbe in the north, and the Danube in the south. The Danube forms a marshy delta on the Black Sea coast. The region is agricultural as well as industrial, producing vegetables and fruit. Tourists love to visit the historical cities of Warsaw, Kraków, Prague, and Budapest.

COUNTRIES

CZECH REPUBLIC
AREA: 78,864 SQ KM (30,449 SQ MI)
POPULATION: 10.3 MILLION
CAPITAL: PRAGUE

ESTONIA
AREA: 45,100 SQ KM (17,413 SQ MI)
POPULATION: 1.4 MILLION
CAPITAL: TALLINN

HUNGARY
AREA: 93,030 SQ KM (35,919 SQ MI)
POPULATION: 10.1 MILLION
CAPITAL: BUDAPEST

LATVIA
AREA: 63,700 SQ KM (24,595 SQ MI)
POPULATION: 2.4 MILLION
CAPITAL: RIGA

LITHUANIA
AREA: 65,200 SQ KM (25,174 SQ MI)
POPULATION: 3.7 MILLION
CAPITAL: VILNIUS

POLAND
AREA: 312,758 SQ KM (120, 756 SQ MI)
POPULATION: 38.7 MILLION
CAPITAL: WARSAW

ROMANIA
AREA: 237,500 SQ KM (91,699 SQ MI)
POPULATION: 22.5 MILLION
CAPITAL: BUCHAREST

SLOVAKIA
AREA: 49,011 SQ KM (18,923 SQ MI)
POPULATION: 5.4 MILLION
CAPITAL: BRATISLAVA

PEOPLES OF THE REGION

Finno-Ugric languages are spoken by the Estonians of the Baltic and the Magyars of Hungary. The Lithuanians and Latvians are Baltic peoples, while the Poles, Czechs, and Slovaks are Slavs. Romanians include people of varied descent, but their common language is related to Italian, for this was once part of the Roman Empire. Many Gypsies, known as Roma, live in Central Europe. Only a few of them still manage to live as nomadic travellers.

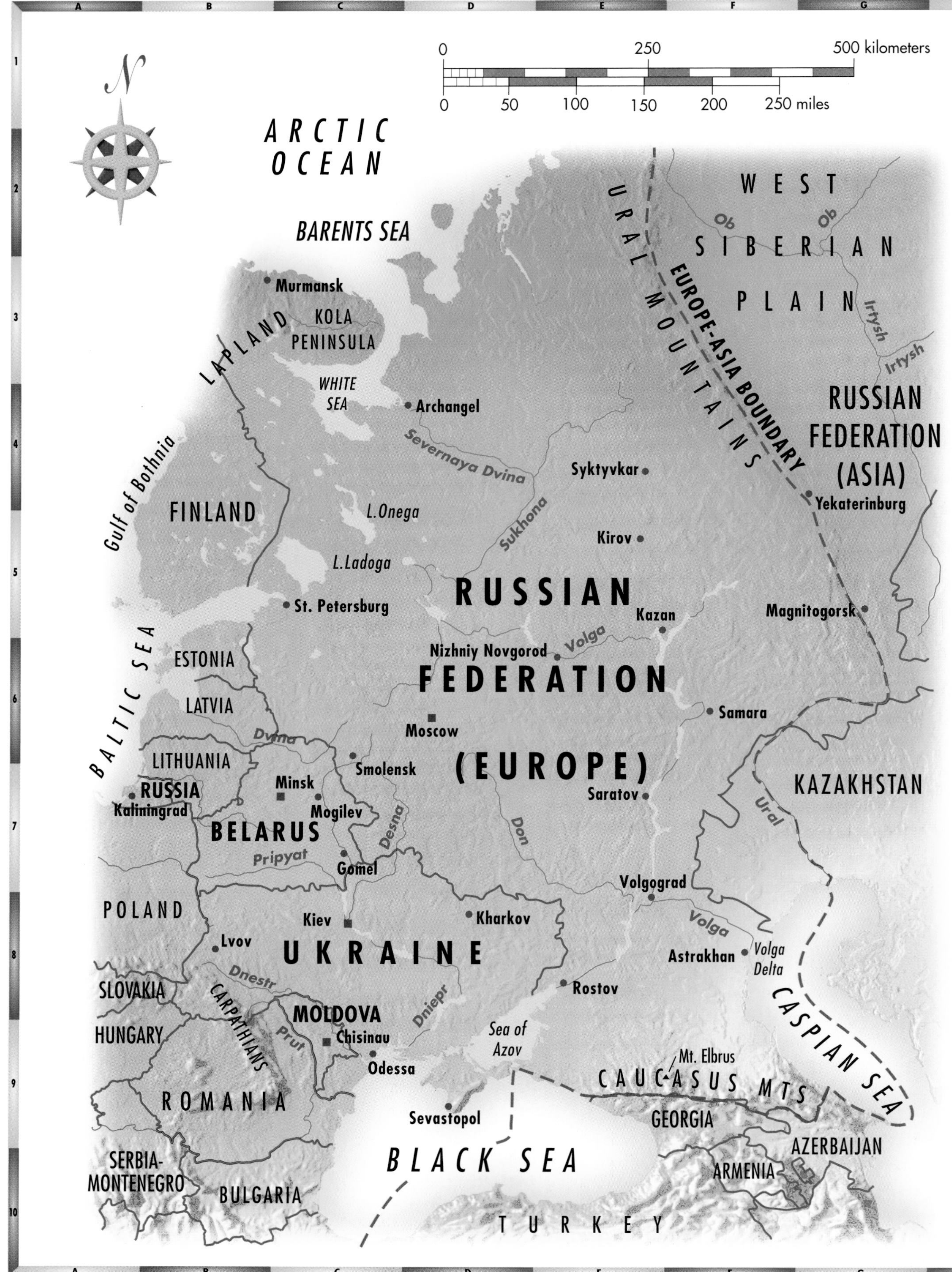
A
B
C
D
E
F
G
H
1
2
3
4
5
6
7
8
9
10
N
0
250
500 kilometers
0
50
100
150
200
250 miles
ARCTIC OCEAN
BARENTS SEA
WEST SIBERIAN PLAIN
Ob
Ob
Irtysh
Irtysh
URAL MOUNTAINS
EUROPE-ASIA BOUNDARY
Murmansk
KOLA PENINSULA
LAPLAND
WHITE SEA
Archangel
RUSSIAN FEDERATION (ASIA)
Severnaya Dvina
Syktyvkar
Yekaterinburg
Gulf of Bothnia
FINLAND
L. Onega
Sukhona
Kirov
L. Ladoga
RUSSIAN FEDERATION (EUROPE)
St. Petersburg
Kazan
Magnitogorsk
Nizhniy Novgorod
Volga
BALTIC SEA
ESTONIA
LATVIA
Samara
Moscow
Dvina
LITHUANIA
Smolensk
KAZAKHSTAN
RUSSIA
Kaliningrad
Minsk
Mogilev
Saratov
Ural
BELARUS
Desna
Don
Pripyat
Gomel
Volgograd
POLAND
Kiev
Kharkov
Volga
Lvov
UKRAINE
Astrakhan
Volga Delta
Dnestr
SLOVAKIA
CARPATHIANS
Dniepr
Rostov
CASPIAN SEA
MOLDOVA
HUNGARY
Prut
Chisinau
Sea of Azov
Odessa
Mt. Elbrus
CAUCASUS MTS
ROMANIA
Sevastopol
GEORGIA
AZERBAIJAN
SERBIA-MONTENEGRO
BLACK SEA
ARMENIA
BULGARIA
TURKEY

EASTERN EUROPE

COUNTRIES

BELARUS
AREA: 207,599 SQ KM (80,154 SQ MI)
POPULATION: 10.2 MILLION
CAPITAL: MINSK

MOLDOVA
AREA: 33,700 SQ KM (13,012 SQ MI)
POPULATION: 4.3 MILLION
CAPITAL: CHISINAU

RUSSIAN FEDERATION
EUROPEAN AND ASIAN RUSSIA
AREA: 17,075,383 SQ KM (6,592,812 SQ MI)
POPULATION: 146.5 MILLION
CAPITAL: MOSCOW

UKRAINE
AREA: 603,700 SQ KM (233,089 SQ MI)
POPULATION: 49.8 MILLION
CAPITAL: KIEV

Even in summer, the Russian Arctic can be bleak and cold. At the same time Eastern European vacationers may be sunbathing on the warm beaches of the Black Sea, far to the south.

Much of Eastern Europe is a vast plain. It is drained by great rivers such as the Dvina, Volga, and Don. The border with Asia is formed by the long, low range of the Ural Mountains in the east and by the massive peaks of the Caucasus Mountains to the south. The icy tundra of the Arctic coast is fringed by a broad belt of mixed spruce and birch forest, warm in summer but bitterly cold in winter. In the southwest are the Steppes. They are rolling grasslands with a rich black soil that is ideal for growing wheat. Eastern Europe is heavily industrialized.

From 1922 until 1991 this region was part of one country, the Soviet Union. Today, the Russian Federation, Belarus, Ukraine, and Moldova are separate independent states, although all belong to an economic union called the Commonwealth of Independent States (CIS). The Russian Federation is the world's biggest country, stretching eastward through Asia to the Pacific Ocean.

PEOPLES OF THE REGION

The Moldovans have close historical ties with the Romanians. The Russians, Belarussians, and Ukrainians are all Slavs, speaking closely related languages. The Cossacks, riders of the Steppes, have their own traditions and customs. So do peoples of the Arctic such as the Komi and Nentsi. The Chechen people of the Caucasus region were in armed conflict with the Russians throughout the 1990s, as they were in the 1700s and 1800s.

DID YOU KNOW?

St. Petersburg changed its name three times in less than one hundred years. In 1900, it was called St. Petersburg. In 1914 it became Petrograd. In 1924, it was renamed Leningrad. In 1991, it returned to its original name. St. Petersburg is a beautiful city, built on islands at the mouth of the Neva River. It is the second biggest city in the Russian Federation, and a former capital city. It is so far north that at midsummer it experiences the famous White Nights—remaining light all night long.

ASIA

One of the terra-cotta soldiers guarding a Chinese emperor's tomb, buried since 210 B.C.

Asia is the biggest continent in the world. It takes up one-third of the Earth's land surface. Six out of every ten people live there. It stretches all the way from the frozen Arctic Ocean to the tropical islands of the East Indies. It is bordered in the west by Russia's Ural Mountains, the Black Sea, and the Mediterranean Sea. In the east it forms the Pacific rim, breaking up into the volcanic islands of Japan and the Philippines.

The Himalaya range is a natural divide between north and south. It includes the world's highest mountains. The lands to the south are called the "subcontinent."

Asia includes gigantic countries, such as the Russian Federation, Kazakhstan, China, and India. Some of these have huge populations—1.25 billion people live in China, almost a billion in India. Parts of Asia are very crowded, such as southern China and Bangladesh. In Japan, the cities of Tokyo and Yokohama have grown together to create the biggest urban area in the world. Other areas of Asia remain wilderness, with very few inhabitants.

ARCTIC CIRCLE
EUROPE
ASIA
TROPIC OF CANCER
AFRICA
INDIAN OCEAN
EQUATOR
TROPIC OF CAPRICORN

ANCIENT & MODERN

Asia gave the world some of its first cities and civilizations, dating back over 5,000 years. They grew up in the Middle East, in the Indus River valley, and in China. Asia gave us the first writing and the world's major religions—Buddhism, Christianty, Hinduism, Islam, Judaism, and Taoism. Asia remains a land of tradition, but it is also a land of modern industry and business, with gleaming skyscrapers rising from cities in Japan, China, and Southeast Asia.

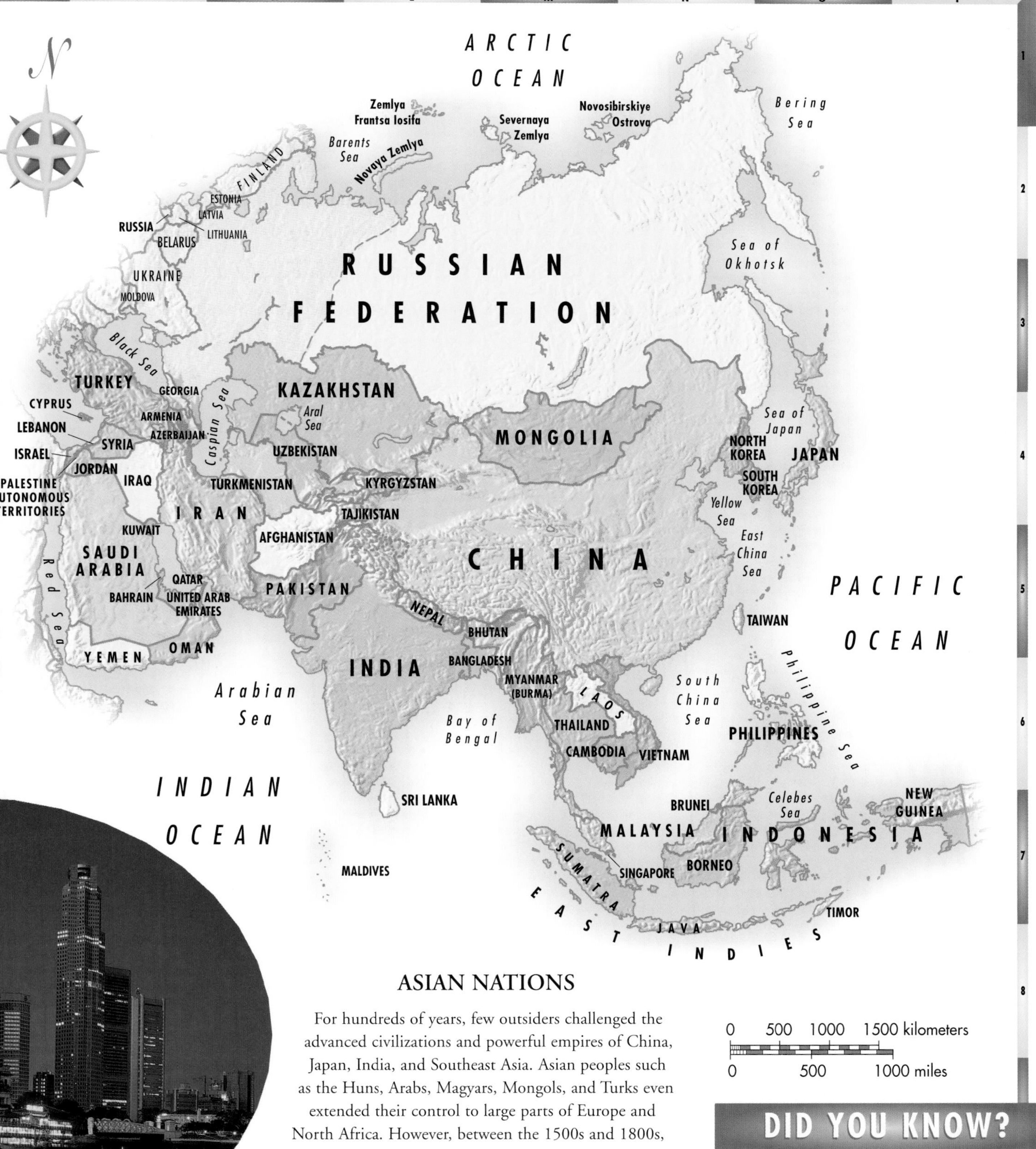
ARCTIC OCEAN
Zemlya Frantsa Iosifa
Barents Sea
Novaya Zemlya
Severnaya Zemlya
Novosibirskiye Ostrova
Bering Sea
FINLAND
ESTONIA
LATVIA
LITHUANIA
RUSSIA
BELARUS
UKRAINE
MOLDOVA
RUSSIAN FEDERATION
Sea of Okhotsk
Black Sea
TURKEY
GEORGIA
ARMENIA
AZERBAIJAN
Caspian Sea
KAZAKHSTAN
Aral Sea
CYPRUS
LEBANON
SYRIA
ISRAEL
JORDAN
PALESTINE AUTONOMOUS TERRITORIES
IRAQ
UZBEKISTAN
TURKMENISTAN
KYRGYZSTAN
TAJIKISTAN
MONGOLIA
Sea of Japan
NORTH KOREA
SOUTH KOREA
JAPAN
Yellow Sea
East China Sea
IRAN
KUWAIT
AFGHANISTAN
CHINA
SAUDI ARABIA
QATAR
BAHRAIN
UNITED ARAB EMIRATES
PAKISTAN
NEPAL
BHUTAN
Red Sea
YEMEN
OMAN
INDIA
BANGLADESH
TAIWAN
PACIFIC OCEAN
Arabian Sea
MYANMAR (BURMA)
LAOS
THAILAND
CAMBODIA
VIETNAM
Bay of Bengal
South China Sea
PHILIPPINES
Philippine Sea
INDIAN OCEAN
SRI LANKA
BRUNEI
Celebes Sea
NEW GUINEA
MALAYSIA
INDONESIA
MALDIVES
SUMATRA
SINGAPORE
BORNEO
TIMOR
JAVA
EAST INDIES
0 500 1000 1500 kilometers
0 500 1000 miles

ASIAN NATIONS

For hundreds of years, few outsiders challenged the advanced civilizations and powerful empires of China, Japan, India, and Southeast Asia. Asian peoples such as the Huns, Arabs, Magyars, Mongols, and Turks even extended their control to large parts of Europe and North Africa. However, between the 1500s and 1800s, Europeans such as the Portuguese, Dutch, Russians, French, and British began to seize control of Asian trade and territory. During World War II (1939–45), Japan tried to dominate Asia, but was defeated. After the war, the Europeans withdrew. New independent Asian nations emerged.

DID YOU KNOW?

There are 1,196 coral islands in the Maldive Islands group, south of India. Their average height above sea level is just 1.8 meters (6 feet). Floods are common and fresh water is hard to come by. Only 203 of the islands are inhabited. If the level of the world's oceans rises, then the Maldives could disappear under the waves.

ASIA

Asia includes extremes of wealth and poverty. There are oil-rich princes in Saudi Arabia and Brunei and desperately poor people living on the streets of India. Asia is a region struggling to feed and care for a rapidly growing population. It is also a region of long-standing political conflicts, from the Middle East to Kashmir (a region claimed by both India and Pakistan) to the Korean peninsula. Southeast Asia faces problems with the environment, too. Illegal logging clears precious rain forest and fires fill the skies with choking smog.

• GENERAL FACTS •

HIGHEST POINT
MT. EVEREST, 8,848 M (29,029 FT), CHINA-NEPAL

LOWEST POINT
DEAD SEA, -394 M (-1,293 FT), ISRAEL-JORDAN

LONGEST RIVER
CHANG (YANGTZE), 6,380 KM (3,965 MI), CHINA

BIGGEST LAKE
CASPIAN SEA, 371,800 SQ KM (143,552 SQ MI), IRAN-TURKMENISTAN-KAZAKHSTAN-RUSSIAN FEDERATION-AZERBAIJAN

HIGHEST WATERFALL
JOG (GERSOPPA), 253 M (830 FT), INDIA

BIGGEST ISLAND
BORNEO, 757,050 SQ KM (292,297 SQ MI), INDIAN OCEAN

BIGGEST DESERT
GOBI, 1,040,000 SQ KM (401,544 SQ MI), MONGOLIA-CHINA

POPULATION OF CONTINENT
3,637 MILLION (1999)

MOST POPULOUS COUNTRY
CHINA, 1,254.1 MILLION (1999)

MOST DENSELY POPULATED COUNTRY
SINGAPORE, 6,449 PER SQ KM (16,706 PER SQ MI) (1999)

MOST POPULOUS CITY
TOKYO, JAPAN, 27.2 MILLION (1999)

POPULATION LIVING IN CITIES
35 PERCENT

INFANT MORTALITY
56 DEATHS PER 1,000 CHILDREN UNDER AGE 1

LIFE EXPECTANCY
MALE 65 YEARS; FEMALE 68 YEARS

WEALTH
GROSS DOMESTIC PRODUCT PER PERSON U.S. $6,110

LITERACY RATE
MALE 82 PERCENT; FEMALE 71 PERCENT

• VEGETATION •

Treeless tundra borders the Arctic Ocean. Below this region lies the great belt of northern forest, or taiga. Southward again are steppe grasslands, giving way to desert. The vegetation of the mountains changes with altitude. Melting snows from the high peaks irrigate the fertile plains of eastern China, northern India, and the valleys of Southeast Asia. India has regions of desert, grassland, and forest. The tropical forests and fields of South and Southeast Asia are fed by heavy monsoon rains.

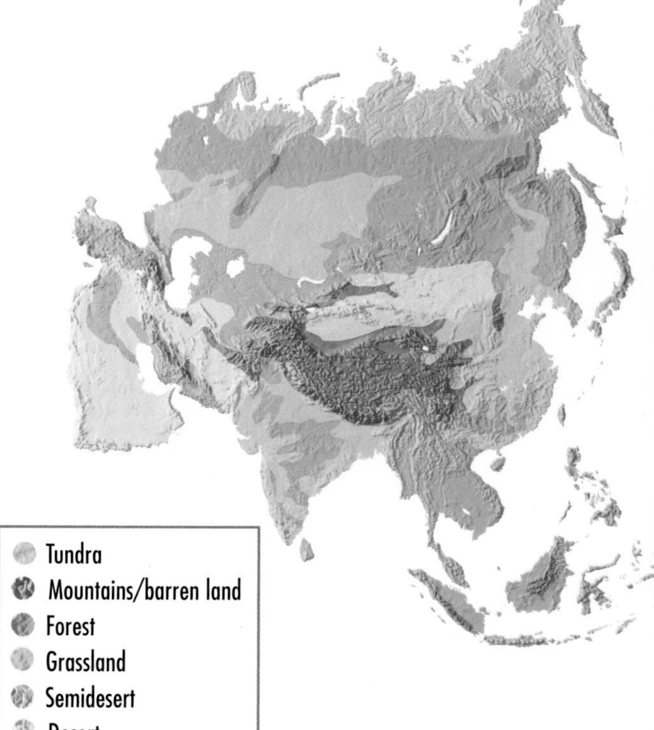
Tundra
Mountains/barren land
Forest
Grassland
Semidesert
Desert

• LANGUAGE •

Standard Chinese is spoken by more people than any other language on Earth. Other forms of Chinese, such as Cantonese, have developed into different languages. There are 407 languages in India. Many languages of northern, central, and southern Asia are part of the great Eurasian language family known as Indo-European.

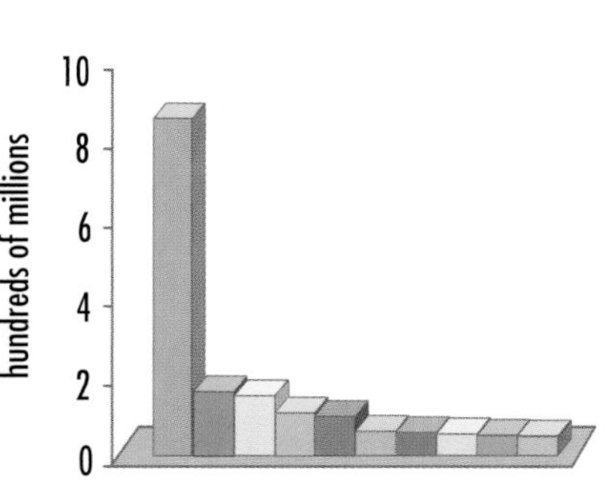
hundreds of millions
10
8
6
4
2
0

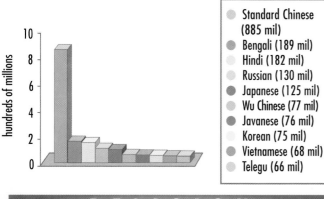

- Standard Chinese (885 mil)
- Bengali (189 mil)
- Hindi (182 mil)
- Russian (130 mil)
- Japanese (125 mil)
- Wu Chinese (77 mil)
- Javanese (76 mil)
- Korean (75 mil)
- Vietnamese (68 mil)
- Telegu (66 mil)

• RELIGION •

Muslims live throughout Southwest and Central Asia. Hindus live in India, Nepal, Sri Lanka, and on the island of Bali, in Indonesia. Buddhism started in Nepal and India, spreading to Sri Lanka, China, Japan, and Southeast Asia. There are Christians in Asiatic Russia, China, India, Sri Lanka, East Timor, and the Philippines.

9.2%
8.6%
31.2%
6.4%
22.2%
22.4%

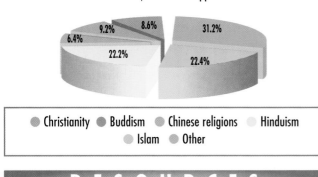

- Christianity
- Buddhism
- Chinese religions
- Hinduism
- Islam
- Other

• RESOURCES •

Oil is the "black gold" that brings wealth to Saudi Arabia, the Persian Gulf states, Iraq, Iran, Central Asia, and Indonesia. Asiatic Russia is rich in minerals. Japan, Asia's leading economic power, has to import oil and minerals for its manufacturing industries.

COAL: *China, India, Russian Federation*

GOLD: *Armenia, China, India, Indonesia, Japan, Russian Federation, Uzbekistan*

IRON: *China, India, Iran, Korea, Russian Federation*

OIL: *China, Indonesia, Iran, Iraq, Kazakhstan, Kuwait, Oman, Qatar, Russian Federation, Saudi Arabia, United Arab Emirates, Uzbekistan*

TIN: *China, Indonesia, Malaysia, Thailand*

• CLIMATE •

Almost every type of climate can be found in Asia. Asiatic Russia has bitterly cold winters. There are hot deserts in Arabia and India, and cool deserts in Central Asia. There are high, cold plateaus in the Himalayan region of Tibet. There are temperate zones in Japan and warm, mild climates on the Mediterranean coast. Southern Asia has intensely hot and dry seasons followed by a seasonal deluge of rain brought by the monsoon winds.

JANUARY

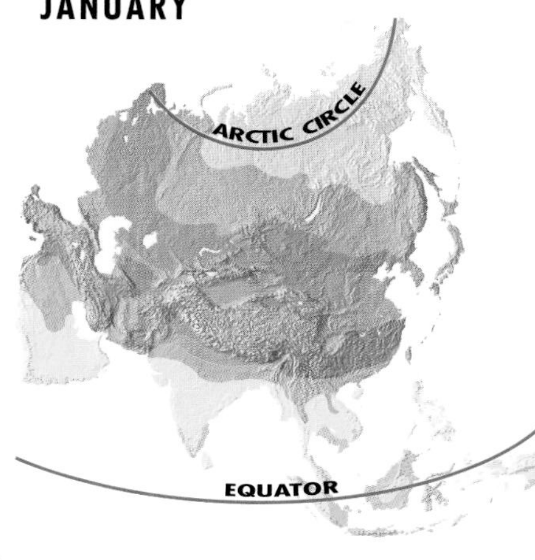
ARCTIC CIRCLE
EQUATOR

JULY

ARCTIC CIRCLE
EQUATOR

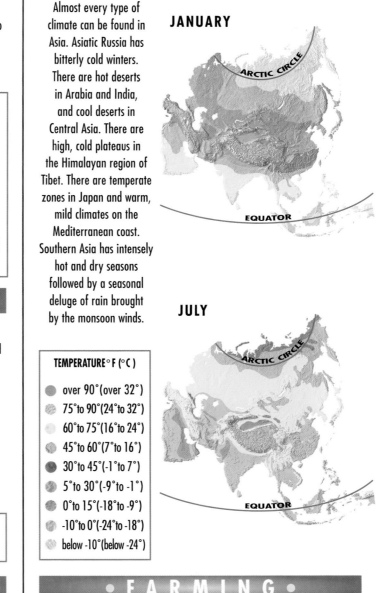

TEMPERATURE° F (°C)

- over 90° (over 32°)
- 75° to 90° (24° to 32°)
- 60° to 75° (16° to 24°)
- 45° to 60° (7° to 16°)
- 30° to 45° (-1° to 7°)
- 5° to 30° (-9° to -1°)
- 0° to 15° (-18° to -9°)
- -10° to 0° (-24° to -18°)
- below -10° (below -24°)

• FARMING •

Although wheat is widely grown in northern Asia, rice is the chief food crop of the continent. Bangladesh specializes in growing jute, a fiber crop used for making sacks and coarse cloth. Malaysia specializes in growing natural rubber.

FRUITS: *Armenia, China, Israel, Turkey*

RICE: *Bangladesh, China, India, Indonesia, Japan, Malaysia, Philippines, Thailand, Vietnam*

SUGARCANE: *India, China, Indonesia, Philippines*

TEA: *China, India, Indonesia, Japan, Sri Lanka*

WHEAT: *China, India, Russian Federation*

ASIA
A Growing Continent

Asia is a beautiful land, with shimmering deserts, misty bamboo forests, and smoldering volcanic islands. Its ancient buildings can match nature's beauty, from the moonlit marble of India's Taj Mahal to the golden roofs of the Shwe Dagon Pagoda in Burma (Myanmar).

Asia's ancient civilizations were made possible by farming, and most of its landscapes include people at work—Balinese families planting rice in terraced fields, a Mongolian horseman galloping after his flock of sheep, Hong Kong businesswomen traveling to their offices by ferry, crowds in colorful dress scrambling onto an Indian train. The population of Asia will double in the next 50 years, so it is certain that Asia's future will affect the world as much as its past has done.

A HOLY MAN

Sadhus are Hindus who have given up worldly possessions, living off charity. They may pray, meditate, or teach. Some go on pilgrimages to holy sites in the Himalaya Mountains or attend religious festivals beside the sacred Ganges River in India.

MARKET DAY, VIETNAM

Fresh produce is laid out for sale in Da Nang market. Sights like this are common on riverbanks and roadsides all over Vietnam. The women wear broad, cone-shaped hats. These are ideal for keeping off hot sun or monsoon rains. After fighting long wars with France in the 1950s and with the United States in the 1960s and 1970s, today the Vietnamese are enjoying peace.

FLOODED FIELDS

Wild rice first grew in river valleys, and rice farmers still plant rice seedlings in flooded paddy fields. Rice is Asia's most important food crop. It is eaten with almost every meal across the southern half of the continent.

EAST MEETS WEST

Topkapi, the old palace of the Turkish sultans, dates back to the year 1462. It stands on the shores of the Bosporus strait, in European Istanbul, and looks across to the rest of the city on the Asian shore. Istanbul is Turkey's largest city and sits in both Europe and Asia. The Bosporus strait acts as a natural divide between the two continents.

PEOPLES OF ASIA

Japanese schoolgirls visit the Asakusa Kannon Temple in Tokyo. The Japanese are one of the many different ethnic groups living in Asia. These include Arabs, Turks, Iranians, Russians, Arctic peoples, Mongols, Chinese, Tibetans, Burmans, Dravidians, Sinhalese, Thais, and Malays.

TIGERS IN DANGER

The biggest of the big cats, the magnificent tiger was once found from Siberia to the Caspian Sea, from China to India, and on the islands of Sumatra and Bali. The tiger has been hunted ruthlessly for thousands of years, and its natural habitats are still being destroyed. It desperately needs the protection it receives in the jungle reserves of Nepal, India, and Bangladesh.

COUNTRIES

ARMENIA
AREA: 29,800 SQ KM (11,506 SQ MI)
POPULATION: 3.8 MILLION
CAPITAL: YEREVAN

AZERBAIJAN
AREA: 86,599 SQ KM (33,436 SQ MI)
POPULATION: 7.7 MILLION
CAPITAL: BAKU

GEORGIA
AREA: 69,700 SQ KM (26,911 SQ MI)
POPULATION: 5.4 MILLION
CAPITAL: TBILISI

KAZAKHSTAN
AREA: 2,715,097 SQ KM (1,048,300 SQ MI)
POPULATION: 15.4 MILLION
CAPITAL: ASTANA

KYRGYZSTAN
AREA: 198,500 SQ KM (76,641 SQ MI)
POPULATION: 4.7 MILLION
CAPITAL: BISHKEK

RUSSIAN FEDERATION
ASIAN & EUROPEAN RUSSIA
AREA: 17,075,383 SQ KM (6,592,812 SQ MI)
POPULATION: 146.5 MILLION
CAPITAL: MOSCOW

TAJIKISTAN
AREA: 143,100 SQ KM (55,251 SQ MI)
POPULATION: 5.75 MILLION
CAPITAL: DUSHANBE

TURKMENISTAN
AREA: 488,100 SQ KM (188,455 SQ MI)
POPULATION: 4.8 MILLION
CAPITAL: ASHKHABAD

UZBEKISTAN
AREA: 449,601 SQ KM (173,591 SQ MI)
POPULATION: 24.4 MILLION
CAPITAL: TASHKENT

SIBERIA & CENTRAL ASIA

The whole of Asia's ice-bound coast on the Arctic Ocean is taken up by the Russian Federation, which extends beyond the Ural Mountains into Europe. Most of Asian Russia forms the region of Siberia, with its great northern forests, known as taiga. It is bitterly cold in winter.

Western Siberia is a vast plain, lying between the Ob River and the Yenisey River. A central plateau extends eastward to the Lena River. Eastern Siberia rises to uplands, the Verkhoyanski Mountains and the volcanic Kamchatka peninsula. Russia's chief port on the Pacific coast is Vladivostok. Southern Siberia is bordered by the Amur River. High peaks rise to the south of Lake Baikal, the world's deepest lake.

Central Asian nations include Kyrgyzstan, Tajikistan, Uzbekistan, Turkmenistan, and Kazakhstan. They are made up of deserts, steppe grasslands, and mountains. They surround three large, salty lakes—Lake Balkhash, the Aral Sea, and the Caspian Sea. The mountain states of Azerbaijan, Georgia, and Armenia occupy the Caucasus range. Until 1991, Central Asia and the Caucasus were united with Russia within the Soviet Union. Since the breakup of the Soviet Union, these countries maintain economic links through the Commonwealth of Independent States (C.I.S.).

PEOPLES OF THE REGION

Siberia has a harsh climate, and the people who live there must be tough. They include Nenet reindeer herders, Chukchee hunters, the Yakuts of the taiga, the Evenks of the plateau and uplands, and the Buryats and Tuvinians of southern Siberia. Russians have settled in Siberia since they conquered the region in the years between 1581 and 1639. Central Asian peoples include farmers and herders, relatives of the Turks and Mongols. The Caucasus Mountains are home to Armenians, Georgians and Azeris.

0 500 1000 1500 kilometers
0 500 1000 miles
ARCTIC OCEAN
Bering Sea
East Siberian Sea
Novosibirskiye Ostrova
Severnaya Zemlya
Zemlya Frantsa Iosifa
Barents Sea
Novaya Zemlya
Kara Sea
Laptev Sea
Anadyr
Kolyma
Kolyma Lowland
KAMCHATKA
Nordvik
Dikson
FINLAND
LATVIA
ESTONIA
RUSSIA
LITHUANIA
BELARUS
RUSSIAN FEDERATION (EUROPE)
URAL MOUNTAINS
EUROPE-ASIA BOUNDARY
Salekhard
Ob
Siberian Lowland
Yenisey
CENTRAL SIBERIAN PLATEAU
Lena
VERKHOYANSKI MOUNTAINS
Magadan
Petropavlovsk-Kamchatskiy
Yakutsk
Sea of Okhotsk
Olekminsk
Lensk
ALDANSKOYE NAGOR'YE
Sakhalin
RUSSIAN FEDERATION (ASIA)
UKRAINE
Tobol
Tobolsk
Chelyabinsk
Ural
Orsk
Omsk
Tomsk
Novosibirsk
Krasnoyarsk
Irkutsk
Lake Baikal
Ulan-Ude
Amur
Khabarovsk
Yuzhno-Sakhalinsk
Black Sea
CAUCASUS
Batumi
GEORGIA
Tbilisi
ARMENIA
Yerevan
AZERBAIJAN
AZER.
Baku
Caspian Sea
IRAQ
KAZAKHSTAN
Irtysh
Karaganda
Semipalatinsk
Aral Sea
Balkhash
Lake Balkhash
Nukus
Tashauz
UZBEKISTAN
TURKMENISTAN
Tashkent
Bishkek
ASTANA
KYRGYZSTAN
Ashkabad
Bukhara
Dushanbe
TAJIKISTAN
IRAN
AFGHANISTAN
PAKISTAN
MONGOLIA
CHINA
Vladivostok
Sea of Japan
NORTH KOREA
SOUTH KOREA
JAPAN
Yellow Sea

DID YOU KNOW?

The Trans-Siberian railway is the world's longest track, stretching 9,438 kilometers (5,865 miles) from Moscow to the Pacific coast. The journey takes 6 days, and stops at 97 stations. A branch line from Lake Baikal leads south through Mongolia to Beijing, the capital of China.

OIL & GOLD

Central Asia is rich in oil. Siberia has reserves of oil, natural gas, coal, iron ore, and gold. Timber is another important resource. However, the bitter climate and remote locations make transportation costly.

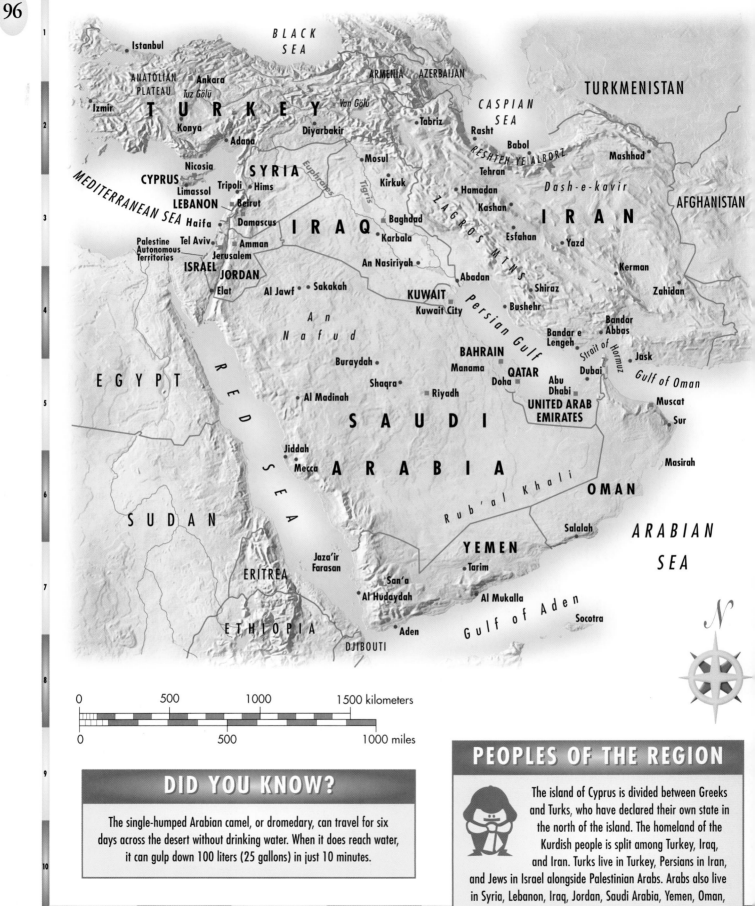

BLACK SEA
Istanbul
ANATOLIAN PLATEAU
Ankara
Tuz Gölü
Izmir
TURKEY
Van Gölü
Konya
Adana
Diyarbakir
ARMENIA
AZERBAIJAN
CASPIAN SEA
Tabriz
Rasht
Babol
RESHTEH-YE ALBORZ
Tehran
TURKMENISTAN
Mashhad
Nicosia
CYPRUS
Limassol
SYRIA
Euphrates
Tigris
Mosul
Kirkuk
Tripoli
Hims
Hamadan
Dash-e-kavir
AFGHANISTAN
MEDITERRANEAN SEA
LEBANON
Beirut
Damascus
Haifa
IRAQ
Baghdad
Kashan
ZAGROS MTNS
IRAN
Esfahan
Palestine Autonomous Territories
Tel Aviv
Amman
Jerusalem
Karbala
Yazd
ISRAEL
JORDAN
An Nasiriyah
Abadan
Kerman
Elat
Al Jawf
Sakakah
KUWAIT
Kuwait City
Shiraz
Zahidan
Bushehr
An Nafud
Persian Gulf
Bandar Abbas
Bandar e Lengeh
Strait of Hormuz
BAHRAIN
Manama
Jask
EGYPT
RED SEA
Buraydah
QATAR
Doha
Dubai
Abu Dhabi
Gulf of Oman
Shaqra
Riyadh
UNITED ARAB EMIRATES
Muscat
Al Madinah
SAUDI ARABIA
Sur
Jiddah
Mecca
Masirah
Rub'al Khali
OMAN
SUDAN
Salalah
ARABIAN SEA
YEMEN
Jaza'ir Farasan
Tarim
ERITREA
San'a
Al Hudaydah
Al Mukalla
Gulf of Aden
Socotra
ETHIOPIA
Aden
DJIBOUTI
N

0 500 1000 1500 kilometers
0 500 1000 miles

DID YOU KNOW?

The single-humped Arabian camel, or dromedary, can travel for six days across the desert without drinking water. When it does reach water, it can gulp down 100 liters (25 gallons) in just 10 minutes.

PEOPLES OF THE REGION

The island of Cyprus is divided between Greeks and Turks, who have declared their own state in the north of the island. The homeland of the Kurdish people is split among Turkey, Iraq, and Iran. Turks live in Turkey, Persians in Iran, and Jews in Israel alongside Palestinian Arabs. Arabs also live in Syria, Lebanon, Iraq, Jordan, Saudi Arabia, Yemen, Oman, the United Arab Emirates, Qatar, Bahrain, and Kuwait.

SOUTHWEST ASIA

Asia Minor, the Levant, the Near East, and the Middle East—all these names have been given to parts of Southwest Asia. This region borders both Europe and Africa. It gave birth to some of the world's first great civilizations.

The island of Cyprus and the Mediterranean coastal countries of Syria, Lebanon, and Israel have a warm, mild climate suitable for growing citrus fruits. Inland, however, landscapes are harsher and climates more extreme. In Turkey the Anatolian plateau and mountains have warm summers but very cold winters. Hot sandy deserts stretch from Syria and Iraq southward across the Arabian peninsula to the Red Sea and the Gulf of Aden. Only small areas are irrigated.

The region depends mostly on oil for its wealth. The Tigris and Euphrates Rivers flow through central Iraq, creating a band of fertile farmland and marshes. Beyond the Zagros Mountains is Iran, another land of desert and mountains, with grassy steppes bordering the Caspian Sea.

A HOLY LAND

Jerusalem, in Israel, is a holy city to three major world religions. To Jews it is the city chosen by King David to be his capital 3,000 years ago, and the site of their ancient temples. To Christians it is the site of the crucifixion and resurrection of Jesus Christ. To Muslims, the Dome of the Rock mosque, completed in A.D.691, marks the place where the Prophet Muhammad ascended to heaven on a winged horse.

COUNTRIES

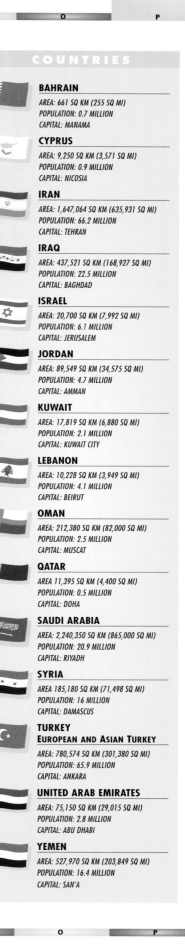

BAHRAIN
AREA: 661 SQ KM (255 SQ MI)
POPULATION: 0.7 MILLION
CAPITAL: MANAMA

CYPRUS
AREA: 9,250 SQ KM (3,571 SQ MI)
POPULATION: 0.9 MILLION
CAPITAL: NICOSIA

IRAN
AREA: 1,647,064 SQ KM (635,931 SQ MI)
POPULATION: 66.2 MILLION
CAPITAL: TEHRAN

IRAQ
AREA: 437,521 SQ KM (168,927 SQ MI)
POPULATION: 22.5 MILLION
CAPITAL: BAGHDAD

ISRAEL
AREA: 20,700 SQ KM (7,992 SQ MI)
POPULATION: 6.1 MILLION
CAPITAL: JERUSALEM

JORDAN
AREA: 89,549 SQ KM (34,575 SQ MI)
POPULATION: 4.7 MILLION
CAPITAL: AMMAN

KUWAIT
AREA: 17,819 SQ KM (6,880 SQ MI)
POPULATION: 2.1 MILLION
CAPITAL: KUWAIT CITY

LEBANON
AREA: 10,228 SQ KM (3,949 SQ MI)
POPULATION: 4.1 MILLION
CAPITAL: BEIRUT

OMAN
AREA: 212,380 SQ KM (82,000 SQ MI)
POPULATION: 2.5 MILLION
CAPITAL: MUSCAT

QATAR
AREA 11,395 SQ KM (4,400 SQ MI)
POPULATION: 0.5 MILLION
CAPITAL: DOHA

SAUDI ARABIA
AREA: 2,240,350 SQ KM (865,000 SQ MI)
POPULATION: 20.9 MILLION
CAPITAL: RIYADH

SYRIA
AREA 185,180 SQ KM (71,498 SQ MI)
POPULATION: 16 MILLION
CAPITAL: DAMASCUS

TURKEY
EUROPEAN AND ASIAN TURKEY
AREA: 780,574 SQ KM (301,380 SQ MI)
POPULATION: 65.9 MILLION
CAPITAL: ANKARA

UNITED ARAB EMIRATES
AREA: 75,150 SQ KM (29,015 SQ MI)
POPULATION: 2.8 MILLION
CAPITAL: ABU DHABI

YEMEN
AREA: 527,970 SQ KM (203,849 SQ MI)
POPULATION: 16.4 MILLION
CAPITAL: SAN'A

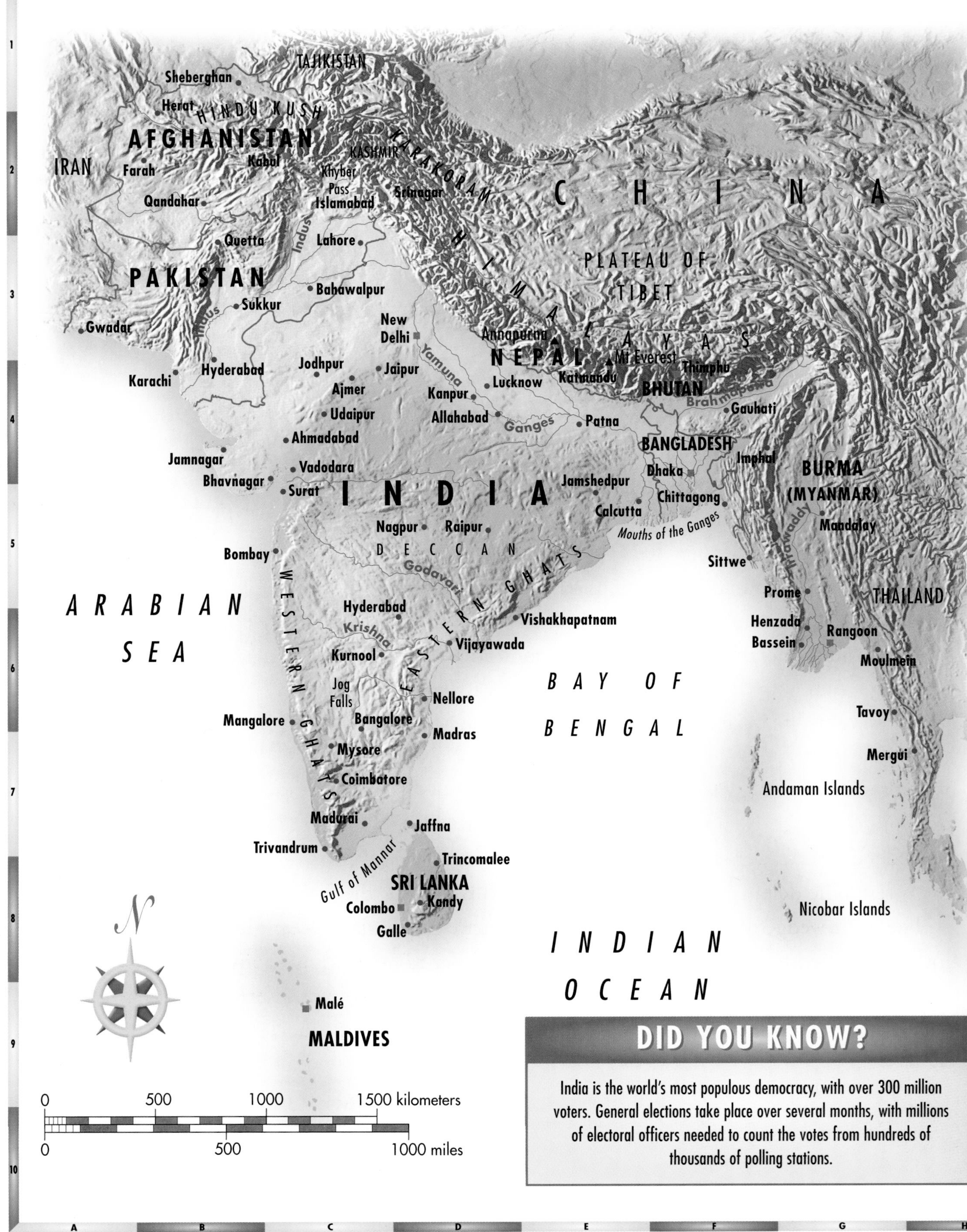
TAJIKISTAN
Sheberghan
Herat
HINDU KUSH
AFGHANISTAN
IRAN
Farah
Kabul
KASHMIR
Khyber Pass
KARAKORAM
Srinagar
Islamabad
Qandahar
CHINA
Quetta
Lahore
Indus
PAKISTAN
PLATEAU OF TIBET
HIMALAYAS
Bahawalpur
Sukkur
Gwadar
New Delhi
Annapurna
Mt Everest
NEPAL
Thimphu
Karachi
Hyderabad
Jodhpur
Jaipur
Yamuna
Lucknow
Katmandu
BHUTAN
Ajmer
Kanpur
Brahmaputra
Gauhati
Udaipur
Allahabad
Ganges
Patna
Ahmadabad
BANGLADESH
Imphal
Jamnagar
Vadodara
Dhaka
BURMA (MYANMAR)
Bhavnagar
Surat
INDIA
Jamshedpur
Chittagong
Calcutta
Mandalay
Nagpur
Raipur
Mouths of the Ganges
DECCAN
Bombay
Sittwe
Godavari
Irrawaddy
WESTERN GHATS
EASTERN GHATS
Prome
THAILAND
ARABIAN SEA
Hyderabad
Vishakhapatnam
Henzada
Rangoon
Krishna
Bassein
Vijayawada
Moulmein
Kurnool
BAY OF BENGAL
Jog Falls
Nellore
Tavoy
Mangalore
Bangalore
Madras
Mysore
Mergui
Coimbatore
Andaman Islands
Madurai
Jaffna
Trivandrum
Trincomalee
Gulf of Mannar
SRI LANKA
Colombo
Kandy
Nicobar Islands
Galle
N
INDIAN OCEAN
Malé
MALDIVES
0
500
1000
1500 kilometers
0
500
1000 miles

DID YOU KNOW?

India is the world's most populous democracy, with over 300 million voters. General elections take place over several months, with millions of electoral officers needed to count the votes from hundreds of thousands of polling stations.

HIMALAYAS TO THE OCEAN

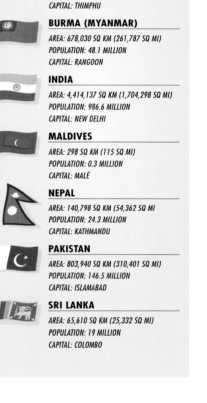

A great arc of mountains divides the Asian subcontinent from the rest of Asia. The Karakoram Range lies to the west of the Indus River. To the east lie the Himalayas. These ranges include the world's highest peaks, many of them over 8,000 meters (26,000 feet).

Melting snows feed the great rivers—the Indus, Ganges, Brahmaputra, and Irrawaddy—that flow across the plains of Pakistan, northern India, Bangladesh, and Burma (Myanmar). Crops include rice, sugarcane, tea, and jute.

Afghanistan is a land of deserts, snowy mountains, and gorges plunging to dizzying depths. The misty lakes and mountains of Kashmir lie on both sides of the border between India and Pakistan, but the entire region is claimed by both countries. Nepal and Bhutan are two small mountain kingdoms. They rise from hills covered with forests of scarlet rhododendron through high valleys to the great mountains. Pakistan flanks India to the northwest. The delta lands of Bangladesh and Burma flank the region to the northeast.

The great wedge of India extends southward into the Indian Ocean. It is extremely hot and parched for most of the year but refreshed by rain-shedding monsoon winds. Below the fertile northern plains, the Deccan plateau is bordered by two coastal ranges, the Eastern and Western Ghats. Islands of the Indian Ocean include green, forested Sri Lanka and the long coral chain of the Maldives.

COUNTRIES

AFGHANISTAN
AREA: 649,507 SQ KM (250,775 SQ MI)
POPULATION: 25.8 MILLION
CAPITAL: KABUL

BANGLADESH
AREA: 142,776 SQ KM (55,126 SQ MI)
POPULATION: 125.7 MILLION
CAPITAL: DHAKA

BHUTAN
AREA: 41,440 SQ KM (16,000 SQ MI)
POPULATION: 0.8 MILLION
CAPITAL: THIMPHU

BURMA (MYANMAR)
AREA: 678,030 SQ KM (261,787 SQ MI)
POPULATION: 48.1 MILLION
CAPITAL: RANGOON

INDIA
AREA: 4,414,137 SQ KM (1,704,298 SQ MI)
POPULATION: 986.6 MILLION
CAPITAL: NEW DELHI

MALDIVES
AREA: 298 SQ KM (115 SQ MI)
POPULATION: 0.3 MILLION
CAPITAL: MALÉ

NEPAL
AREA: 140,798 SQ KM (54,362 SQ MI
POPULATION: 24.3 MILLION
CAPITAL: KATHMANDU

PAKISTAN
AREA: 803,940 SQ KM (310,401 SQ MI)
POPULATION: 146.5 MILLION
CAPITAL: ISLAMABAD

SRI LANKA
AREA: 65,610 SQ KM (25,332 SQ MI)
POPULATION: 19 MILLION
CAPITAL: COLOMBO

PEOPLES OF THE REGION

Hundreds of ethnic groups live in this region of Asia, including Pushtus, Baluchis, Sherpas, Newars, Drukpa, Nagas, Punjabis, Rajasthanis, Gujaratis, Bengalis, Tamils, and Sinhalese. Many define themselves by their religious tradition—Muslim, Buddhist, Hindu, Sikh, Parsee, or Jain.

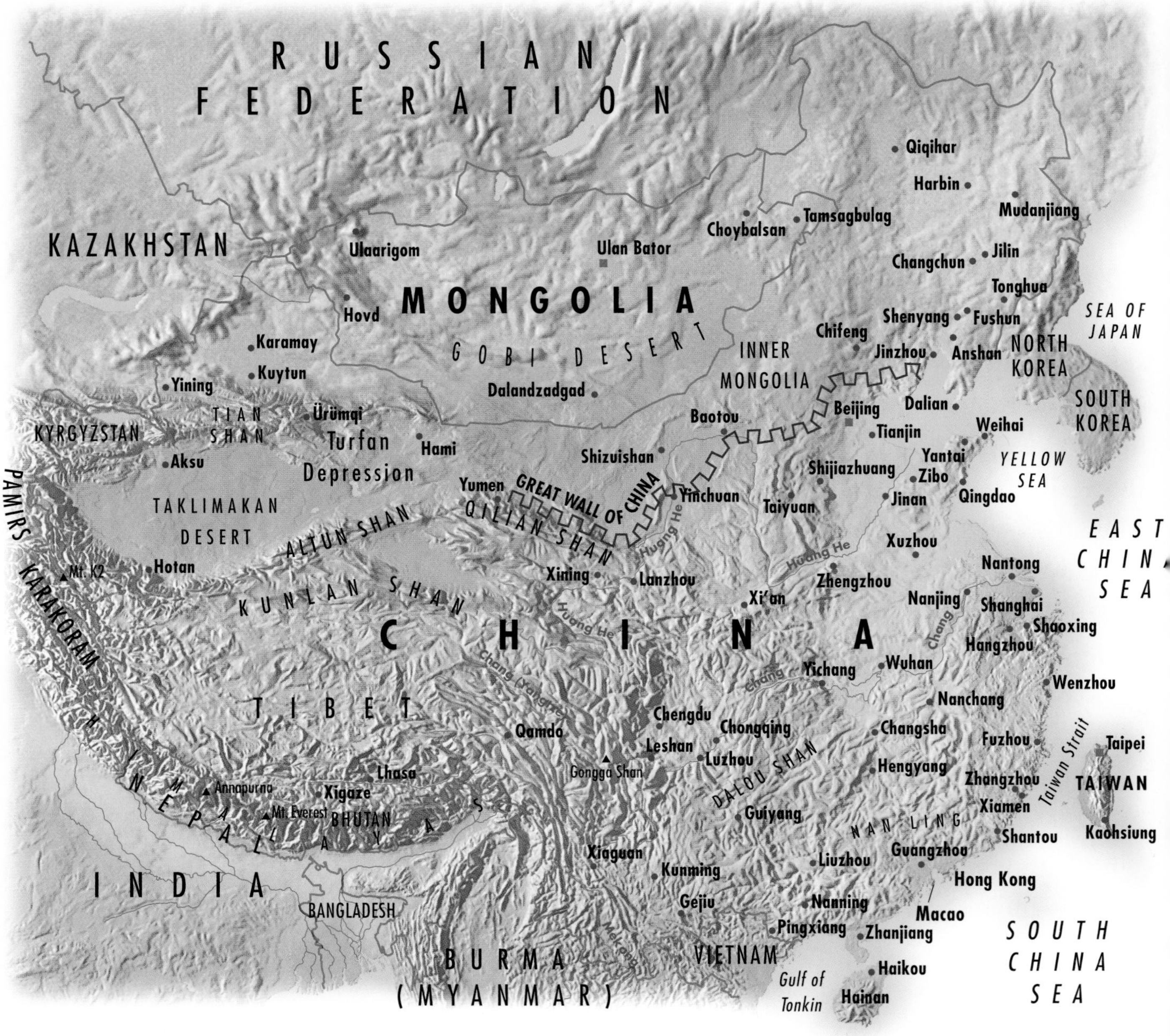

RUSSIAN FEDERATION
KAZAKHSTAN
Ulaarigom
Ulan Bator
Choybalsan
Tamsagbulag
Qiqihar
Harbin
Mudanjiang
Jilin
Changchun
Tonghua
MONGOLIA
Hovd
GOBI DESERT
Shenyang
Fushun
SEA OF JAPAN
Karamay
Kuytun
Yining
Chifeng
INNER MONGOLIA
Jinzhou
Anshan
NORTH KOREA
Dalandzadgad
Dalian
SOUTH KOREA
KYRGYZSTAN
TIAN SHAN
Ürümqi
Turfan Depression
Hami
Baotou
Beijing
Tianjin
Weihai
Aksu
Shizuishan
Shijiazhuang
Yantai
Zibo
YELLOW SEA
PAMIRS
TAKLIMAKAN DESERT
Yumen
GREAT WALL OF CHINA
QILIAN SHAN
Yinchuan
Taiyuan
Jinan
Qingdao
ALTUN SHAN
Huang He
Xuzhou
EAST CHINA SEA
Hotan
Mt. K2
KARAKORAM
Xining
Lanzhou
Zhengzhou
Nantong
KUNLAN SHAN
Xi'an
Nanjing
Shanghai
CHINA
Shaoxing
Hangzhou
Chang (Yangtze)
Chang
Yichang
Wuhan
Wenzhou
TIBET
Nanchang
Chengdu
Qamdo
Chongqing
Changsha
Fuzhou
Taipei
Leshan
Luzhou
Gongga Shan
DALOU SHAN
Hengyang
Lhasa
HIMALAYAS
Annapurna
Xigaze
NEPAL
Mt. Everest
BHUTAN
Zhangzhou
Taiwan Strait
TAIWAN
Xiamen
Guiyang
NAN LING
Shantou
Kaohsiung
Xiaguan
Guangzhou
Liuzhou
Kunming
Hong Kong
INDIA
Gejiu
Nanning
BANGLADESH
Macao
Pingxiang
Zhanjiang
SOUTH CHINA SEA
BURMA (MYANMAR)
Mekong
VIETNAM
Haikou
Gulf of Tonkin
Hainan

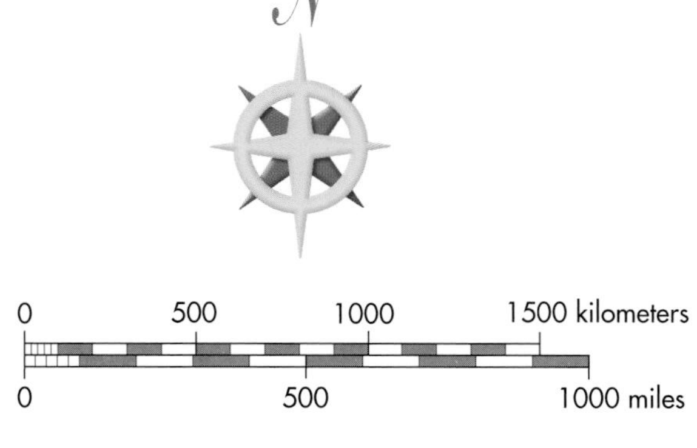
N
0
500
1000
1500 kilometers
0
500
1000 miles

DID YOU KNOW?

For hundreds of years the Chinese Empire produced the most advanced technology in the world. Chinese inventions include the decimal system of counting, paper, silk, cast iron, ships' rudders, printing, compasses, kites, gunpowder, fireworks, rockets, paper money, earthquake recorders, and many more items that we now take for granted.

THE FAR EAST

COUNTRIES

CHINA
AREA: 9,583,000 SQ KM (3,699,996 SQ MI)
POPULATION: 1,254.1 MILLION
CAPITAL: BEIJING

MONGOLIA
AREA: 1,565,000 SQ KM (604,247 SQ MI)
POPULATION: 2.4 MILLION
CAPITAL: ULAN BATOR

TAIWAN
NATIONALIST CHINESE GOVERNMENT
AREA: 35,990 SQ KM (13,896 SQ MI)
POPULATION: 22 MILLION
CAPITAL: TAIPEI

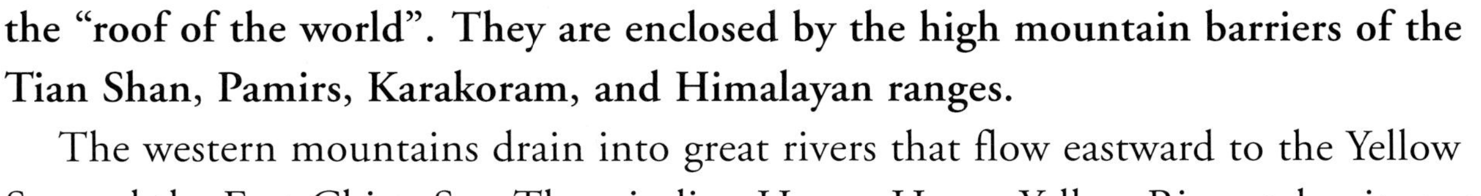

China covers an area slightly larger than the United States. It shares borders with thirteen other Asian countries. Western regions include the Taklimakan desert and the bleak, icy plateau of Tibet, known as the "roof of the world". They are enclosed by the high mountain barriers of the Tian Shan, Pamirs, Karakoram, and Himalayan ranges.

The western mountains drain into great rivers that flow eastward to the Yellow Sea and the East China Sea. The winding Huang He, or Yellow River, takes its name from the wind-blown yellow soil of the north, which muddies its flood waters. The Chang (Yangtze), the world's third longest river, crosses the fertile plains of the east. Southern China is a tropical region, where rice is grown rather than wheat. It takes in Hong Kong and Macao, which used to be British and Portuguese colonies. Another southern territory is the island of Taiwan. In 1948, supporters of China's Nationalist government fled here to set up a rival state after they had been defeated by the Communists in a civil war. Since then, the Chinese Communist government has claimed Taiwan as part of China.

Mongolian herders live around the Gobi Desert and the thinly populated grasslands of the far north. Their ancient homeland is divided between China and the independent Republic of Mongolia.

PEOPLES OF THE REGION

The Mongols live in the autonomous Chinese region of Inner Mongolia and also in the independent country of Mongolia (called Outer Mongolia). Ninety-three percent of the Chinese population are known as Han Chinese, but there are dozens of minority peoples within China's borders, including the Hui, Uygurs, Zhuang, Li, Dai, Dong, and Tibetans.

CHINA
RUSSIAN FEDERATION
SEA OF JAPAN
NORTH KOREA
SOUTH KOREA
JAPAN
HOKKAIDO
HONSHU
SHIKOKU
KYUSHU
PACIFIC OCEAN
YELLOW SEA
Korea Bay
Korea Strait
KII CHANNEL
BUNGO STRAIT
Imjin
Naktong
Wakkanai
Abashiri
Asahigawa
Sapporo
Kushiro
Obihiro
Muroran
Hakodate
Aomori
Hirosaki
Hachinohe
Akita
Kamaishi
Sendai
Niigata
Fukushima
Nagaoka
Koriyama
Toyama
Kanazawa
Hitachi
Fukui
Matsumoto
Mito
Kofu
Tokyo
Fuji-san
Gifu
Yokohama
Matsue
Kyoto
Nagoya
Odawara
Yokosuka
Toyota
Okayama
Kobe
Toyohashi
Shizuoka
Hiroshima
Osaka
Hamamatsu
Kure
Takamatsu
Wakayama
Kita-kyushu
Fukuoka
Matsuyama
Kochi
Sasebo
Omuta
Kumamoto
Nagasaki
Miyazaki
Kagoshima
Tsushima
Sasuna
Unggi
Najin
Chongjin
Kapsan
Kilchu
Songjin
Pukch'ong
Sinuiju
Hamhung
Hungnam
Anju
P'yongyang
Yonghung
Wonsan
Sariwon
Kosong
Haeju
Kaeson
Yanggu
Chunchon
Inch'on
Kangyang
Seoul
Chingju
Samchok
Ullung do
Taejon
Andong
Kunsan
Puhang
Chonju
Taegu
Kwangju
Chinju
Masan
Pusan
Mokp'o
Chin-do
Cheju
Cheju do
N
0 100 200 300 400 500 kilometers
0 100 200 300 miles

DID YOU KNOW?

Japan's sumo wrestlers are the heavyweights of the world. They often weigh in at about 135 kilograms (298 pounds). A sumo wrestling match is often preceded by religious ceremonies, such as scattering salt around the ring. The wrestlers eye each other up for several minutes before a fight begins. One wrestler normally claims victory in just a few seconds, having toppled his opponent.

THE NORTH PACIFIC

COUNTRIES

JAPAN
AREA: 371,973 SQ KM (143,619 SQ MI)
POPULATION: 126.7 MILLION
CAPITAL: TOKYO

NORTH KOREA
AREA: 120,717 SQ KM (46,609 SQ MI)
POPULATION: 21.4 MILLION
CAPITAL: PYONGYANG

SOUTH KOREA
AREA: 98,477 SQ KM (38,022 SQ MI)
POPULATION: 46.9 MILLION
CAPITAL: SEOUL

The Korean peninsula stretches southward from northeast China, dividing the Yellow Sea from the Sea of Japan. Following World War II, the region was divided. North Korea was set up as a communist state in 1945, and remains a bitter enemy of South Korea. The division was made official in 1953.

Japan is made up of volcanic islands lying in a long chain off Asia's North Pacific coast. It is cold and snowy in the north but warm in the south. From north to south, the chief islands are Hokkaido, Honshu, Shikoku, and Kyushu. They are densely populated, especially in the center and south. Most people live on the narrow coastal plains, since the islands are very mountainous inland.

The Japanese are great rice growers and ocean fishers. Although Japan faced economic problems in the 1990s, it remains the world's second largest economic power, a leading manufacturer of cars and electrical goods. It has few natural resources and has to import most of its fuel.

PEOPLES OF THE REGION

Peoples of the North Pacific rim include the Koreans, the Japanese, and a small number of Ainu in northern Japan. The Ainu are descended from the original inhabitants of the islands. The Japanese follow various forms of Buddhism, as well as a religion called Shinto ("the way of the gods"). Korean religions include Buddhism, Christianity, and the Taoist and Confucian teachings of China.

Traditional Japan, with its fine old castles and spring blossoms, impresses visitors, and silk robes called kimonos are still worn for special occasions. However, Japan is also a land of bright city lights and computer games.

SOUTHEAST ASIA

COUNTRIES

BRUNEI
AREA: 5,765 SQ KM (2,225 SQ MI)
POPULATION: 0.3 MILLION
CAPITAL: BANDAR SERI BEGAWAN

CAMBODIA
AREA: 181,000 SQ KM (69,894 SQ MI)
POPULATION: 11.9 MILLION
CAPITAL: PHNOM PENH

INDONESIA
AREA: 2,019,358 SQ KM (779,675 SQ MI)
POPULATION: 211.8 MILLION
CAPITAL: JAKARTA

LAOS
AREA: 236,795 SQ KM (91,428 SQ MI)
POPULATION: 5 MILLION
CAPITAL: VIENTIANE

MALAYSIA
AREA: 333,403 SQ KM (128,727 SQ MI)
POPULATION: 22.7 MILLION
CAPITAL: KUALA LUMPUR

PHILIPPINES
AREA: 299,536 SQ KM (115,651 SQ MI)
POPULATION: 74.7 MILLION
CAPITAL: MANILA

SINGAPORE
AREA: 583 SQ KM (225 SQ MI)
POPULATION: 4 MILLION
CAPITAL: SINGAPORE

THAILAND
AREA: 514,000 SQ KM (198,455 SQ MI)
POPULATION: 61.8 MILLION
CAPITAL: BANGKOK

VIETNAM
AREA: 337, 912 SQ KM (130, 468 SQ MI)
POPULATION: 79.5 MILLION
CAPITAL: HANOI

The bulge of land lying between the Indian Ocean and the South China Sea is often called Indochina. This is a land of forested hills, mountains, rivers, plains, and rice paddies. The climate is hot and tropical, with monsoon winds sweeping in heavy rains from the ocean.

Indochina has a fascinating history. Ruins and old temples bear witness to the splendor of its ancient kingdoms. Modern history brought terrifying warfare to the region, but recent years have been more peaceful. The four countries of this region are Thailand, Cambodia, Laos, and Vietnam.

A long arm of land stretches southward from Thailand to the peninsula of Malaysia and the small city-state of Singapore. Beyond lies the great island of Borneo, divided among Malaysia, Indonesia, and oil-rich Brunei. Farther still are the two groups of smaller islands that make up Indonesia and the Philippines. Massive volcanic eruptions are frequently seen in these islands. They are part of the "ring of fire" that encircles the Pacific Ocean.

Southeast Asia produces rice, timber, natural rubber, and spices such as cloves. Tourism is a growing industry. Cities such as Singapore and Kuala Lumpur are international centers of business.

PEOPLES OF THE REGION

Southeast Asia presents a rich tapestry of ancient cultures. Its peoples include Chinese, Indians, Thais, Karens, Hmong, Lao, Annamese, Malays, Filipinos, Dayak, Javanese, Balinese, and many more. Indochina is mostly Buddhist. Indonesia is the most populous Muslim country in the world, although the islanders of Bali follow a form of Hinduism. Most Filipinos and Timorese are Roman Catholic Christians.

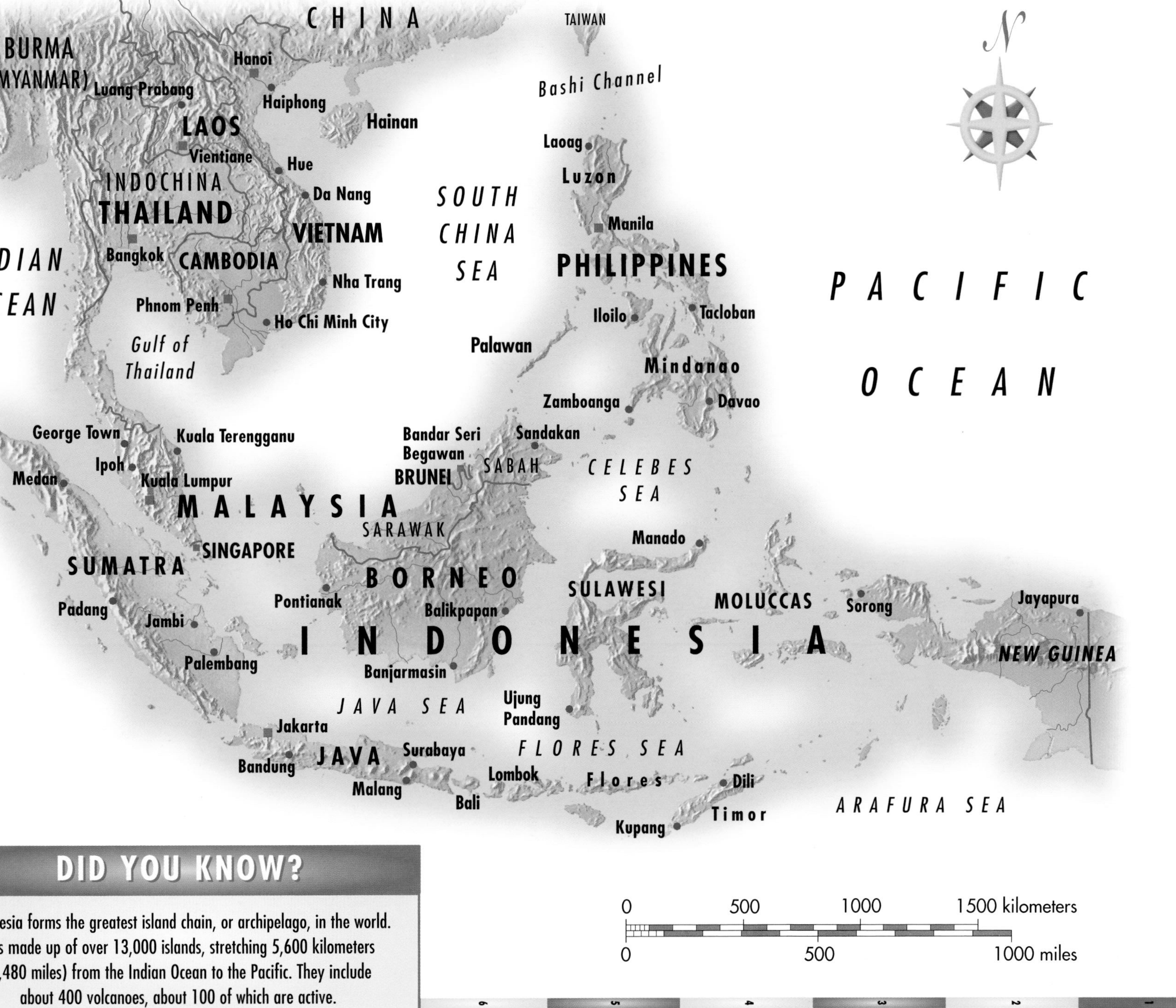
CHINA
TAIWAN
Bashi Channel
BURMA (MYANMAR)
Hanoi
Luang Prabang
Haiphong
Hainan
LAOS
Vientiane
Hue
INDOCHINA
Da Nang
THAILAND
VIETNAM
SOUTH CHINA SEA
Laoag
Luzon
Manila
PHILIPPINES
INDIAN OCEAN
Bangkok
CAMBODIA
Nha Trang
Phnom Penh
Ho Chi Minh City
Gulf of Thailand
Iloilo
Tacloban
Palawan
Mindanao
Zamboanga
Davao
PACIFIC OCEAN
George Town
Kuala Terengganu
Bandar Seri Begawan
Sandakan
BRUNEI
SABAH
CELEBES SEA
Ipoh
Medan
Kuala Lumpur
MALAYSIA
SARAWAK
SINGAPORE
Manado
SUMATRA
BORNEO
SULAWESI
MOLUCCAS
Sorong
Jayapura
Pontianak
Padang
Balikpapan
Jambi
INDONESIA
NEW GUINEA
Palembang
Banjarmasin
JAVA SEA
Ujung Pandang
Jakarta
FLORES SEA
JAVA
Surabaya
Bandung
Lombok
Flores
Dili
Malang
Bali
Timor
ARAFURA SEA
Kupang
0 500 1000 1500 kilometers
0 500 1000 miles

DID YOU KNOW?

Indonesia forms the greatest island chain, or archipelago, in the world. It is made up of over 13,000 islands, stretching 5,600 kilometers (3,480 miles) from the Indian Ocean to the Pacific. They include about 400 volcanoes, about 100 of which are active.

OCEANIA

Australia is too large to be called an island. It is really a continent in its own right. It is often grouped together with Papua New Guinea, New Zealand, and the many islands of the South Pacific. Together they are called Australasia or Oceania. Their combined land area may be smaller than any other continent, but they are spread over a vast area of ocean.

Australia extends from the tropical seas off Cape York Peninsula to the cool ocean waters off the southern island of Tasmania. It is a hot land, in which deserts are bordered by grassland, eucalyptus woodland, and rain forest.

To the north, New Guinea is an island of remote mountain valleys, forests, and rivers. It is divided between the independent Papua New Guinea in the east, and a province of Indonesia in the west. To the east of Australia, across the Tasman Sea, are the volcanic islands of New Zealand. There, the climate is mild and farmland and pasture have been cleared from forest. Countless island chains are scattered across the Pacific Ocean, formed from coral reefs or underwater volcanoes.

THE LAND DOWN UNDER

Uluru (Ayers Rock) casts a dramatic shadow against the sun in the hot desert of central Australia. It is a single block of sandstone, about 340 meters (1,111 feet) high and 9 kilometers (6 miles) around the edge. It is at least 450 million years old. The Anangu Aborigines have lived near the rock for some 20,000 years. It is one of their sacred sites, dating back to the dawn of the world, the mythical "dreamtime." Aborigines were the first Australians. No European had seen Uluru until 1872.

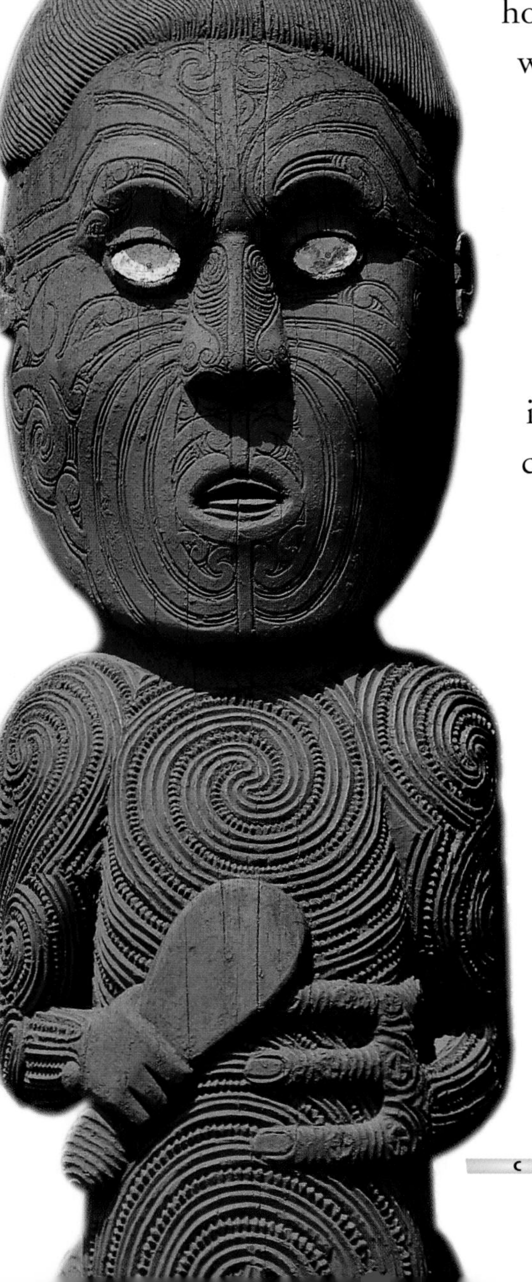

New Zealand's Maori people have developed their own unique style of wood carving and decoration.

THE COUNTRIES OF OCEANIA

In 1787 the British started the modern settlement of Australia. At first they used it as a destination for criminals. They founded several colonies and territories, which today form a single federal nation. New Zealand, the home of the native Maori people, was settled by the British too. It became a colony in 1840. Today, both Australia and New Zealand are powerful independent nations on the Pacific rim. Most of the South Pacific islands also became European colonies in the 1800s. Some still are—or are administered under international agreements—but most have recently grouped together to form small independent nations.

N
NORTH PACIFIC OCEAN
PHILIPPINES
NORTHERN MARIANA ISLANDS
Guam
Marianas Trench
PALAU
MICRONESIA
MELANESIA
POLYNESIA
Caroline Islands
MARSHALL ISLANDS
Johnston Atoll
HAWAIIAN ISLANDS (U.S.)
Line Islands
Kiritimati
Gilbert Islands
KIRIBATI
NAURU
INDONESIA
PAPUA NEW GUINEA
Arafura Sea
SOLOMON ISLANDS
TUVALU
Tokelau
WESTERN SAMOA
American Samoa
VANUATU
FIJI
TONGA
Niue
Cook Islands
French Polynesia
Tahiti
Pitcairn
Coral Sea
Great Barrier Reef
New Caledonia
AUSTRALIA
Norfolk Islands
South West Pacific Basin
Tasman Sea
NEW ZEALAND
INDIAN OCEAN
Chatham Islands
SOUTH PACIFIC OCEAN
0 1000 2000 3000 4000 kilometers
0 1000 2000 miles

DID YOU KNOW?

The world's biggest butterfly may occasionally be seen fluttering high over Papua New Guinea's Popondetta plain. Females of the rare Queen Alexandra's Birdwing species can have a wingspan of over 25 centimeters (10 inches). The females are dark brown with cream patterns. The males are brilliantly colored, but smaller than the female. Over the years, their habitat has been destroyed by logging, farming, and volcanic eruptions.

OCEANIA

Oceania covers an area larger than the Asian continent but the landmass is smaller than Europe's. Its population is the smallest of any continent.

• GENERAL FACTS •

HIGHEST POINT
MT. WILHELM, 4,509 M (14,793 FT), PAPUA NEW GUINEA

LONGEST RIVER
MURRAY-DARLING, 3,750 KM (2,330 MI), AUSTRALIA

BIGGEST LAKE
LAKE EYRE, 9,583 SQ KM (3,700 SQ MI), AUSTRALIA

BIGGEST ISLAND
NEW GUINEA, 808,510 SQ KM (312,166 SQ MI), THE WESTERN HALF IS PART OF THE ASIAN COUNTRY OF INDONESIA. THE EASTERN HALF — PAPUA NEW GUINEA — HAS AN AREA OF 462,840 SQ KM (178,703 SQ MI)

BIGGEST DESERT
GREAT AUSTRALIAN DESERT, 3,800,000 SQ KM (1,467,180 SQ MI), AUSTRALIA

POPULATION OF CONTINENT
30 MILLION (1999)

MOST POPULOUS COUNTRY
AUSTRALIA, 19 MILLION (1999)

MOST DENSELY POPULATED COUNTRY
NAURU, 523 PER SQ KM (1,374 PER SQ MI) (1998)

MOST POPULOUS CITY
SYDNEY, AUSTRALIA 3.7 MILLION (1999)

POPULATION LIVING IN CITIES
70 PERCENT

INFANT MORTALITY
29 DEATHS PER 1,000 CHILDREN UNDER AGE 1

LIFE EXPECTANCY
MALE 71 YEARS; FEMALE 76 YEARS

WEALTH
GROSS DOMESTIC PRODUCT PER PERSON U.S. $5,350

LITERACY RATE
MALE 86 PERCENT; FEMALE 71 PERCENT

• VEGETATION •

The dry lands of the Australian interior are broken by patches of scrub. They give way to tropical rain forest in the northeast, to eucalyptus woods and grasslands in the southeast. Papua New Guinea too has rain forests. Temperate New Zealand has forests of beech and evergreen conifers as well as open grasslands.

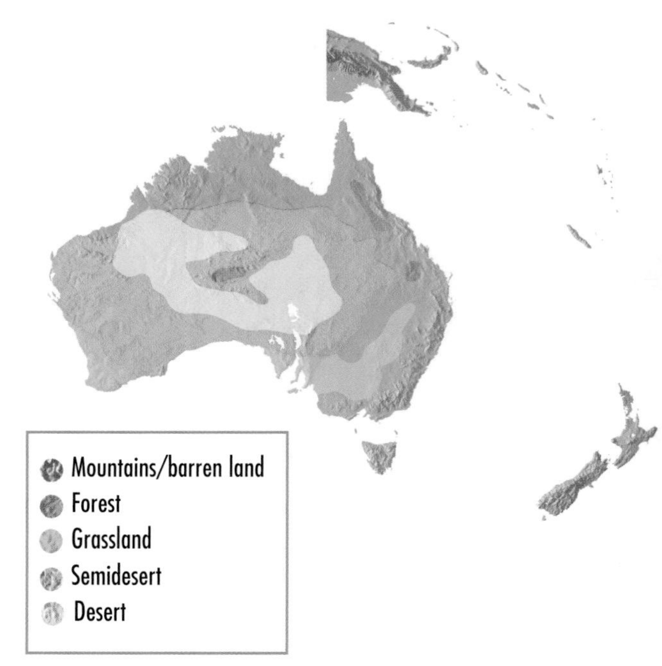
Mountains/barren land
Forest
Grassland
Semidesert
Desert

CLIMATE

The northern belt of Oceania, including Papua New Guinea and northern Queensland, have a hot and humid climate. Central Australia is hot and dry, but the climate becomes milder and more moist to the south. New Zealand has a moderate climate, while the Pacific islands are freshened by ocean winds.

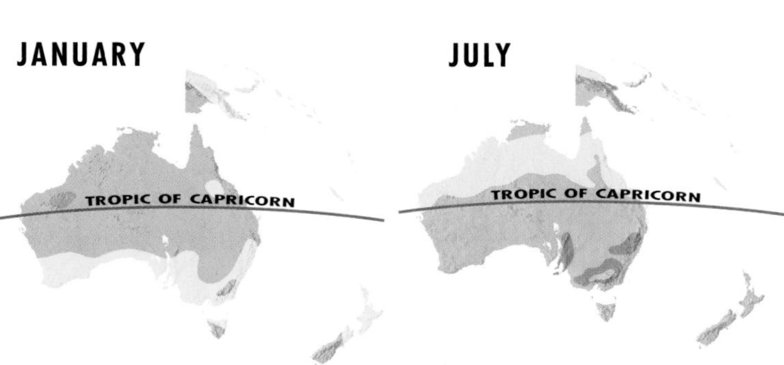
JANUARY
TROPIC OF CAPRICORN
JULY
TROPIC OF CAPRICORN

TEMPERATURE °F (°C)
- over 90° (over 32°)
- 75° to 90° (24° to 32°)
- 60° to 75° (16° to 24°)
- 45° to 60° (7° to 16°)
- 30° to 45° (-1° to 7°)
- 5° to 30° (-9° to -1°)

OCEANIA: *A Continent Apart*

SYDNEY'S SAILS

Sydney Opera House, with its sail-like roofs, looks like a huge ship entering the blue waters of Sydney Harbour. Since it was completed in 1973, this building in Australia's biggest city has become Oceania's most famous landmark.

UNIQUE WILDLIFE

A koala clings to the trunk of a eucalyptus tree. This furry, bear-like creature lives in Australia. It is a marsupial, which means that the mother cares for her baby in a pouch for the first six months of its life. Australia separated from the other landmasses so long ago that the marsupials developed without a challenge from other mammals.

The first Australians were the Aborigines, whose presence on the continent goes back to before 50,000 B.C. The seafarers who colonized the thousands of Pacific islands were Polynesians (such as New Zealand's Maori, the Tahitians, Tongans, and Samoans), Micronesians (of the Caroline and Marshall Islands), and Melanesians (of Papua New Guinea, Fiji, and New Caledonia).

In the 1800s, outsiders poured into Oceania—British, French, Germans, Dutch, Indians. Much of the region was colonized by European countries. Today, Australia and New Zealand have a rich mixture of ethnic groups, including Greeks, Lebanese, Italians, Chinese, Thais, Vietnamese, and Indians. Increasingly, Oceania is breaking away from its colonial past and creating a Pacific economy that extends northward to Indonesia and Japan and eastward to the Americas. Australia and New Zealand are the economic giants of the region. For many of the smaller islands, resources are scant, apart from fish—and the natural beauty that attracts tourists.

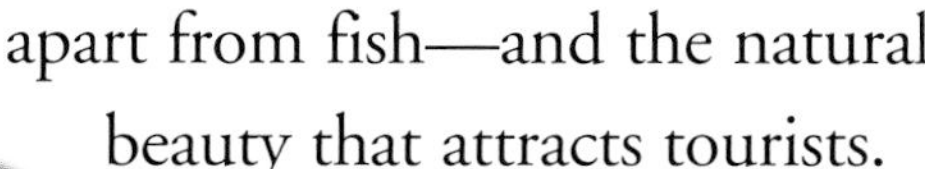

NEW ZEALAND

The beautiful mountains, forests and coasts of New Zealand, and the pleasant climate, attract many people who enjoy outdoor activities, such as climbing, hiking, and sailing.

ANCIENT TRADITION

Descendants of Australia's first inhabitants, the Aborigines have guarded many of their ancient rituals and traditions. Today there is more international interest than ever in Aboriginal painting, music, and dance.

AUSTRALIA

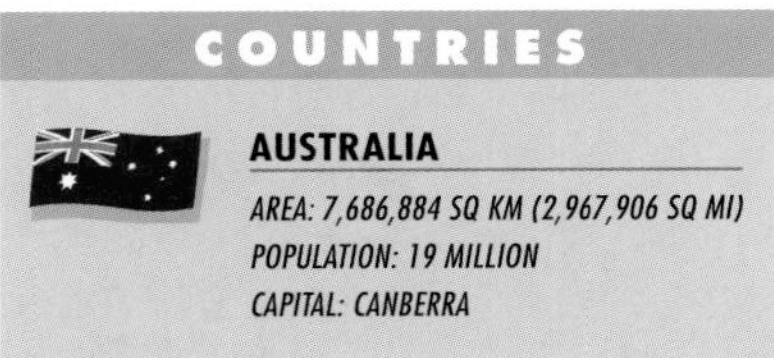
COUNTRIES
AUSTRALIA
AREA: 7,686,884 SQ KM (2,967,906 SQ MI)
POPULATION: 19 MILLION
CAPITAL: CANBERRA

Two-thirds of Australia is taken up by a great western plateau, made up of dry or desert landscapes with ranges of low mountains. It is a sparsely populated continent, with scattered settlements of Aborigines and miners.

A central plain stretches from the Gulf of Carpentaria south-southwest to the Great Australian Bight. Cattle can be raised over large areas, thanks to wells that tap underground water reserves. Running parallel to the eastern coast is the Great Dividing Range, which rises to 2,234 meters (7,329 feet) at Mount Kosciusko. These peaks drain into the Murray-Darling River system. South Australia produces wine, while northern Queensland is a land of tropical rain forests, where farmers can grow sugarcane, pineapples, and bananas. The Pacific coast is shielded by the world's biggest bank of coral, the Great Barrier Reef. New South Wales and Victoria have eucalyptus forests and grasslands where huge flocks of sheep are raised. Across the Bass Strait is the island of Tasmania, with a more temperate climate and extensive forests.

MINES & MINERS

A lucky strike in 1851 started a gold rush in Victoria and New South Wales. Miners and prospectors rushed to Australia from all over the world. Today, Australia produces gold, copper, iron ore, bauxite, coal, and gemstones called opals.

Australia's dusty interior is known as the "outback." It is a land of Aboriginal myths and of tales about the old European pioneers. However 85 percent of modern Australians live near such cities as Brisbane, Sydney, Melbourne, Adelaide, and Perth. Australia's capital is the small city of Canberra, in Australian Capital Territory (ACT). The city was founded and built to serve as the capital.

PEOPLES OF THE REGION

The first Australians — the Torres Strait islanders and the many different Aboriginal peoples — were not officially recognized as citizens of their own country until 1967. They now make up just one percent of the population, outnumbered by the Europeans who have settled in the country over the last 200 years and by more recent immigrants from Asia.

ARAFURA SEA
Torres Strait
Cape York
PACIFIC OCEAN
TIMOR SEA
Melville Island
Darwin
INDIAN OCEAN
Arnhem Land
Cape Arnhem
Gulf of Carpentaria
Cape York Peninsula
Great Barrier Reef
CORAL SEA
Wellesley Island
Cape Lévêque
Broome
Kimberley Plateau
NORTHERN TERRITORY
Cairns
GREAT DIVIDING RANGE
Townsville
Proserpine
Mackay
Barrow Island
Dampier
Great Sandy Desert
MACDONNELL RANGES
Alice Springs
QUEENSLAND
Rockhampton
Mt. Bruce
Gibson Desert
Bundaberg
Lake Macleod
Uluru (Ayers Rock)
Simpson Desert
Fraser Island
Carnarvon
WESTERN AUSTRALIA
MUSGRAVE RANGES
Great Victoria Desert
Lake Eyre
Warrego
Toowoomba
Brisbane
Dirk Hartog Island
SOUTH AUSTRALIA
Cooper Creek
Culgoa
Laverton
Geraldton
Grafton
Lake Torrens
Coffs Harbour
Nullarbor Plain
Lake Everard
NEW SOUTH WALES
Kalgoorlie-Boulder
Ceduna
Darling
Maitland
Perth
Great Australian Bight
Lake Gairdner
Newcastle
Freemantle
Lachlan
Mildura
Sydney
Bunbury
Whidbay Point
Adelaide
Wagga Wagga
Wollongong
Cape Naturaliste
Port Lincoln
Murray
Canberra
AUSTRALIAN CAPITAL TERRITORY
Cape Leeuwin
Albany
Kangaroo Island
VICTORIA
Mt. Kosciusko
Mount Gambier
Geelong
Melbourne
SOUTHERN OCEAN
Cape Otway
Bass Strait
Flinders Island
TASMAN SEA
King Island
Burnie
Cape Barren Island
Davenport
Launceston
Queenstown
TASMANIA
Hobart
South East Cape
0
500
1000
1500 kilometers
0
500
1000 miles

DID YOU KNOW?

Many Australian animals are found nowhere else on Earth. Perhaps the strangest of them all is the platypus. It has a snout like a duck's beak, no teeth, and a tail like a beaver. It spends large amounts of time underwater—where it keeps its eyes tightly shut. It is a mammal, but some of its body is more like that of a reptile, and it lays eggs. Platypuses live in muddy creeks.

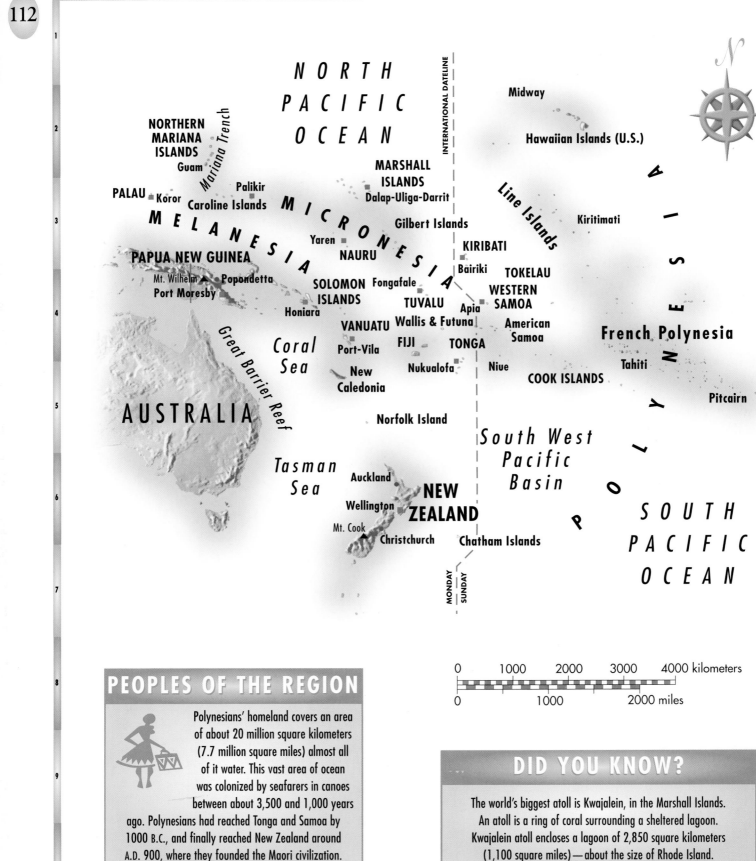

NORTH PACIFIC OCEAN

INTERNATIONAL DATELINE

N

Midway

Hawaiian Islands (U.S.)

NORTHERN MARIANA ISLANDS

Mariana Trench

Guam

PALAU

Koror

Palikir

Caroline Islands

MARSHALL ISLANDS

Dalap-Uliga-Darrit

MICRONESIA

MELANESIA

Line Islands

Kiritimati

Gilbert Islands

Yaren

NAURU

KIRIBATI

Bairiki

PAPUA NEW GUINEA

Mt. Wilhelm

Popondetta

Port Moresby

SOLOMON ISLANDS

Honiara

Fongafale

TUVALU

TOKELAU

WESTERN SAMOA

Apia

American Samoa

Wallis & Futuna

VANUATU

Port-Vila

FIJI

TONGA

Nukualofa

Niue

COOK ISLANDS

French Polynesia

Tahiti

Pitcairn

POLYNESIA

Great Barrier Reef

Coral Sea

New Caledonia

AUSTRALIA

Norfolk Island

South West Pacific Basin

Tasman Sea

Auckland

Wellington

NEW ZEALAND

Mt. Cook

Christchurch

Chatham Islands

MONDAY

SUNDAY

SOUTH PACIFIC OCEAN

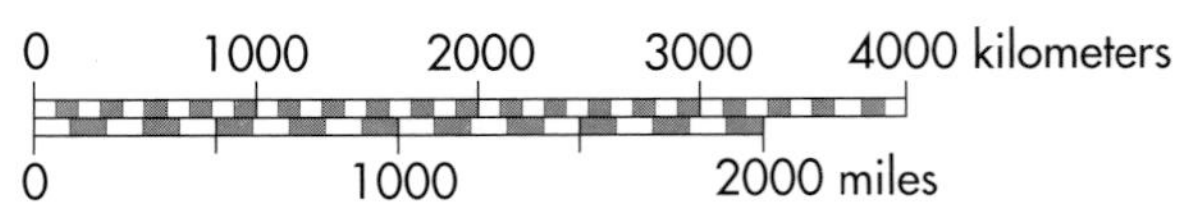
0 1000 2000 3000 4000 kilometers
0 1000 2000 miles

PEOPLES OF THE REGION

Polynesians' homeland covers an area of about 20 million square kilometers (7.7 million square miles) almost all of it water. This vast area of ocean was colonized by seafarers in canoes between about 3,500 and 1,000 years ago. Polynesians had reached Tonga and Samoa by 1000 B.C., and finally reached New Zealand around A.D. 900, where they founded the Maori civilization.

DID YOU KNOW?

The world's biggest atoll is Kwajalein, in the Marshall Islands. An atoll is a ring of coral surrounding a sheltered lagoon. Kwajalein atoll encloses a lagoon of 2,850 square kilometers (1,100 square miles)—about the size of Rhode Island.

NEW ZEALAND & PACIFIC ISLANDS

New Zealand lies in the South Pacific Ocean, about 2,000 kilometers (1,243 miles) east of Australia. Most New Zealanders live on North Island, an area of great volcanic activity, with hot springs and geysers.

South Island is dominated by Mount Cook, a 3,764-meter (12,349-foot) peak in the spectacular Southern Alps. Glaciers have carved out deep sea inlets in the southwest. The chief farming areas are the Canterbury Plains and the Otago plateau. New Zealand exports dairy products, lamb, and fruit such as apples.

Papua New Guinea lies in warmer regions, to the north of Australia. It is a producer of copper, gold, timber, coffee, and cocoa. The villagers of its remote mountains and valleys wear feathers, paint, and traditional costumes for festivals and rituals. The beautiful islands of the South Pacific Ocean have rich cultural traditions and are famous for their singing, dancing, and feasting. Islanders grow coconuts, bananas, and taro (a root crop). They also raise pigs and fish in the lagoons. Phosphate mining has reduced most of the island nation of Nauru to desert. Many island groups gained their independence in the 1970s and 1980s. Some of the new island nations are very small and face economic struggle.

COUNTRIES & DEPENDENCIES

FIJI
LAND AREA: 18,330 SQ KM (7,077 SQ MI)
POPULATION: 0.8 MILLION
CAPITAL: SUVA

KIRIBATI
LAND AREA: 717 SQ KM (277 SQ MI)
POPULATION: 0.08 MILLION
CAPITAL: TARAWA

MARSHALL ISLANDS
LAND AREA: 181 SQ KM (70 SQ MI)
POPULATION: 0.1 MILLION
CAPITAL: DALAP-ULIGA-DARRIT (ON MAJURO ATOLL)

MICRONESIA
LAND AREA: 702 SQ KM (271 SQ MI)
POPULATION: 0.1 MILLION
CAPITAL: PALIKIR

NAURU
LAND AREA: 21 SQ KM (8 SQ MI)
POPULATION: 0.01 MILLION
SEAT OF GOVERNMENT: YAREN

NEW ZEALAND
AREA: 268,676 SQ KM (103,736 SQ MI)
POPULATION: 3.8 MILLION
CAPITAL: WELLINGTON

PALAU
LAND AREA: 495 SQ KM (191 SQ MI)
POPULATION: 0.02 MILLION
CAPITAL: KOROR

PAPUA NEW GUINEA
LAND AREA: 461,693 SQ KM (178,260 SQ MI)
POPULATION: 4.7 MILLION
CAPITAL: PORT MORESBY

SOLOMON ISLANDS
LAND AREA: 29,785 SQ KM (11,500 SQ MI)
POPULATION: 0.4 MILLION
CAPITAL: HONIARA

TONGA
LAND AREA: 699 SQ KM (270 SQ MI)
POPULATION: 0.1 MILLION
CAPITAL: NUKUALOFA

TUVALU
LAND AREA: 25 SQ KM (10 SQ MI)
POPULATION: 0.01 MILLION
CAPITAL: FONGAFALE

VANUATU
LAND AREA: 14,765 SQ KM (5,701 SQ MI)
POPULATION: 0.2 MILLION
CAPITAL: PORT-VILA

WESTERN SAMOA
LAND AREA: 2,840 SQ KM (1,097 SQ MI)
POPULATION: 0.02 MILLION
CAPITAL: APIA

AMERICAN SAMOA
U.S. DEPENDENCY

COOK ISLANDS
N.Z. DEPENDENCY

FRENCH POLYNESIA
FRENCH OVERSEAS TERRITORY

GUAM
U.S. DEPENDENCY

JOHNSTON ATOLL
U.S. DEPENDENCY

MIDWAY ISLANDS
U.S. DEPENDENCY

NIUE
N.Z. DEPENDENCY

NEW CALEDONIA
FRENCH OVERSEAS TERRITORY

NORFOLK ISLAND
AUSTRALIAN DEPENDENCY

NORTHERN MARIANAS
U.S. COMMONWEALTH

PITCAIRN ISLAND
U.K. DEPENDENCY

TOKELAU
N.Z. DEPENDENCY

WAKE ISLAND
U.S. DEPENDENCY

WALLIS & FUTUNA
FRENCH OVERSEAS TERRITORY

THE ARCTIC

The Arctic tundra springs to life in the brief northern summer.

The Arctic Circle is a line drawn by mapmakers around the northern part of the world. At its center lies the most northerly point on Earth, the North Pole. This lies in the middle of the Arctic Ocean, which is permanently frozen. All three of the northern continents cross into the Arctic Circle—North America (Alaska, Canada, and Greenland), Europe (Scandinavia and Russia), and Asia (Siberian Russia).

The climate of our planet has changed many times. Sometimes, the poles have been completely free of ice. At other periods, known as ice ages, glaciers and frozen seas have spread far beyond their current limits. At present the world's climate seems to be warming again, and polar ice is melting. This time it is happening very quickly, probably as a result of pollution of the air by humans.

• GENERAL FACTS •

OCEANIC AREA
14,056,000 SQ KM (5,427,022 SQ MI)

HIGHEST POINT
MT. GUNNBJØRN, GREENLAND, 3,700 M (12,136 FT)

GREATEST THICKNESS OF ICE CAP
3 KM (2 MI)

BIGGEST RECORDED ICEBERG
167 M (548 FT)

LOWEST RECORDED TEMPERATURE
-68°C (-90.4°F) OIMYAKON, SIBERIA, RUSSIA

POPULATION
1 MILLION INDIGENOUS PEOPLE (APPROX)

NORTHERNMOST VILLAGE
NYÅLESUND, SPITSBERGEN, SVALBARD, NORWAY

MINERALS
BAUXITE, COAL, COPPER, GOLD, NATURAL GAS, NICKEL, OIL, SILVER, URANIUM

VEGETATION ZONES
ICE CAP, TUNDRA, FOREST-TUNDRA

ARCTIC PEOPLE

Rich fishing grounds and wildlife make it possible for humans to survive in these inhospitable regions, and there are scattered settlements around the Arctic coasts. Arctic peoples include the Inuit of North America, the reindeer-herding Saami of Scandinavia, and several ethnic groups in Siberia, such as the Chukchee. They have been joined in more recent years by miners, oil workers, prospectors, explorers, and even tourists.

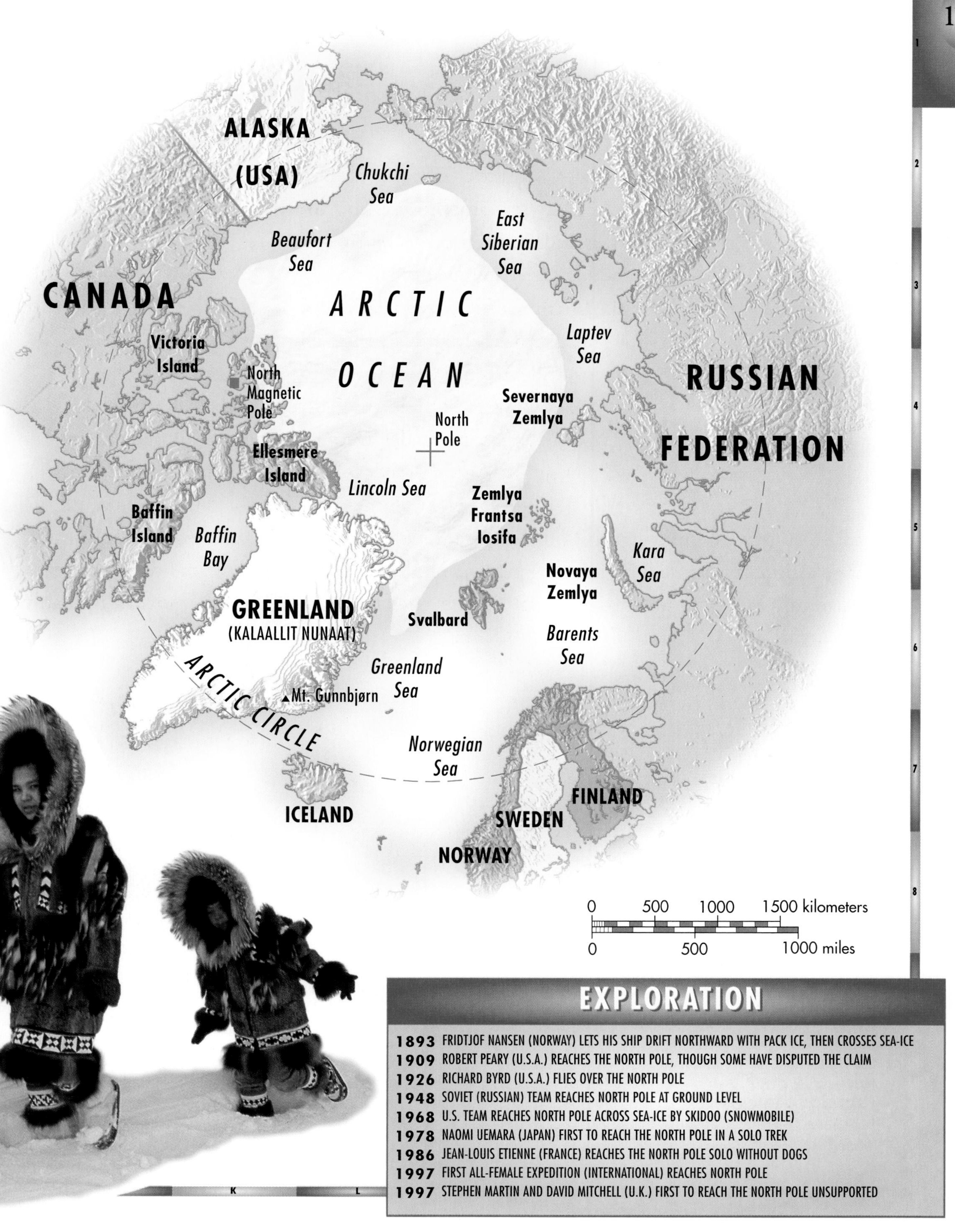

ALASKA (USA)
Chukchi Sea
Beaufort Sea
East Siberian Sea
CANADA
ARCTIC OCEAN
Laptev Sea
Victoria Island
North Magnetic Pole
RUSSIAN FEDERATION
Severnaya Zemlya
North Pole
Ellesmere Island
Lincoln Sea
Zemlya Frantsa Iosifa
Baffin Island
Baffin Bay
Kara Sea
Novaya Zemlya
GREENLAND (KALAALLIT NUNAAT)
Svalbard
Barents Sea
Greenland Sea
Mt. Gunnbjørn
ARCTIC CIRCLE
Norwegian Sea
FINLAND
ICELAND
SWEDEN
NORWAY
0 500 1000 1500 kilometers
0 500 1000 miles

EXPLORATION

1893 FRIDTJOF NANSEN (NORWAY) LETS HIS SHIP DRIFT NORTHWARD WITH PACK ICE, THEN CROSSES SEA-ICE
1909 ROBERT PEARY (U.S.A.) REACHES THE NORTH POLE, THOUGH SOME HAVE DISPUTED THE CLAIM
1926 RICHARD BYRD (U.S.A.) FLIES OVER THE NORTH POLE
1948 SOVIET (RUSSIAN) TEAM REACHES NORTH POLE AT GROUND LEVEL
1968 U.S. TEAM REACHES NORTH POLE ACROSS SEA-ICE BY SKIDOO (SNOWMOBILE)
1978 NAOMI UEMARA (JAPAN) FIRST TO REACH THE NORTH POLE IN A SOLO TREK
1986 JEAN-LOUIS ETIENNE (FRANCE) REACHES THE NORTH POLE SOLO WITHOUT DOGS
1997 FIRST ALL-FEMALE EXPEDITION (INTERNATIONAL) REACHES NORTH POLE
1997 STEPHEN MARTIN AND DAVID MITCHELL (U.K.) FIRST TO REACH THE NORTH POLE UNSUPPORTED

ANTARCTICA

Penguins only live in the southern hemisphere. These Adélie penguins are one of the two species that breed on the Antarctic continent.

Unlike the frozen ocean at the North Pole, the South Pole is located on solid ground. The mountains and valleys of Antarctica are covered in a thick ice cap. Its bays are also frozen over around the coast, forming great shelves of ice.

AFRICA
SOUTH AMERICA
ANTARCTIC CIRCLE
ANTARCTICA
AUSTRALIA

If you were to add the United States of America to Europe, you might begin to get some idea of the vast area covered by Antarctica. It is a land of many mountains, rising to 5,139 meters (16,866 feet) at Vinson Massif. It even has an active volcano, Mount Erebus, on Ross Island. The amount of ice here at the bottom of the world is awesome—perhaps 90 percent of all the ice on the planet, and 70 percent of its fresh water.

• GENERAL FACTS •

LAND AREA
13,340,000 SQ KM (5,150,574 SQ MI)

LOWEST POINT
BENTLEY TRENCH (UNDER THE ICE CAP), -2,538 M (-8,327 FT)

HIGHEST POINT
VINSON MASSIF, 5,139 M (16,860 FT)

HIGHEST VOLCANO
MT. EREBUS, 4,024 M (13,202 FT)

AVERAGE THICKNESS OF ICE CAP
1,880 M (6,168 FT)

BIGGEST RECORDED ICEBERG
31,000 SQ KM (11,969 SQ MI)

LOWEST RECORDED TEMPERATURE
-89.2°C (-128.6°F) VOSTOK BASE

POPULATION
ZERO PERMANENT. APPROXIMATELY 2,500 VISITING SCIENTISTS

SOUTHERNMOST BASE
AMUNDSEN-SCOTT SOUTH POLAR STATION

MINERALS
COAL, OIL, PALLADIUM, PLATINUM

VEGETATION ZONES
ICE CAPS, TUNDRA

AT THE END OF THE WORLD

Antarctica is the coldest place on Earth, with bitter, howling winds and temperatures in the southern winter dropping to -89°C (-129°F). No humans have ever settled here: it is too cold. But explorers do come to test themselves against the forces of nature. Scientists have set up bases to study rocks, penguins or climate. Various countries claim parts of Antarctica as their own, but these claims are not recognized by the international community. Most countries have demanded that the Antarctic be kept as an international nature reserve, unspoiled and free of mining and industry.

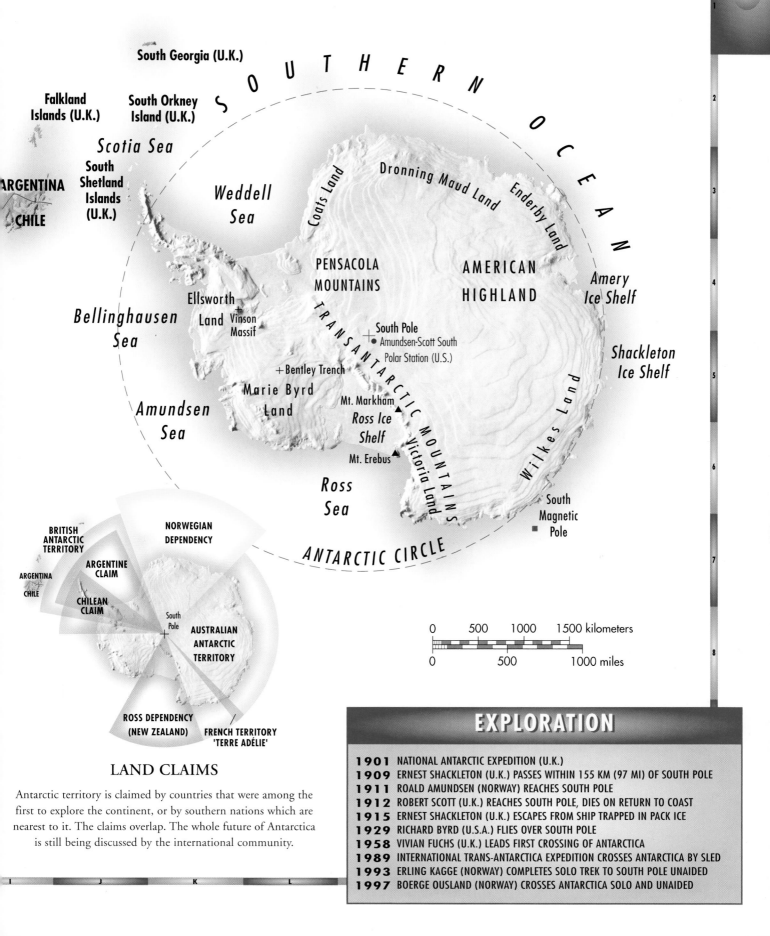

South Georgia (U.K.)
SOUTHERN OCEAN
Falkland Islands (U.K.)
South Orkney Island (U.K.)
Scotia Sea
South Shetland Islands (U.K.)
ARGENTINA
CHILE
Weddell Sea
Coats Land
Dronning Maud Land
Enderby Land
PENSACOLA MOUNTAINS
AMERICAN HIGHLAND
Amery Ice Shelf
Ellsworth Land
Vinson Massif
Bellinghausen Sea
TRANSANTARCTIC MOUNTAINS
South Pole
Amundsen-Scott South Polar Station (U.S.)
Shackleton Ice Shelf
Bentley Trench
Marie Byrd Land
Wilkes Land
Mt. Markham
Amundsen Sea
Ross Ice Shelf
Mt. Erebus
Victoria Land
Ross Sea
South Magnetic Pole
ANTARCTIC CIRCLE
BRITISH ANTARCTIC TERRITORY
NORWEGIAN DEPENDENCY
ARGENTINE CLAIM
ARGENTINA
CHILE
CHILEAN CLAIM
South Pole
AUSTRALIAN ANTARCTIC TERRITORY
ROSS DEPENDENCY (NEW ZEALAND)
FRENCH TERRITORY 'TERRE ADÉLIE'
0 500 1000 1500 kilometers
0 500 1000 miles

LAND CLAIMS

Antarctic territory is claimed by countries that were among the first to explore the continent, or by southern nations which are nearest to it. The claims overlap. The whole future of Antarctica is still being discussed by the international community.

EXPLORATION

1901	NATIONAL ANTARCTIC EXPEDITION (U.K.)
1909	ERNEST SHACKLETON (U.K.) PASSES WITHIN 155 KM (97 MI) OF SOUTH POLE
1911	ROALD AMUNDSEN (NORWAY) REACHES SOUTH POLE
1912	ROBERT SCOTT (U.K.) REACHES SOUTH POLE, DIES ON RETURN TO COAST
1915	ERNEST SHACKLETON (U.K.) ESCAPES FROM SHIP TRAPPED IN PACK ICE
1929	RICHARD BYRD (U.S.A.) FLIES OVER SOUTH POLE
1958	VIVIAN FUCHS (U.K.) LEADS FIRST CROSSING OF ANTARCTICA
1989	INTERNATIONAL TRANS-ANTARCTICA EXPEDITION CROSSES ANTARCTICA BY SLED
1993	ERLING KAGGE (NORWAY) COMPLETES SOLO TREK TO SOUTH POLE UNAIDED
1997	BOERGE OUSLAND (NORWAY) CROSSES ANTARCTICA SOLO AND UNAIDED

FACT FILE

• PLANET EARTH •

Average speed of Earth's orbit: 107,220 km/h (66,627 mph)
Average distance from Sun: 150 million km (93,210,000 mi)
Average distance from Moon: 384,399 km (238,865 mi)
Diameter at Equator: 12,756 km (7,926.41 mi)
Diameter at Poles: 12,714 km (7,899.83 mi)
Mass: 6.6 sextillion tons
Average surface temperature: 15°C (59°F)

• DRY LAND •

Biggest landmass: Eurasia – 54,106,000 sq km (20,890,326 sq mi)
Biggest continent: Asia – 43,608,000 sq km (16,837,048 sq mi)
Northernmost land: Odaaq island (706 km 439 mi from North Pole)
Southernmost land: South Pole
Biggest desert: Sahara (Africa) – 9,000,000 sq km (3,474,900 sq mi)
Longest cave system: Mammoth Caves (North America) – 567 km (352 mi)

• HIGH & LOW •

Lowest exposed point: Dead Sea (Asia) – 400 m (1,311 ft) below sea level
Lowest point under polar ice: Lake Vostok (Antarctica) – 4,000 m (13,123 ft) below sea level
Highest mountain above sea level: Everest (Asia) – 8,848 m (29,028 ft)
Highest mountain from ocean floor: Mauna Kea (Hawaii) – 10,203 m (33,476 ft)
Longest mountain range: Andes (South America) – 7,240 km (4,500 mi)
Widest plateau: Tibet (Asia) – 1,850,000 sq km (714,285 sq mi)
Biggest gorge: Grand Canyon (North America) – 446 km (277 mi) long, 1,600m (1 mi) deep, up to 29 km (18 mi) wide
Most massive active volcano: Mauna Loa (Hawaii) – 42,500 cu km (16,623,450 cu ft)
Highest active volcano: Guallatiri (South America) – 6,060 m (19,882 ft)

• ISLANDS & REEFS •

Biggest oceanic island: Greenland (North America) – 2,175,594 sq km (839,999 sq mi)
Biggest freshwater island: Ilha de Marajó (South America) – 40,150 sq km (15,500 sq mi)
Biggest archipelago or island chain: Indonesia (Asia) – 17,000 islands
Biggest atoll: Kwajalein (Oceania) – 283 km (176 mi) long
Longest reef: Great Barrier Reef (Australia) – 2,027 km (1,260 mi)

WATER & ICE

Deepest seabed: Mariana Trench (Pacific Ocean) – max. 11,033 m (36,198 ft)
Widest ocean: Pacific Ocean – 179,700,000 sq km (6,938,217 sq mi)
Longest river: Nile (Africa) – 6,670 km (4,145 mi)
Biggest river basin: Amazon (South America) – 7,050,000 sq km (2,722,005 sq mi)
Highest waterfall: Angel Falls (South America) – 979 m (3,212 ft) total drop
Biggest inland sea: Caspian Sea (Europe/Asia) – 371,000 sq km (143,243 sq mi)
Biggest freshwater lake: Lake Superior (North America) – 82,350 sq km (31,795 sq mi)
Deepest freshwater lake: Baikal (Asia) – max. 1,637 m (5,371 ft)
Biggest gulf: Gulf of Mexico (North America) – 1,544,000 sq km (596,138 sq mi)
Longest glacier: Lambert-Fisher (Antarctica) – 525 km (326 mi)

CLIMATE

Highest recorded temperature: Libya (Africa) – 58°C (136°F)
Lowest recorded temperature: Vostok base (Antarctica) – -89°C (-192°F)
Heaviest annual rainfall: Meghalaya (India) – 2,646 cm (1,042 in)
Driest place: Atacama desert (South America) – zero rainfall
Windiest place: Commonwealth Bay (Antarctica) – 320 km/h (199 mph)

VEGETATION

Largest surviving rain forest: Amazonia – 330,000,000 ha (1,274,130 sq mi)
Tallest tree: coastal redwood (North America) – height of 112 m (367 ft)
Most massive tree: giant sequoia (North America) – girth of 31 m (102 ft)
Biggest flower: rafflesia (Asia) – 91 cm (36 in) diameter
Oldest plant: King's holly (Oceania) – 40,000 years

WORLD WILDLIFE

Biggest animal: blue whale (oceanic) – 33.5 m (110 ft) long, 130 tons (286,599 lbs)
Biggest land animal: African elephant (Africa) – 12 tons (26,455 lbs)
Smallest mammal: Kitti's hog-nosed bat (Asia) – 29 mm (11.4 in) long
Biggest bird: ostrich (Africa) – 274 cm (9 ft) tall
Biggest fish: whale shark (oceanic) – 12.7 m (42 ft) long
Longest snake: reticulated python (Asia) – 10 m (33 ft) long
Heaviest insect: Goliath beetle (Africa) – 100 g (3.5 oz)

HUMAN WORLD

Biggest nation: Russian Federation (Europe/Asia) – 17,075,383 sq km (6,592,812 sq mi)
Smallest nation: Vatican City State (Europe) – 0.4 sq km (0.15 sq mi)
Most populous country: China (Asia) – 1,254,100,000 people
Most crowded country: Monaco (Europe) – 32,100 per sq km (12,394 per sq mi)
Most spoken language: Standard Chinese (worldwide) – 1,070,000,000 speakers

INDEX

Picture Credits: t=top, b=bottom, c=centre, l=left, r=right, OFC=outside front cover, OBC=outside back cover, IFC=inside front cover

AKG Photos; 56tl, 88tl. B. C. Alexander; 114tl, 116br. Bridgeman Art Library; 60/61bc. e. t. archive; 44tl. Image Select; 9tr, 19tr, 44br, 48tl, 48bl, 49tr, 49br, 60bl, 70br, 74bl, 75br, 92bl, 109b. NASA; 6/7c. Pictor; 8tl, 14/15c, 18br, 19tl, 19bc, 19br, 19cr, 20br, 24cl, 24br, 38tl, 38br, 48/49c, 49cl, 61br, 61cl, 62br, 74/75c, 75tl, 75cr, 88/89c, 92/93c, 92br, 93tl, 93cr, 93br, 106bl, 106br, 109tr, 109cl, 109tr. PIX; 56bc. Still Pictures; 30cl, 114/115bc, 116tl. Spectrum; 70tl. Telegraph Colour Library; 60/61tc, 61tr.